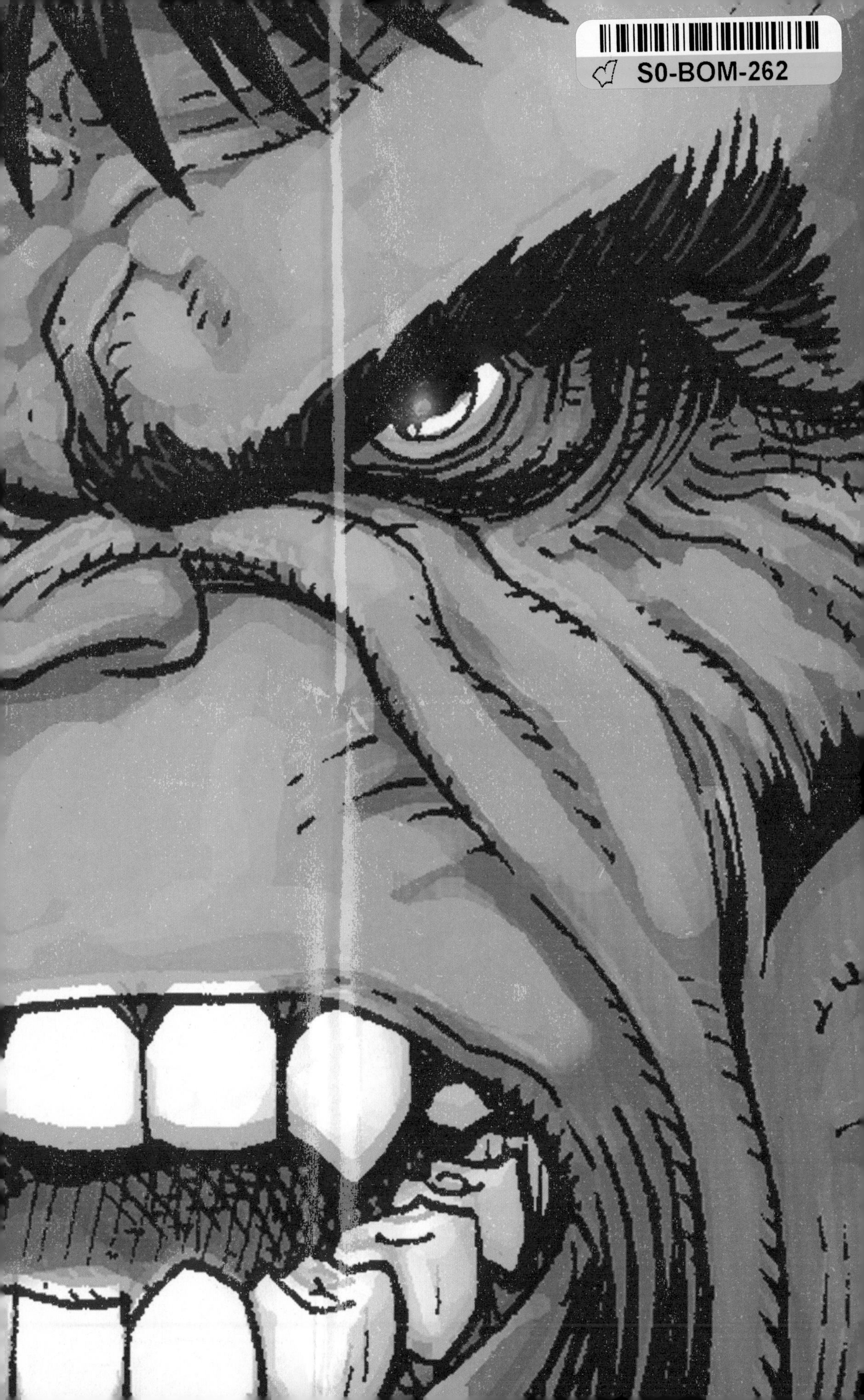

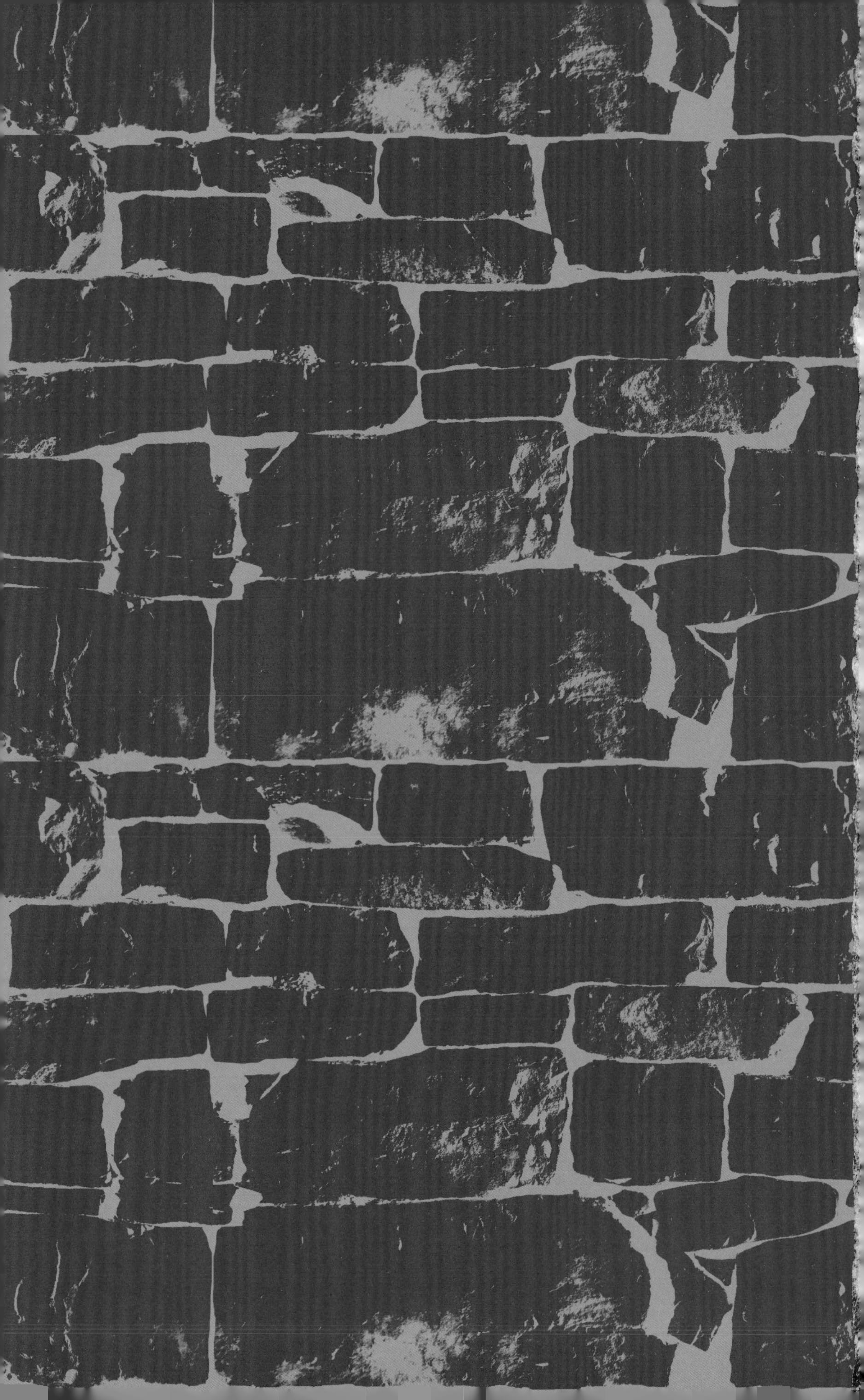

VOLUME   ISSUES   PAGES

2   4   120

LOEB ★ ADAMS ★ CHO

HULK

MARVEL COMICS ★ PRESENTS ★

★ STARRING: ★

WRITER JEPH LOEB

★ ROUND ONE ★

PENCILER ART ADAMS

VS.

INKER WALDEN WONG

COLORS BY JASON KEITH AND
ASPEN'S PETER STEIGERWALD

★ ROUND TWO ★

ARTIST FRANK CHO

VS.

COLORIST JASON KEITH and CURV EFX

LK

★ VOLUME TWO ★
RED & GREEN

★ ROUND THREE ★
ARTIST **HERB TRIMPE**

— VS. —

COLORIST **EDGAR DELGADO**
of STUDIO F

RICHARD STARKINGS
and COMICRAFT'S
ALBERT DESCHESNE
★ CORNERMEN ★

★ ON THE UNDERCARD ★
WRITER **AUDREY LOEB**
— AND —
ARTIST & LETTERER CHRIS
GIARRUSSO

"HULK WEB" ★ "HULK
AIRPORT" ★ "HULK ICE"

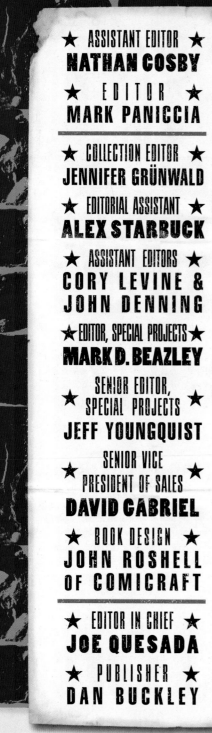

★ ASSISTANT EDITOR ★
NATHAN COSBY

★ EDITOR ★
MARK PANICCIA

★ COLLECTION EDITOR ★
JENNIFER GRÜNWALD

★ EDITORIAL ASSISTANT ★
ALEX STARBUCK

★ ASSISTANT EDITORS ★
CORY LEVINE & JOHN DENNING

★ EDITOR, SPECIAL PROJECTS ★
MARK D. BEAZLEY

★ SENIOR EDITOR, SPECIAL PROJECTS ★
JEFF YOUNGQUIST

★ SENIOR VICE PRESIDENT OF SALES ★
DAVID GABRIEL

★ BOOK DESIGN ★
JOHN ROSHELL OF COMICRAFT

★ EDITOR IN CHIEF ★
JOE QUESADA

★ PUBLISHER ★
DAN BUCKLEY

HULK VOL. 2: RED & GREEN. Contains material originally published in magazine form as HULK #7-9 and KING-SIZE HULK #1. First printing 2009. ISBN# 978-0-7851-2883-0. Published by MARVEL PUBLISHING, INC., a subsidiary of MARVEL ENTERTAINMENT, INC. OFFICE OF PUBLICATION: 417 5th Avenue, New York, NY 10016. Copyright © 2008 and 2009 Marvel Characters, Inc. All rights reserved. $19.99 per copy in the U.S. (GST #R127032852); Canadian Agreement #40668537. All characters featured in this issue and the distinctive names and likenesses thereof, and all related indicia are trademarks of Marvel Characters, Inc. No similarity between any of the names, characters, persons, and/or institutions in this magazine with those of any living or dead person or institution is intended, and any such similarity which may exist is purely coincidental. **Printed in the U.S.A.** ALAN FINE, CEO Marvel Toys & Publishing Divisions and CMO Marvel Characters, Inc.; JIM SOKOLOWSKI, Chief Operating Officer; DAVID GABRIEL, SVP of Publishing Sales & Circulation; DAVID BOGART, SVP of Business Affairs & Talent Management; MICHAEL PASCIULLO, VP Merchandising & Communications; JIM O'KEEFE, VP of Operations & Logistics; DAN CARR, Executive Director of Publishing Technology; JUSTIN F. GABRIE, Director of Publishing & Editorial Operations; SUSAN CRESPI, Editorial Operations Manager; ALEX MORALES, Publishing Operations Manager; STAN LEE, Chairman Emeritus. For information regarding advertising in Marvel Comics or on Marvel.com, please contact Mitch Dane, Advertising Director, at mdane@marvel.com. For Marvel subscription inquiries, please call 800-217-9158.

10 9 8 7 6 5 4 3 2 1

ROUND ★ ONE

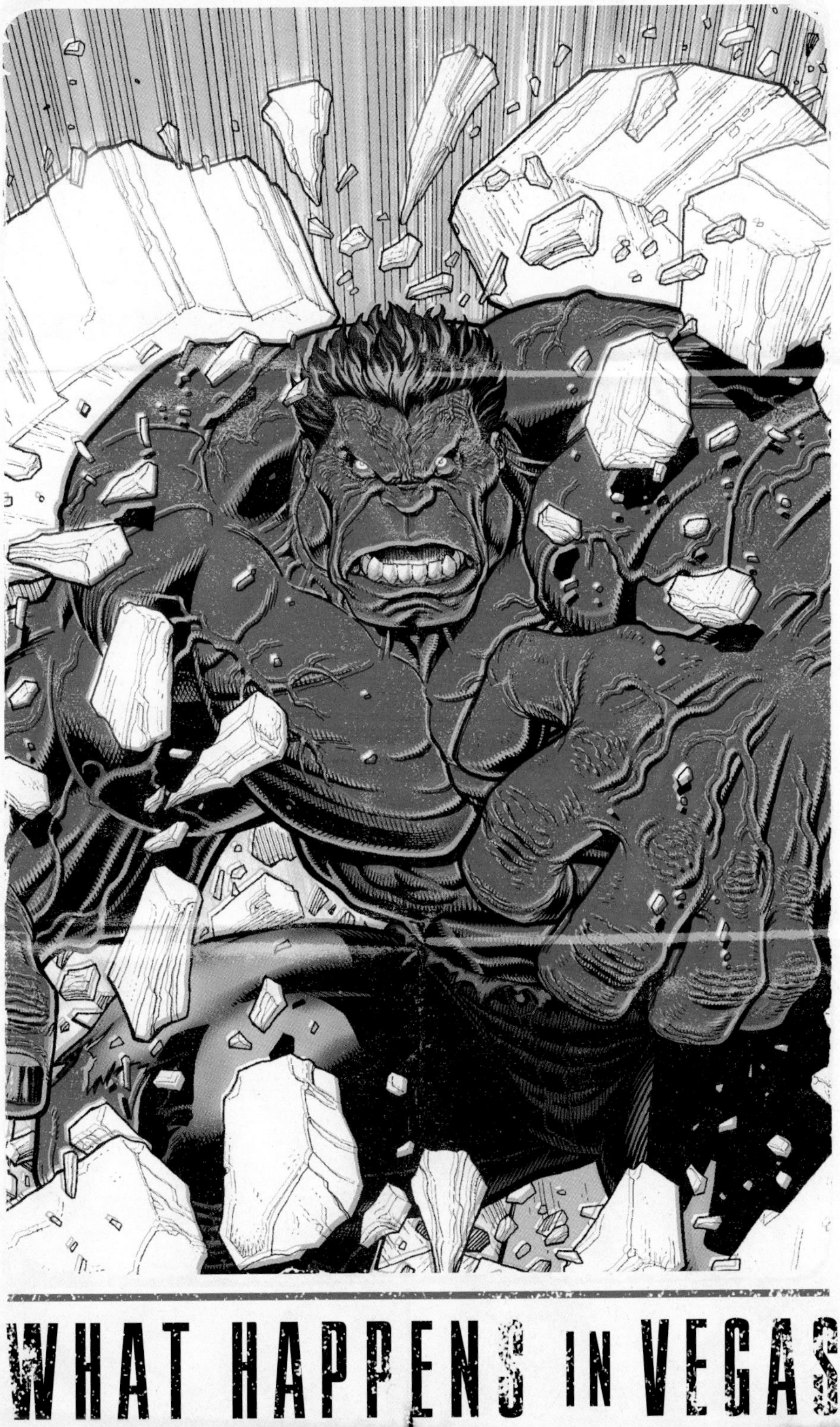

WHAT HAPPENS IN VEGAS

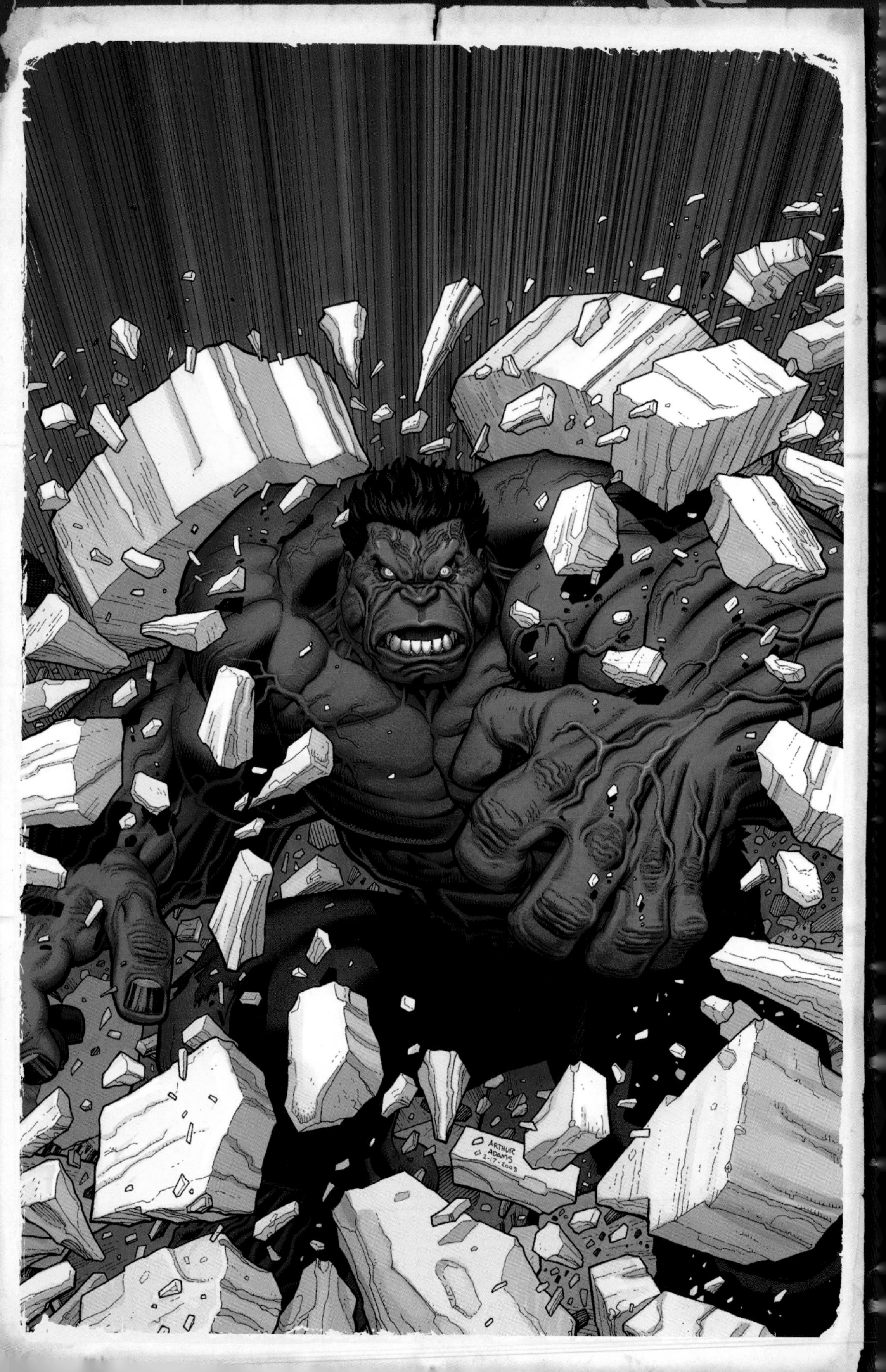
ARTHUR ADAMS 2-17-2008

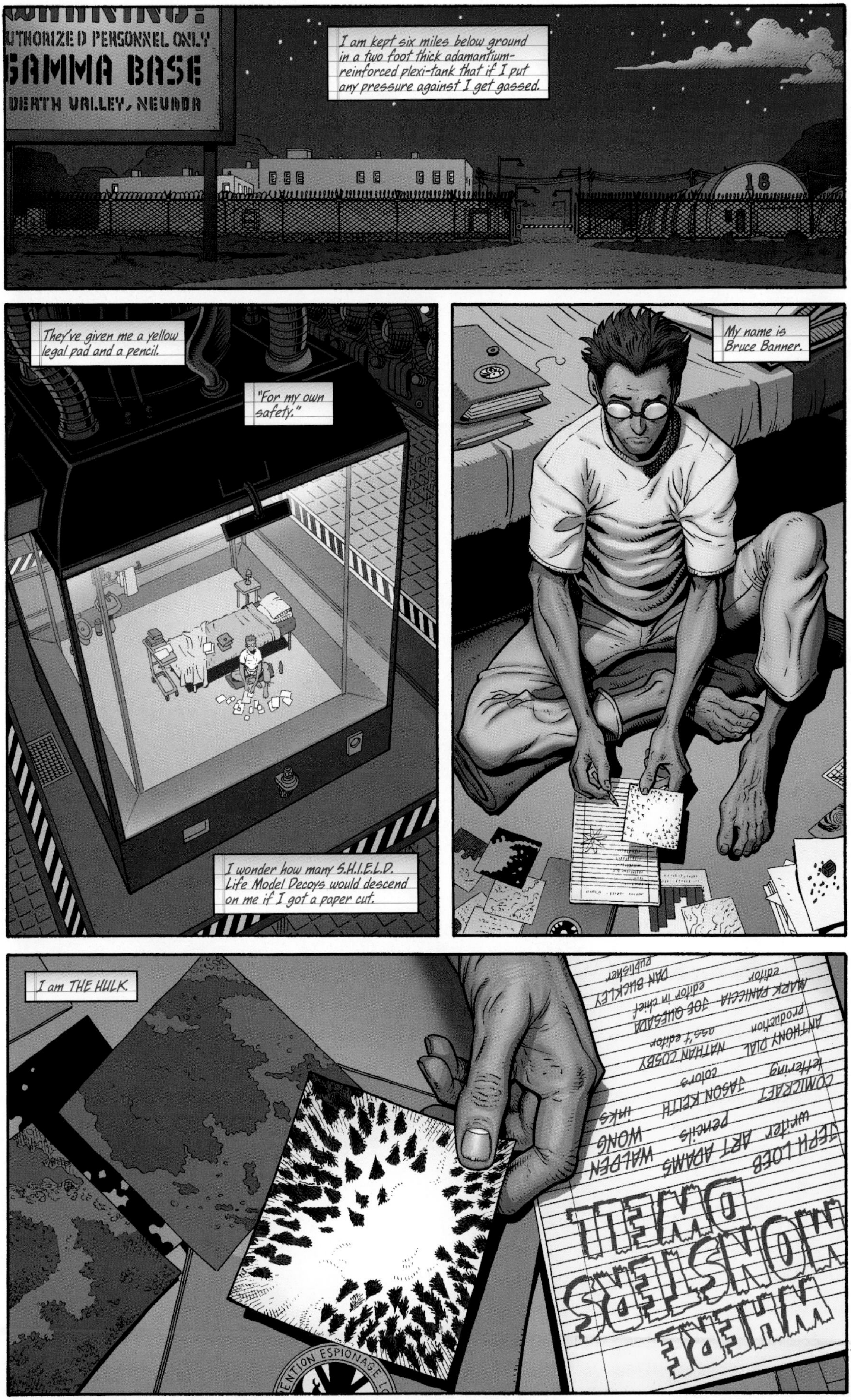
UTHORIZED PERSONNEL ONLY
AMMA BASE
EATH VALLEY, NEVADA
I am kept six miles below ground in a two foot thick adamantium-reinforced plexi-tank that if I put any pressure against I get gassed.
18
They've given me a yellow legal pad and a pencil.
"For my own safety."
I wonder how many S.H.I.E.L.D. Life Model Decoys would descend on me if I got a paper cut.
My name is Bruce Banner.
I am THE HULK.
WHERE MONSTERS DWELL
JEPH LOEB writer
ART ADAMS pencils
WALDEN WONG inks
JASON KEITH colors
COMICRAFT lettering
NATHAN COSBY ass't editor
ANTHONY DIAL production
MARK PANICCIA editor
JOE QUESADA editor in chief
DAN BUCKLEY publisher

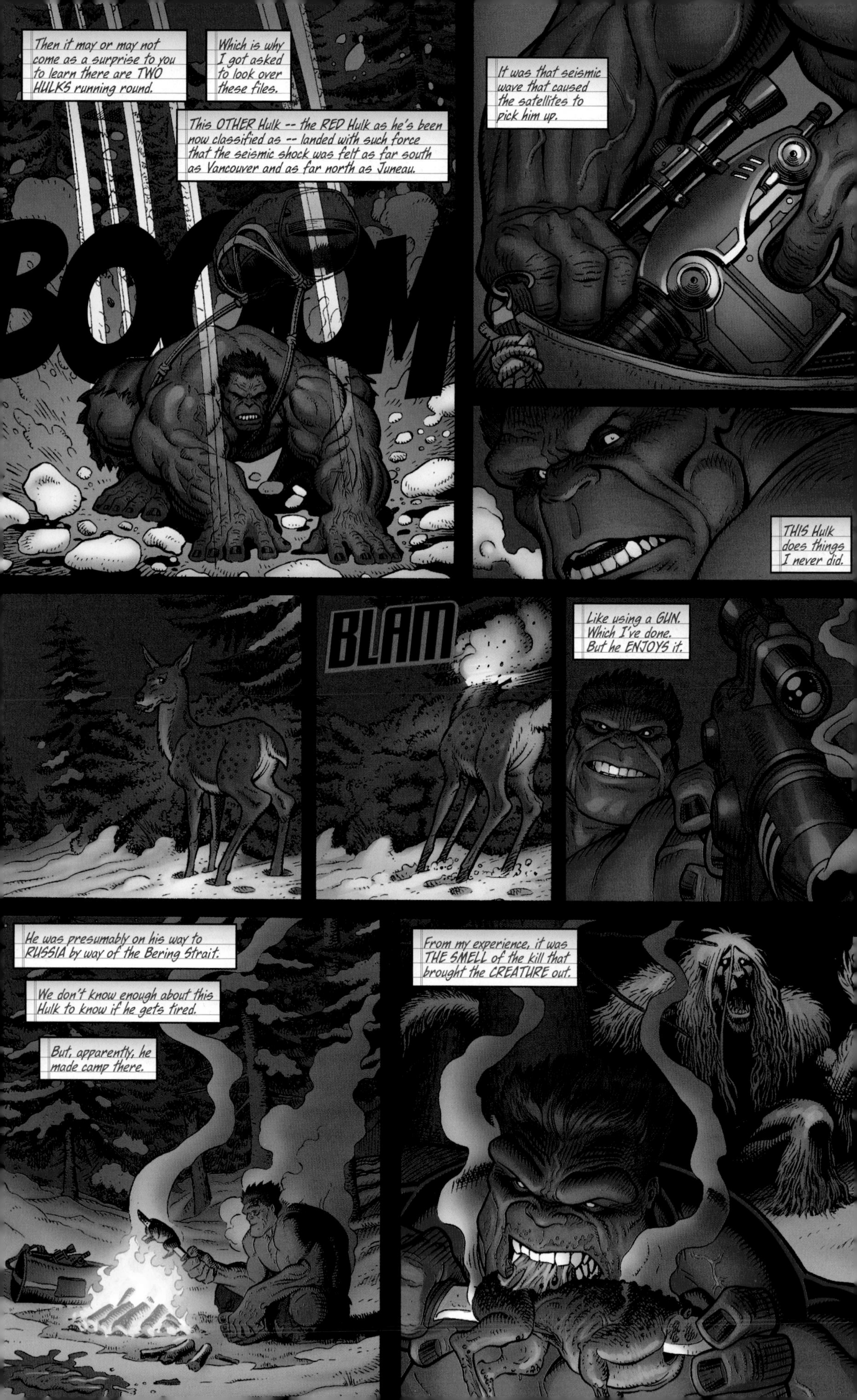
Then it may or may not come as a surprise to you to learn there are TWO HULKS running round.
Which is why I got asked to look over these files.
This OTHER Hulk -- the RED Hulk as he's been now classified as -- landed with such force that the seismic shock was felt as far south as Vancouver and as far north as Juneau.
BOOM
It was that seismic wave that caused the satellites to pick him up.
THIS Hulk does things I never did.
BLAM
Like using a GUN. Which I've done. But he ENJOYS it.
He was presumably on his way to RUSSIA by way of the Bering Strait.
We don't know enough about this Hulk to know if he gets tired.
But, apparently, he made camp there.
From my experience, it was THE SMELL of the kill that brought the CREATURE out.

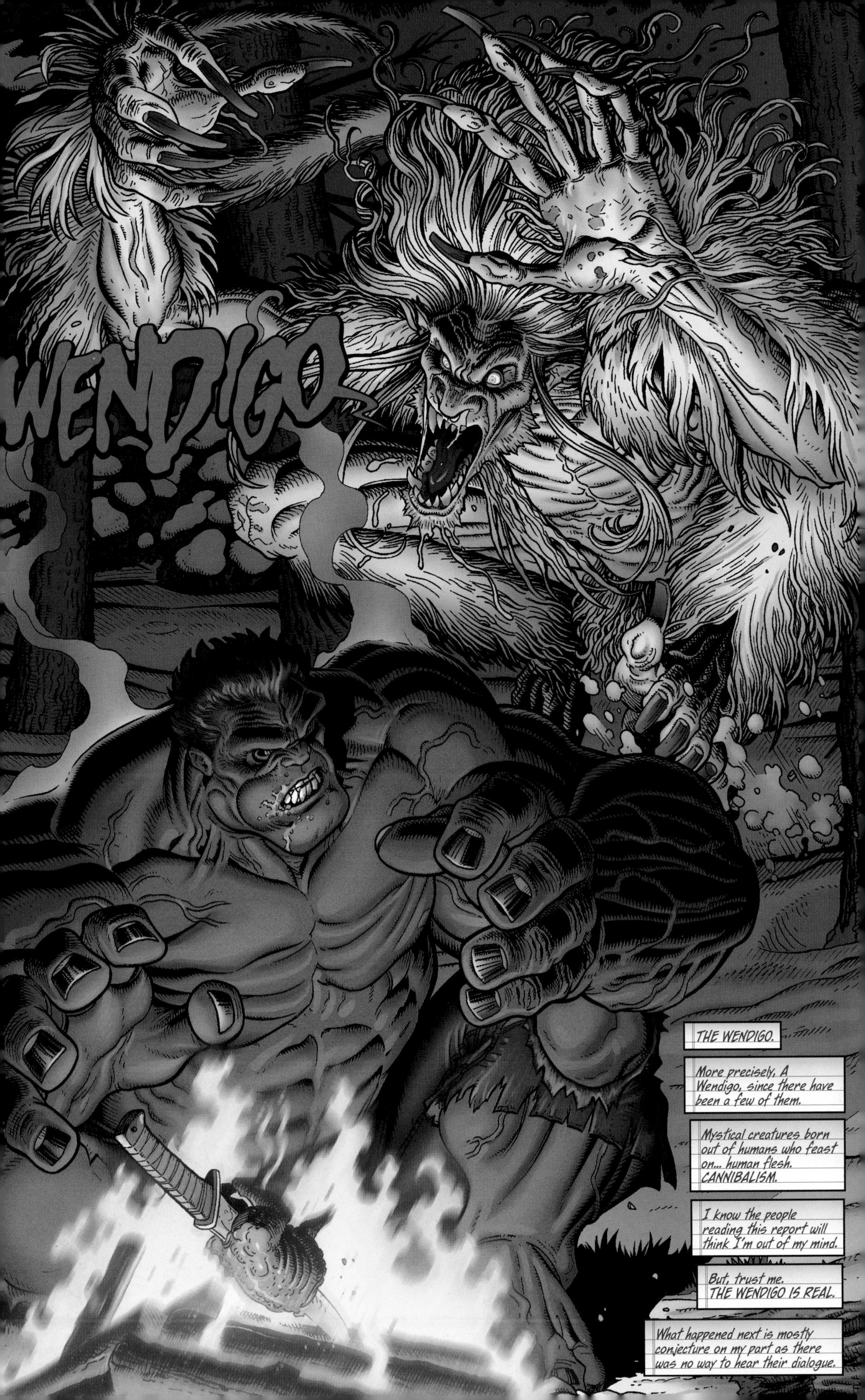
WENDIGO
THE WENDIGO.
More precisely, A Wendigo, since there have been a few of them.
Mystical creatures born out of humans who feast on... human flesh. CANNIBALISM.
I know the people reading this report will think I'm out of my mind.
But, trust me. THE WENDIGO IS REAL.
What happened next is mostly conjecture on my part as there was no way to hear their dialogue.

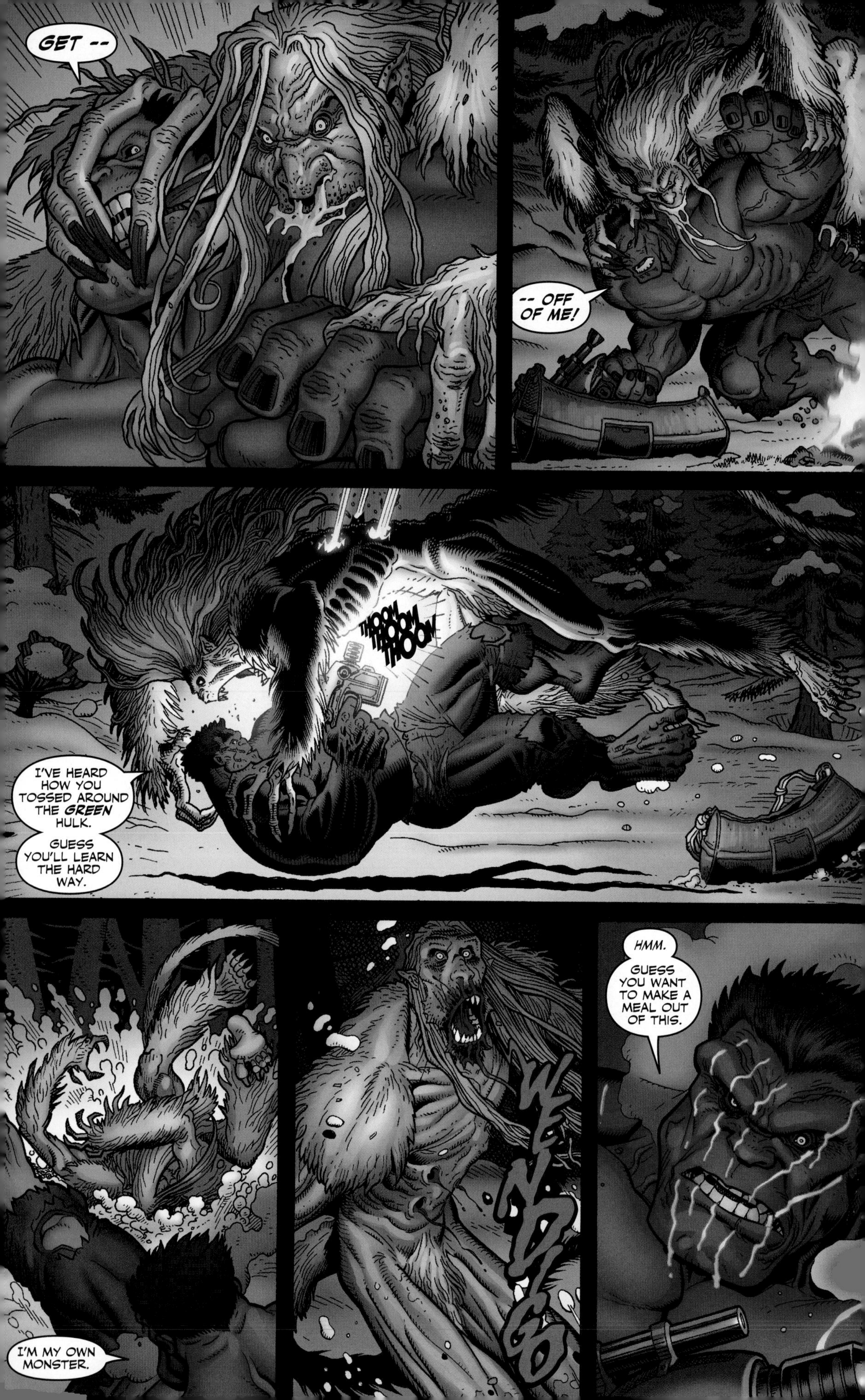
GET --
-- OFF OF ME!
THOOM THOOM THOOM
I'VE HEARD HOW YOU TOSSED AROUND THE GREEN HULK.
GUESS YOU'LL LEARN THE HARD WAY.
I'M MY OWN MONSTER.
WENDIGO
HMM.
GUESS YOU WANT TO MAKE A MEAL OUT OF THIS.

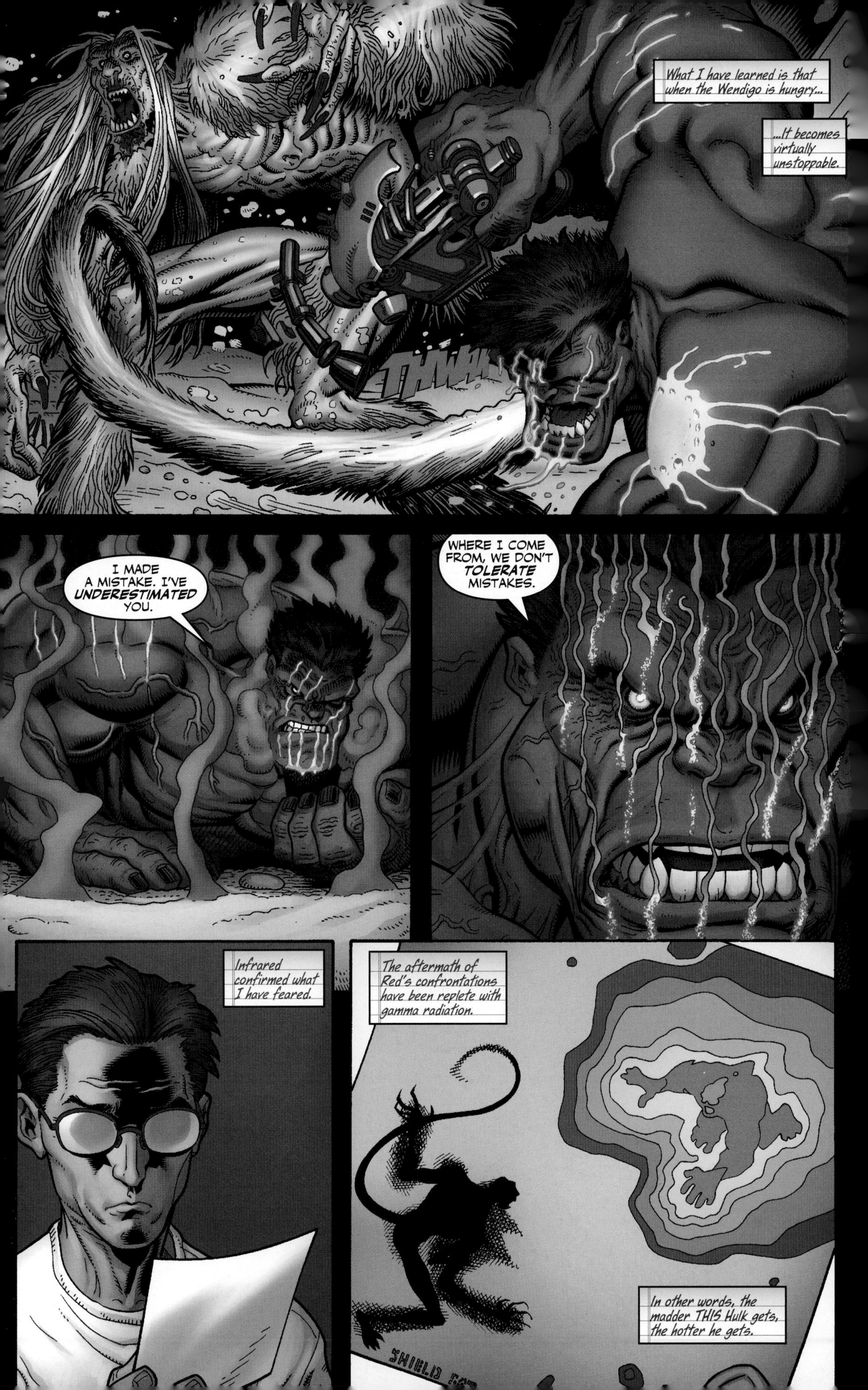
What I have learned is that when the Wendigo is hungry...
...It becomes virtually unstoppable.
THWAK
I MADE A MISTAKE. I'VE UNDERESTIMATED YOU.
WHERE I COME FROM, WE DON'T TOLERATE MISTAKES.
Infrared confirmed what I have feared.
The aftermath of Red's confrontations have been replete with gamma radiation.
In other words, the madder THIS Hulk gets, the hotter he gets.
SHIELD

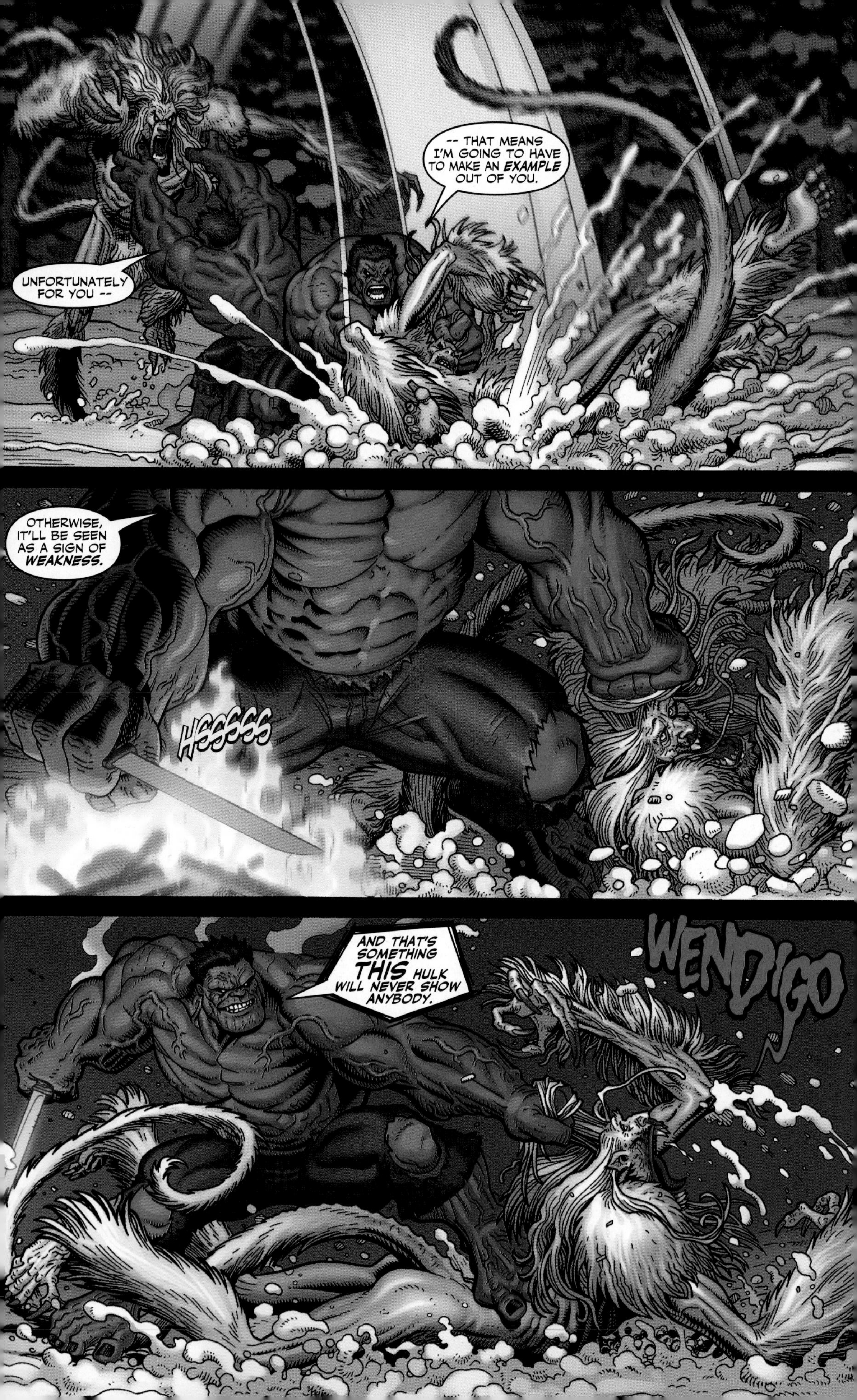
UNFORTUNATELY FOR YOU --
-- THAT MEANS I'M GOING TO HAVE TO MAKE AN EXAMPLE OUT OF YOU.
OTHERWISE, IT'LL BE SEEN AS A SIGN OF WEAKNESS.
HSSSSS
AND THAT'S SOMETHING THIS HULK WILL NEVER SHOW ANYBODY.
WENDIGO

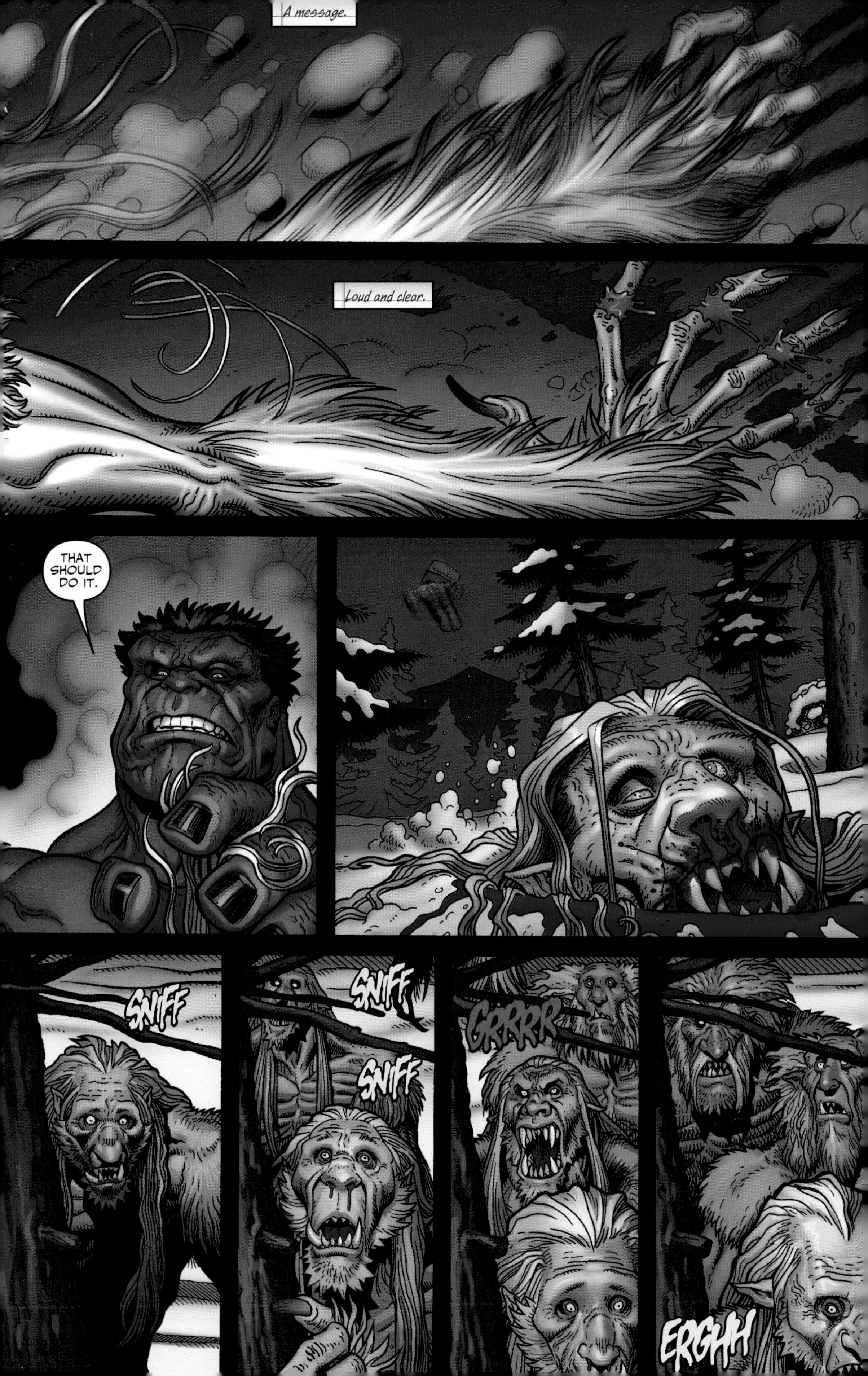
A message.
Loud and clear.
THAT SHOULD DO IT.
SNIFF
SNIFF
SNIFF
GRRRR
ERGHH

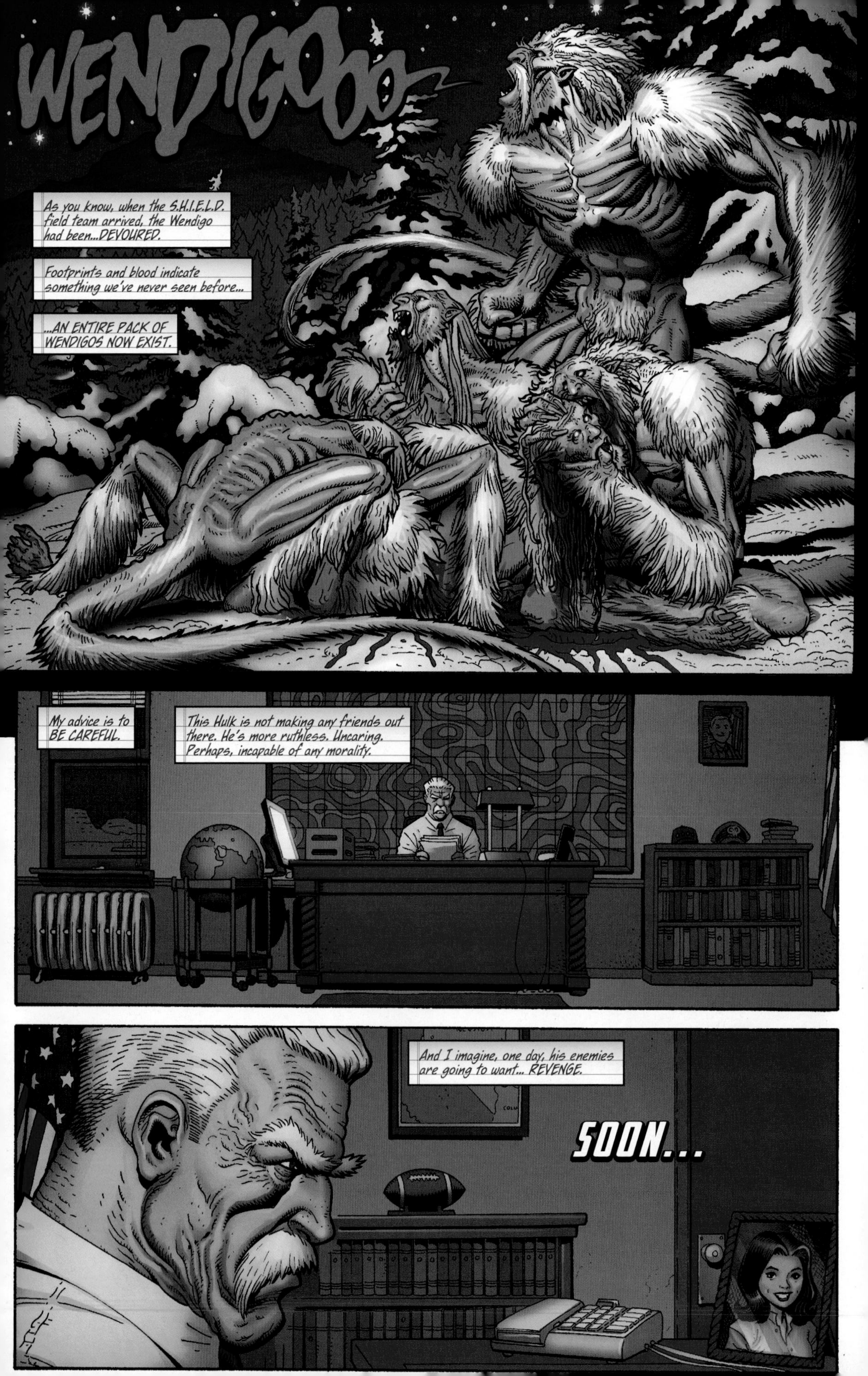
WENDIGOOO
As you know, when the S.H.I.E.L.D. field team arrived, the Wendigo had been...DEVOURED.
Footprints and blood indicate something we've never seen before...
...AN ENTIRE PACK OF WENDIGOS NOW EXIST.
My advice is to BE CAREFUL.
This Hulk is not making any friends out there. He's more ruthless. Uncaring. Perhaps, incapable of any morality.
And I imagine, one day, his enemies are going to want... REVENGE.
SOON...

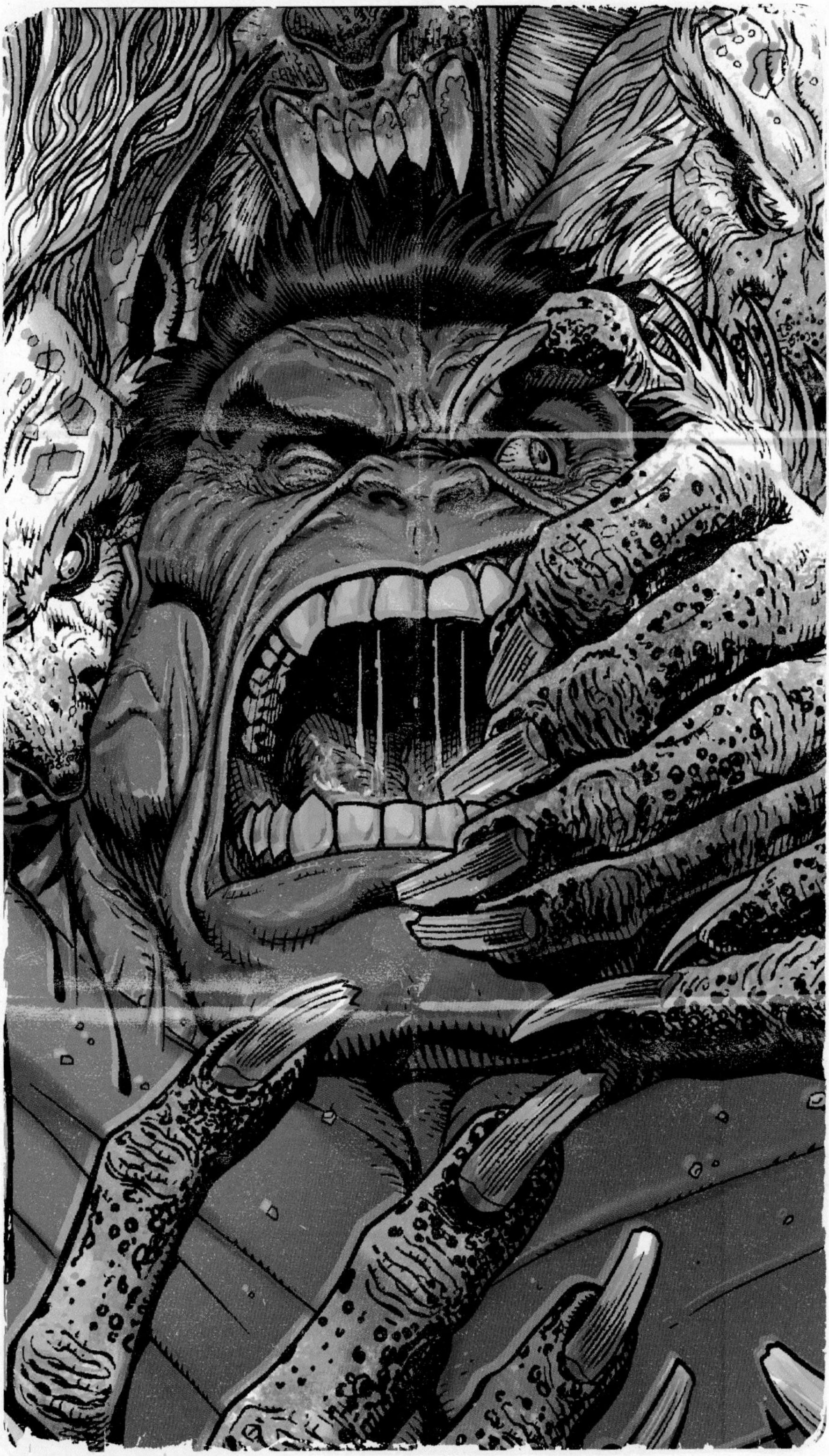

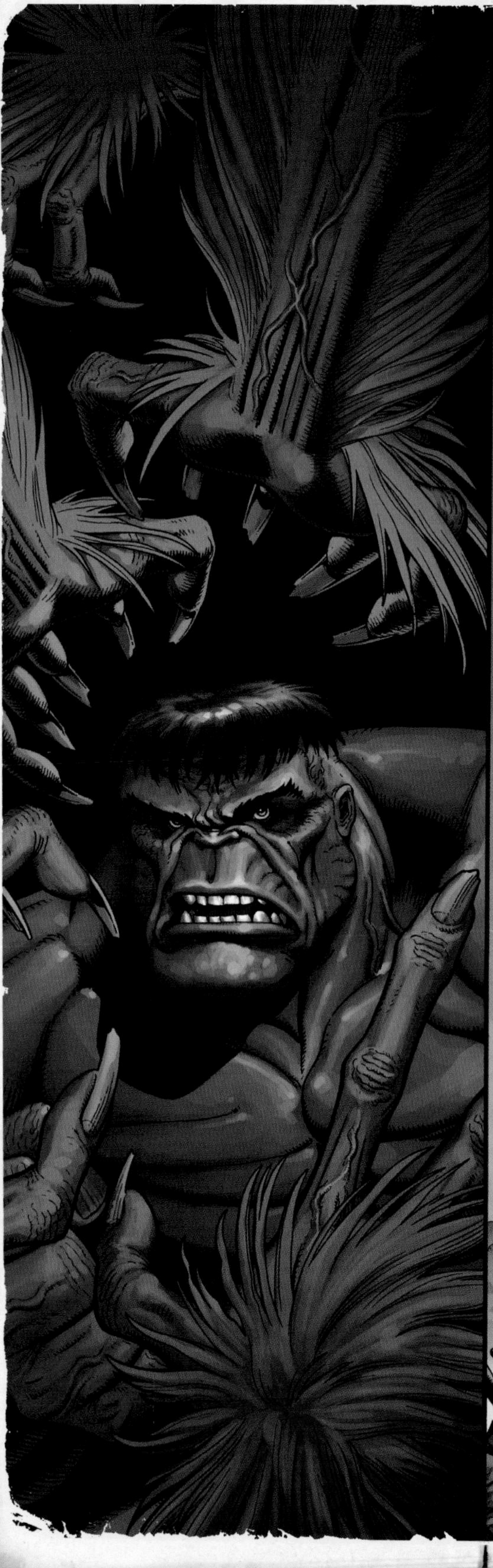

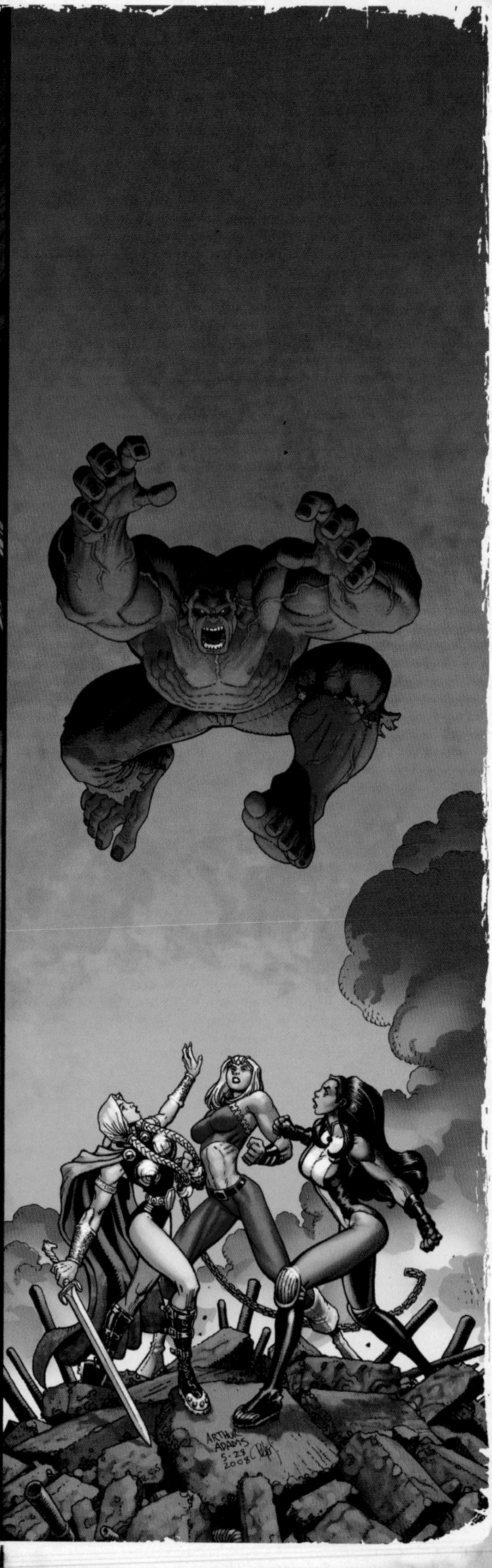
ARTHUR
ADAMS
5-28
2008

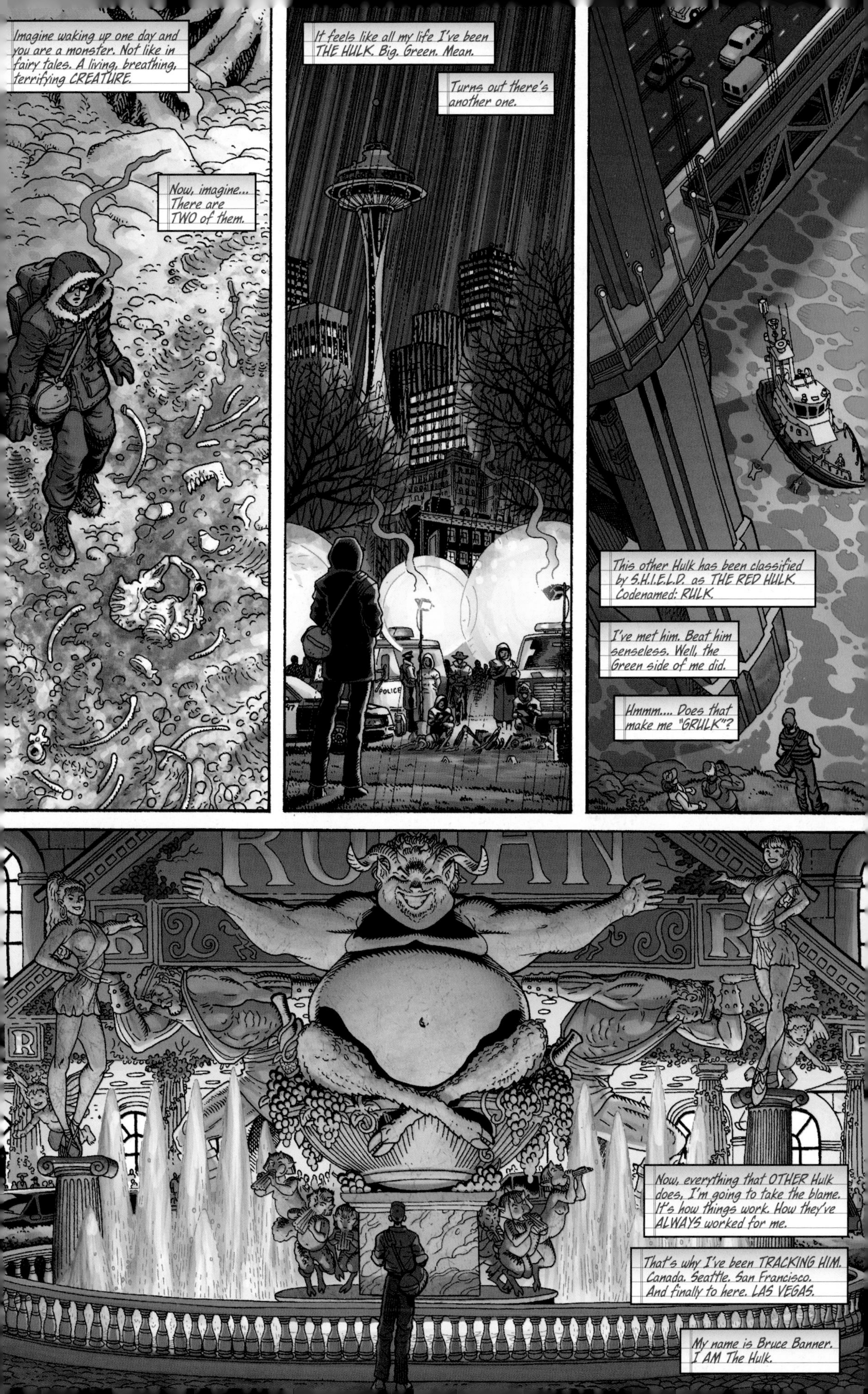
Imagine waking up one day and you are a monster. Not like in fairy tales. A living, breathing, terrifying CREATURE.
Now, imagine... There are TWO of them.
It feels like all my life I've been THE HULK. Big. Green. Mean.
Turns out there's another one.
POLICE
This other Hulk has been classified by S.H.I.E.L.D. as THE RED HULK. Codenamed: RULK.
I've met him. Beat him senseless. Well, the Green side of me did.
Hmmm.... Does that make me "GRULK"?
Now, everything that OTHER Hulk does, I'm going to take the blame. It's how things work. How they've ALWAYS worked for me.
That's why I've been TRACKING HIM. Canada. Seattle. San Francisco. And finally to here. LAS VEGAS.
My name is Bruce Banner. I AM The Hulk.

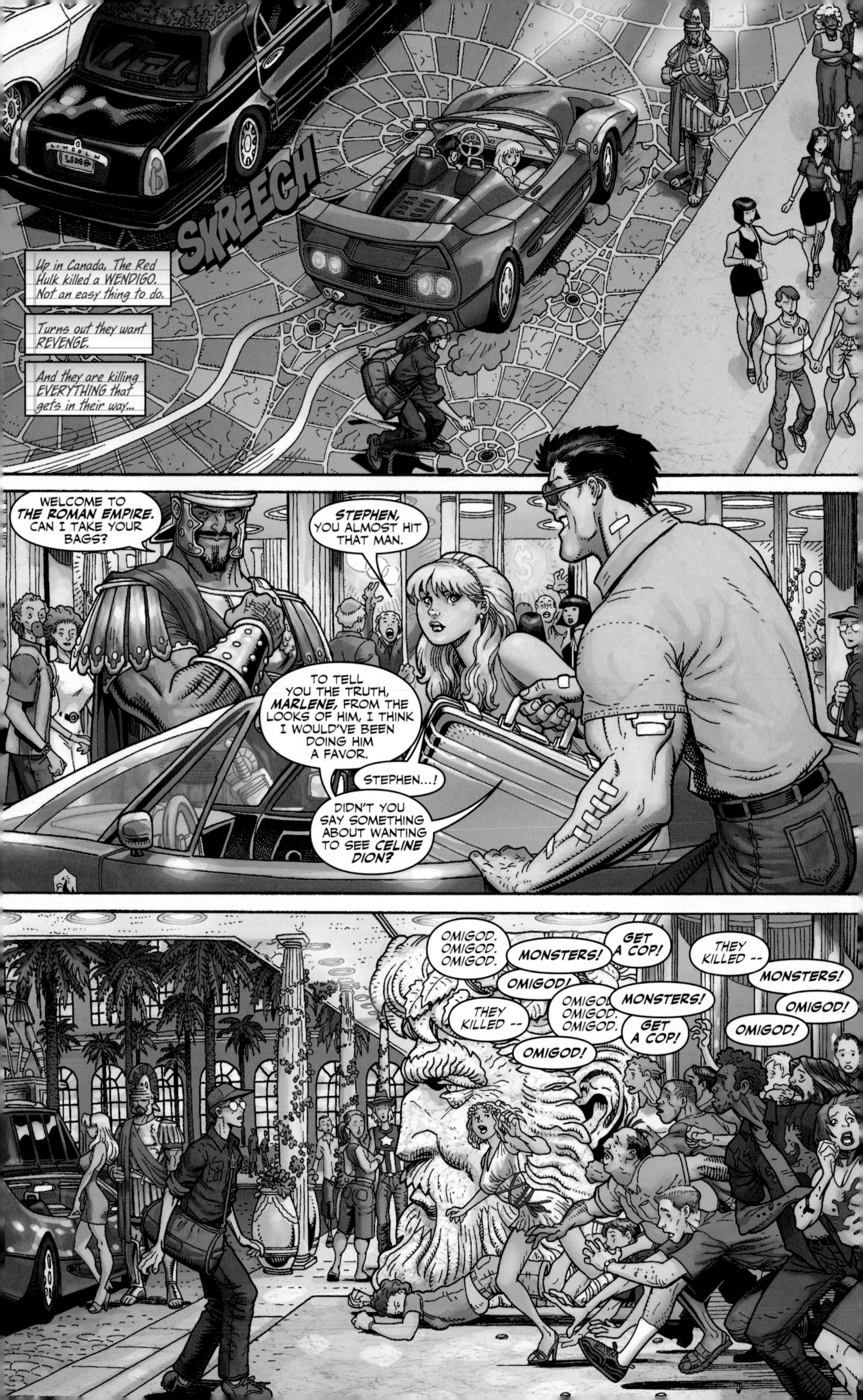
SKREECH
Up in Canada, The Red Hulk killed a WENDIGO. Not an easy thing to do.
Turns out they want REVENGE.
And they are killing EVERYTHING that gets in their way...
WELCOME TO THE ROMAN EMPIRE. CAN I TAKE YOUR BAGS?
STEPHEN, YOU ALMOST HIT THAT MAN.
TO TELL YOU THE TRUTH, MARLENE, FROM THE LOOKS OF HIM, I THINK I WOULD'VE BEEN DOING HIM A FAVOR.
STEPHEN...!
DIDN'T YOU SAY SOMETHING ABOUT WANTING TO SEE CELINE DION?
OMIGOD. OMIGOD. OMIGOD.
MONSTERS!
GET A COP!
THEY KILLED --
MONSTERS!
OMIGOD!
MONSTERS!
THEY KILLED --
OMIGOD. OMIGOD. OMIGOD.
GET A COP!
OMIGOD!
OMIGOD!
OMIGOD!

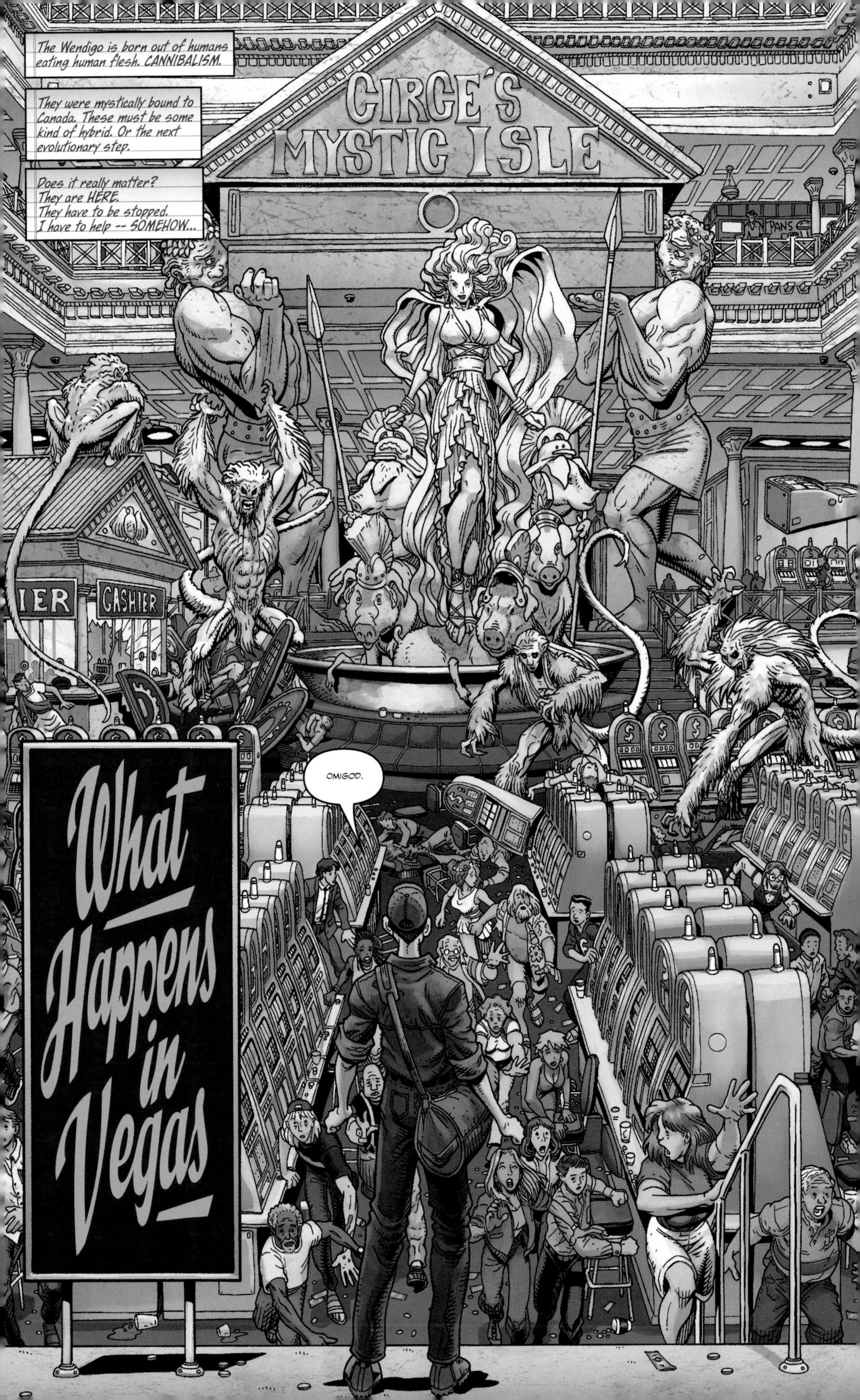
The Wendigo is born out of humans eating human flesh. CANNIBALISM.
They were mystically bound to Canada. These must be some kind of hybrid. Or the next evolutionary step.
Does it really matter? They are HERE. They have to be stopped. I have to help -- SOMEHOW...
CIRCE'S MYSTIC ISLE
CASHIER
IER
OMIGOD.
What Happens in Vegas

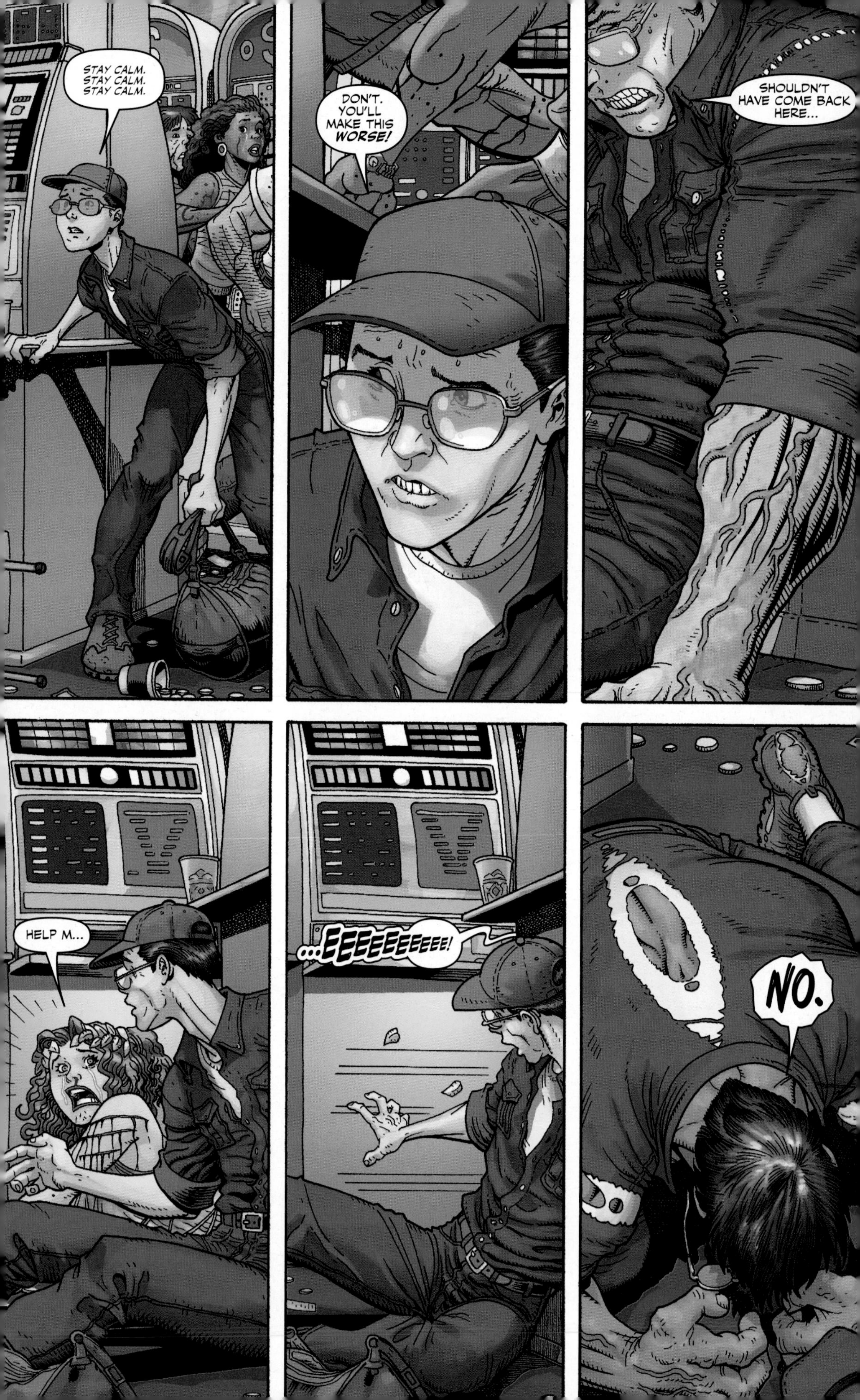
STAY CALM.
STAY CALM.
STAY CALM.
DON'T. YOU'LL MAKE THIS *WORSE!*
SHOULDN'T HAVE COME BACK HERE...
HELP M...
...EEEEEEEEEEE!
NO.

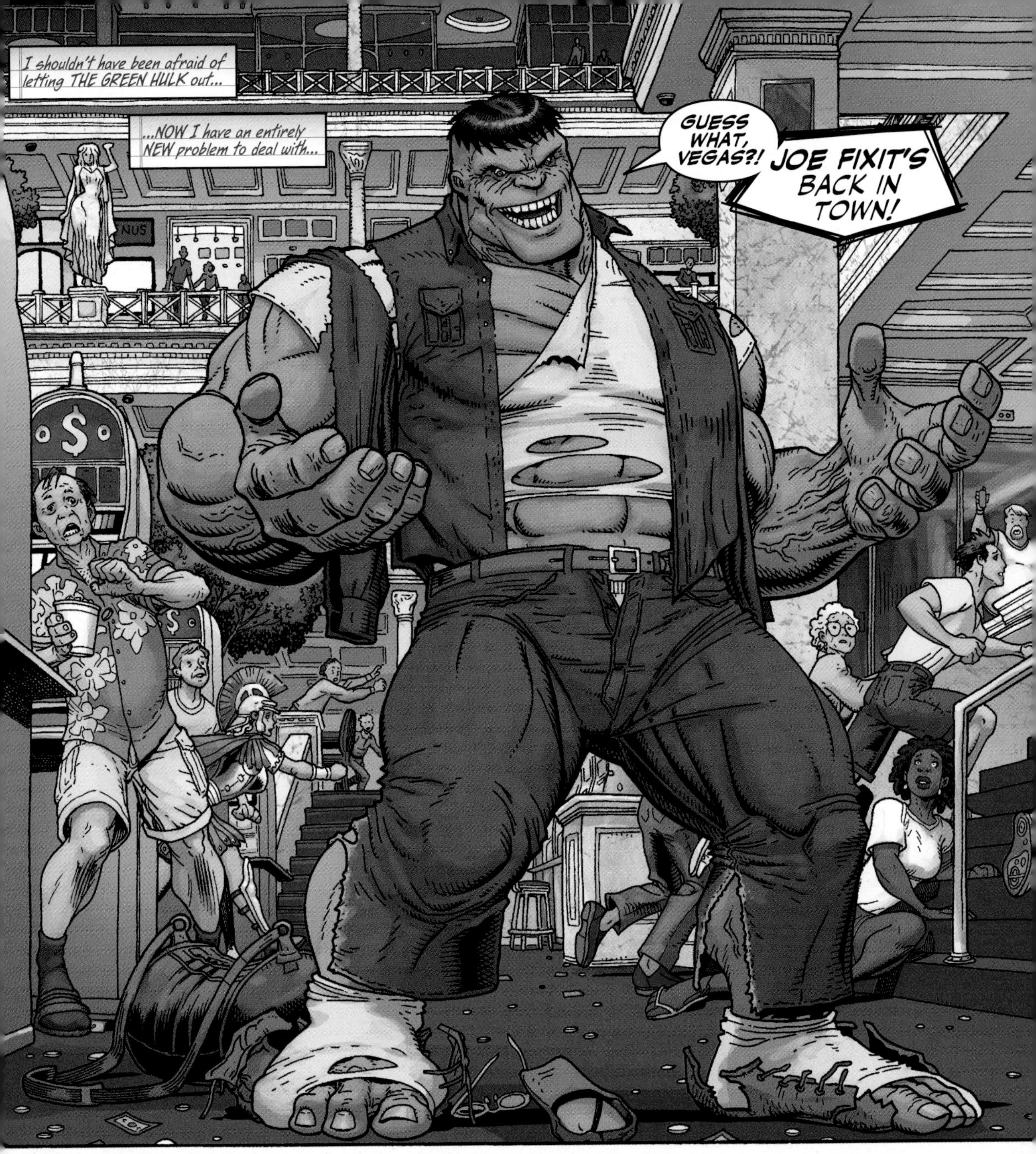
I shouldn't have been afraid of letting THE GREEN HULK out...
...NOW I have an entirely NEW problem to deal with...
GUESS WHAT, VEGAS?!
JOE FIXIT'S BACK IN TOWN!

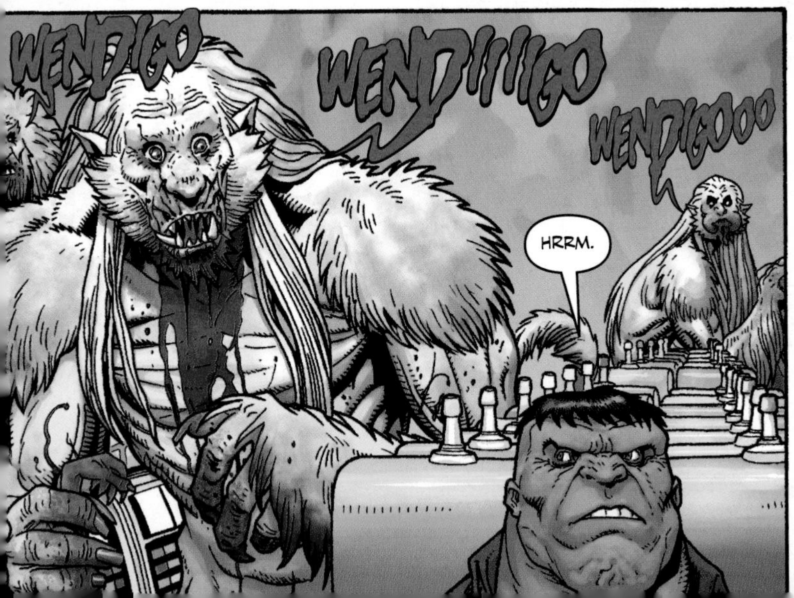
WENDIGO
WENDIIIIGO
WENDIGOOO
HRRM.

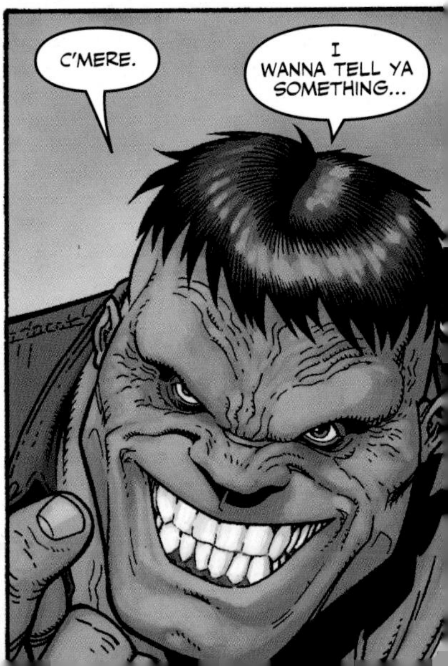
C'MERE.
I WANNA TELL YA SOMETHING...

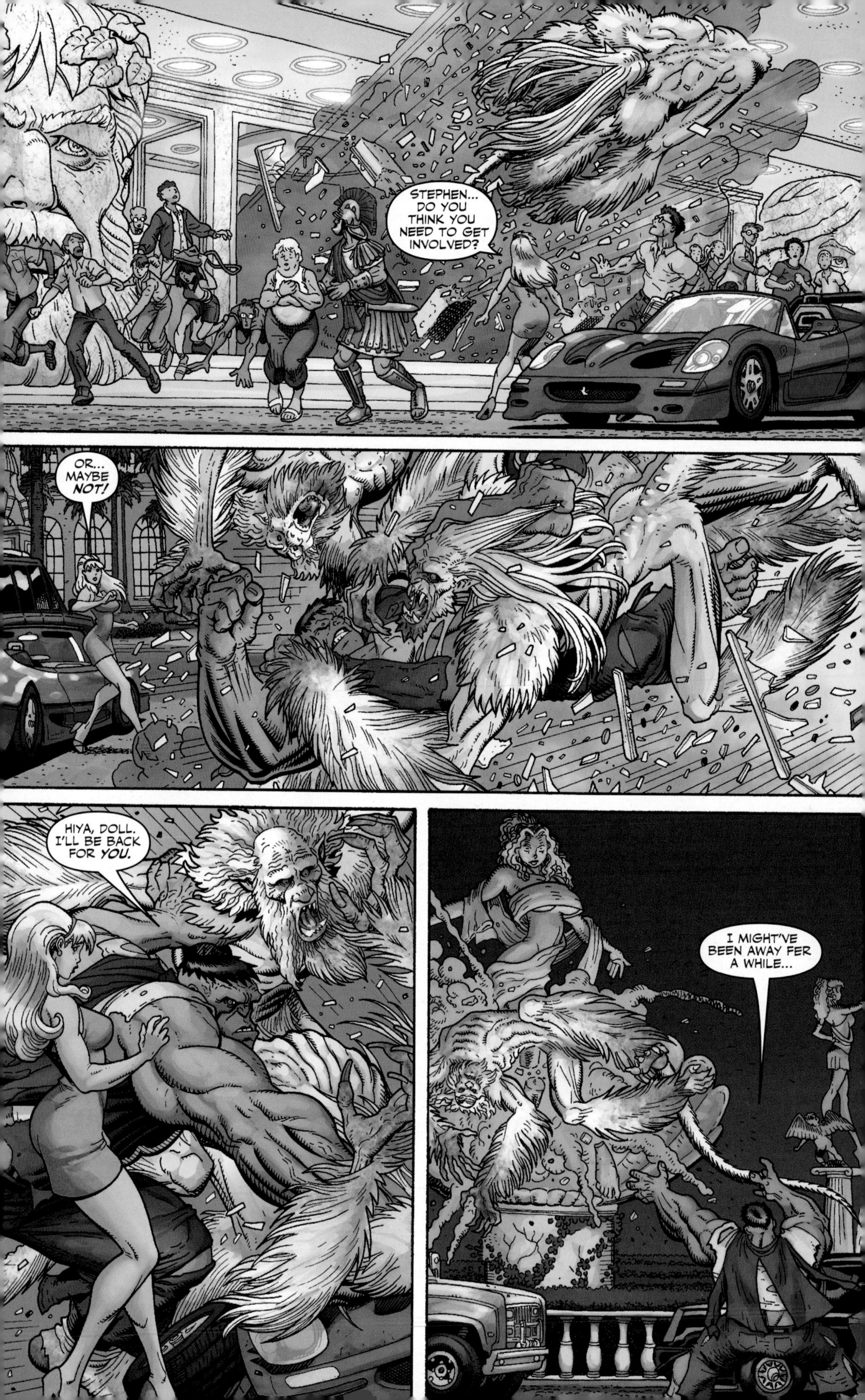
STEPHEN... DO YOU THINK YOU NEED TO GET INVOLVED?
OR... MAYBE NOT!
HIYA, DOLL. I'LL BE BACK FOR YOU.
I MIGHT'VE BEEN AWAY FER A WHILE...

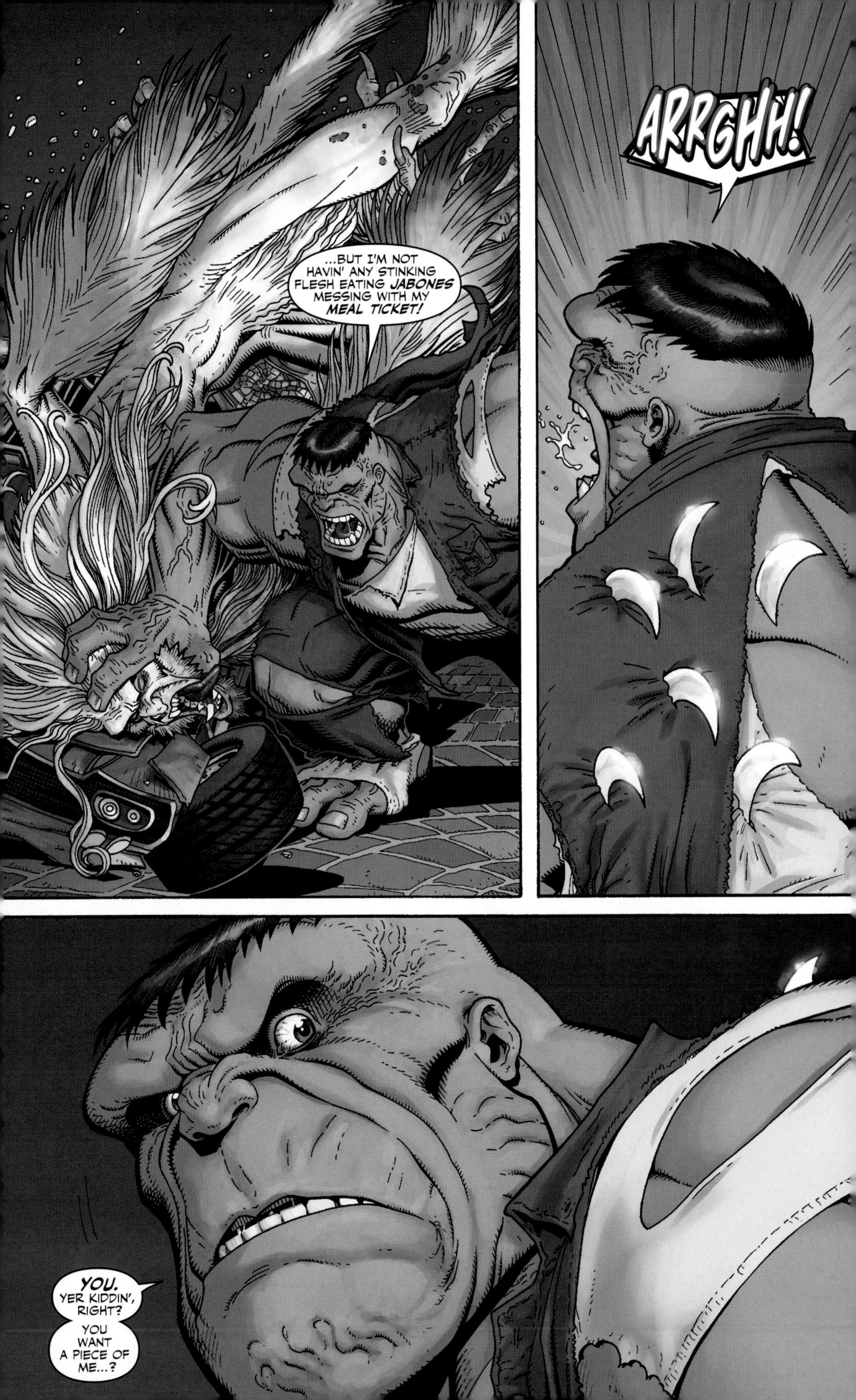
...BUT I'M NOT HAVIN' ANY STINKING FLESH EATING JABONES MESSING WITH MY MEAL TICKET!
ARRGHH!
YOU. YER KIDDIN', RIGHT?
YOU WANT A PIECE OF ME...?

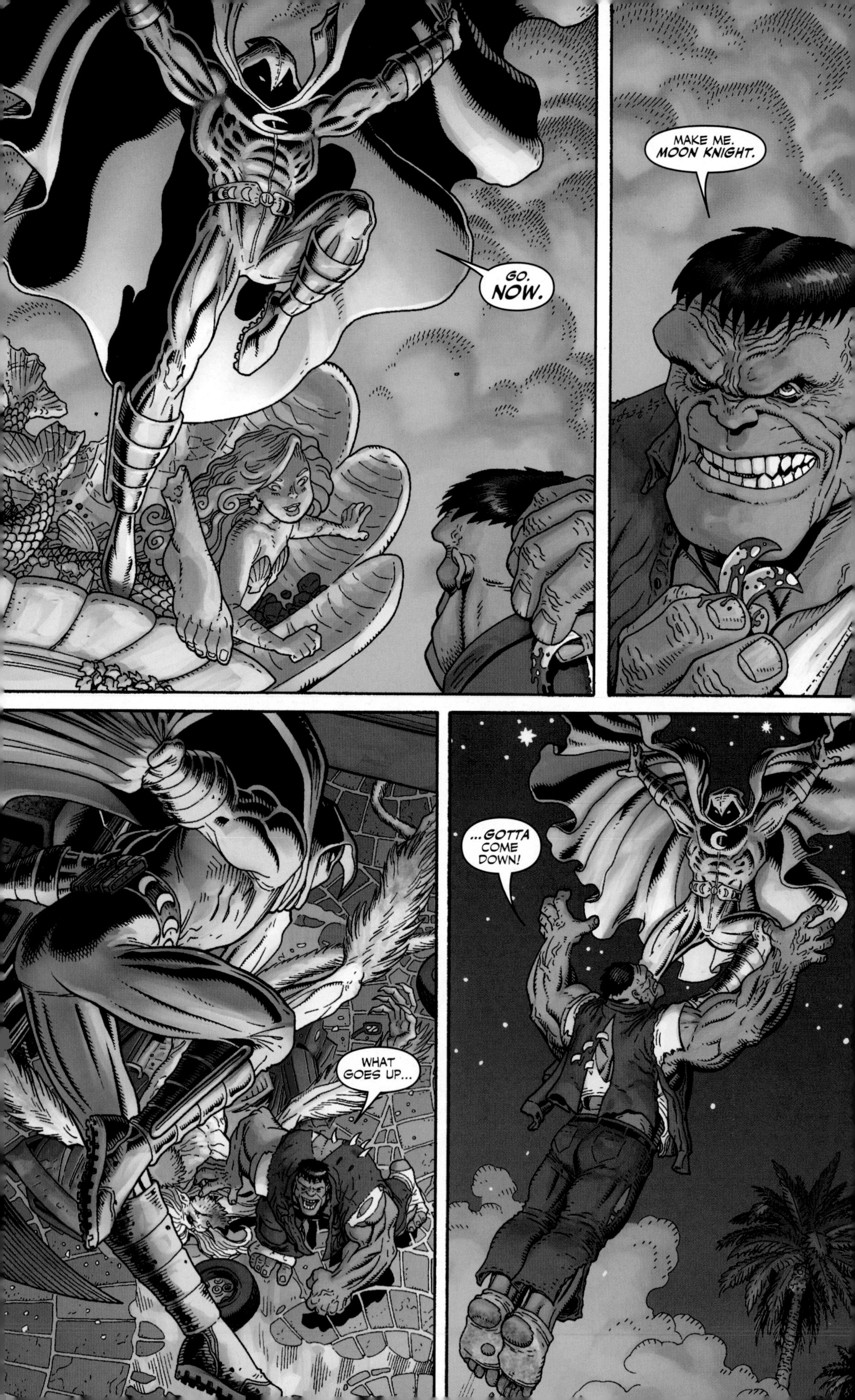
GO. NOW.
MAKE ME. MOON KNIGHT.
WHAT GOES UP...
...GOTTA COME DOWN!

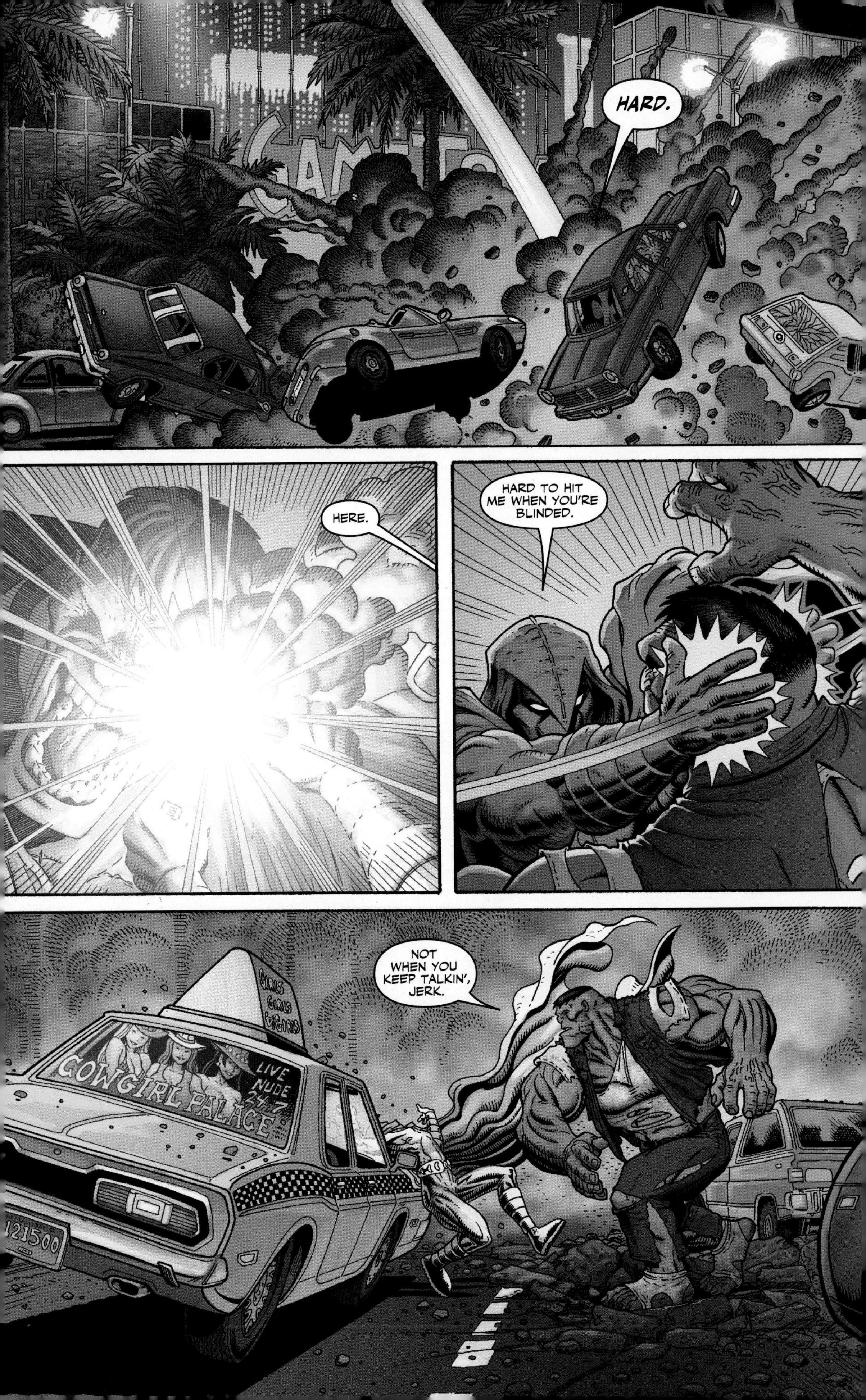
HARD.
HERE.
HARD TO HIT ME WHEN YOU'RE BLINDED.
NOT WHEN YOU KEEP TALKIN', JERK.
GIRLS GIRLS GIRLS
COWGIRL PALACE
LIVE NUDE 24-7
121500

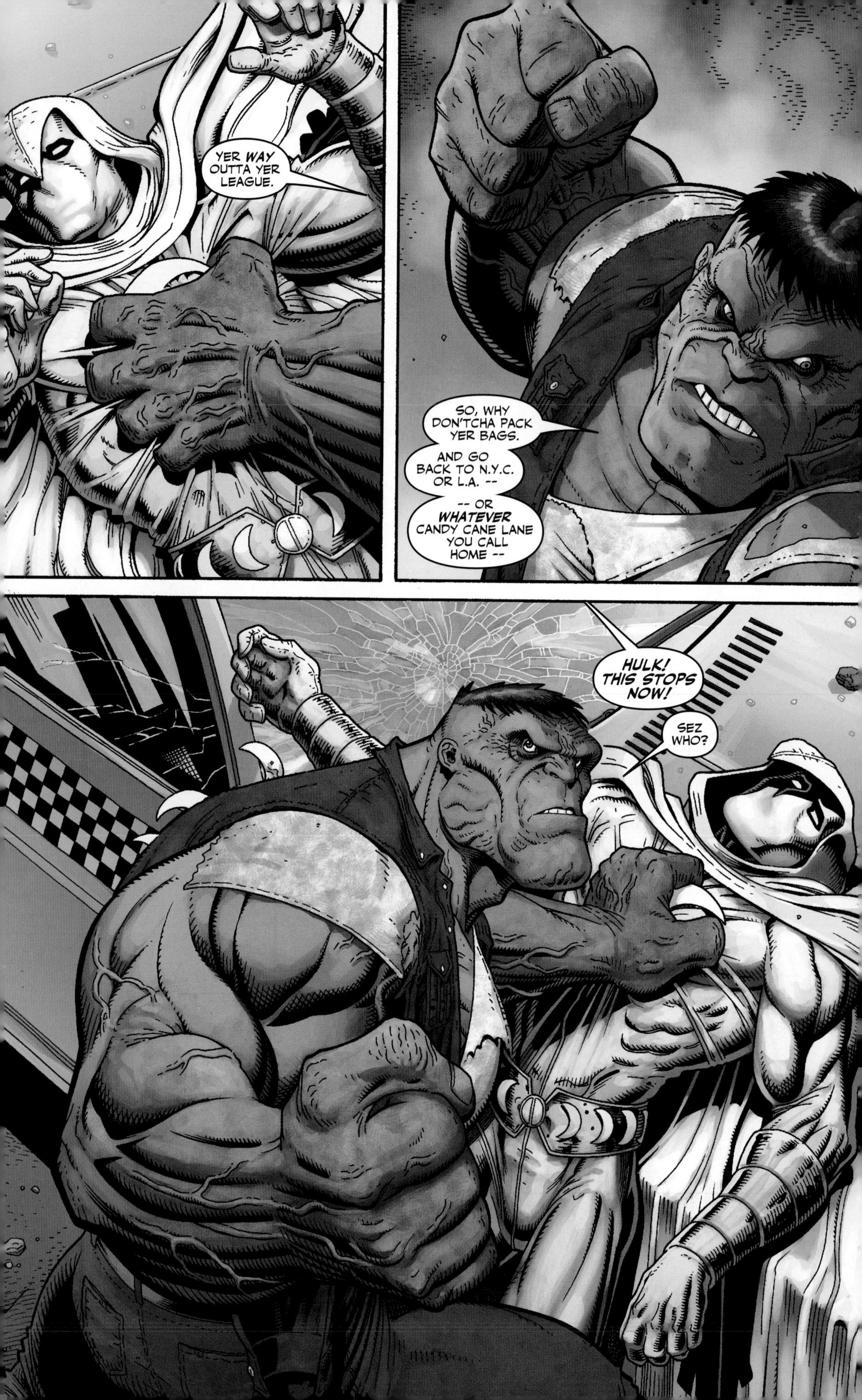
YER WAY OUTTA YER LEAGUE.
SO, WHY DON'TCHA PACK YER BAGS.
AND GO BACK TO N.Y.C. OR L.A. --
-- OR WHATEVER CANDY CANE LANE YOU CALL HOME --
HULK! THIS STOPS NOW!
SEZ WHO?

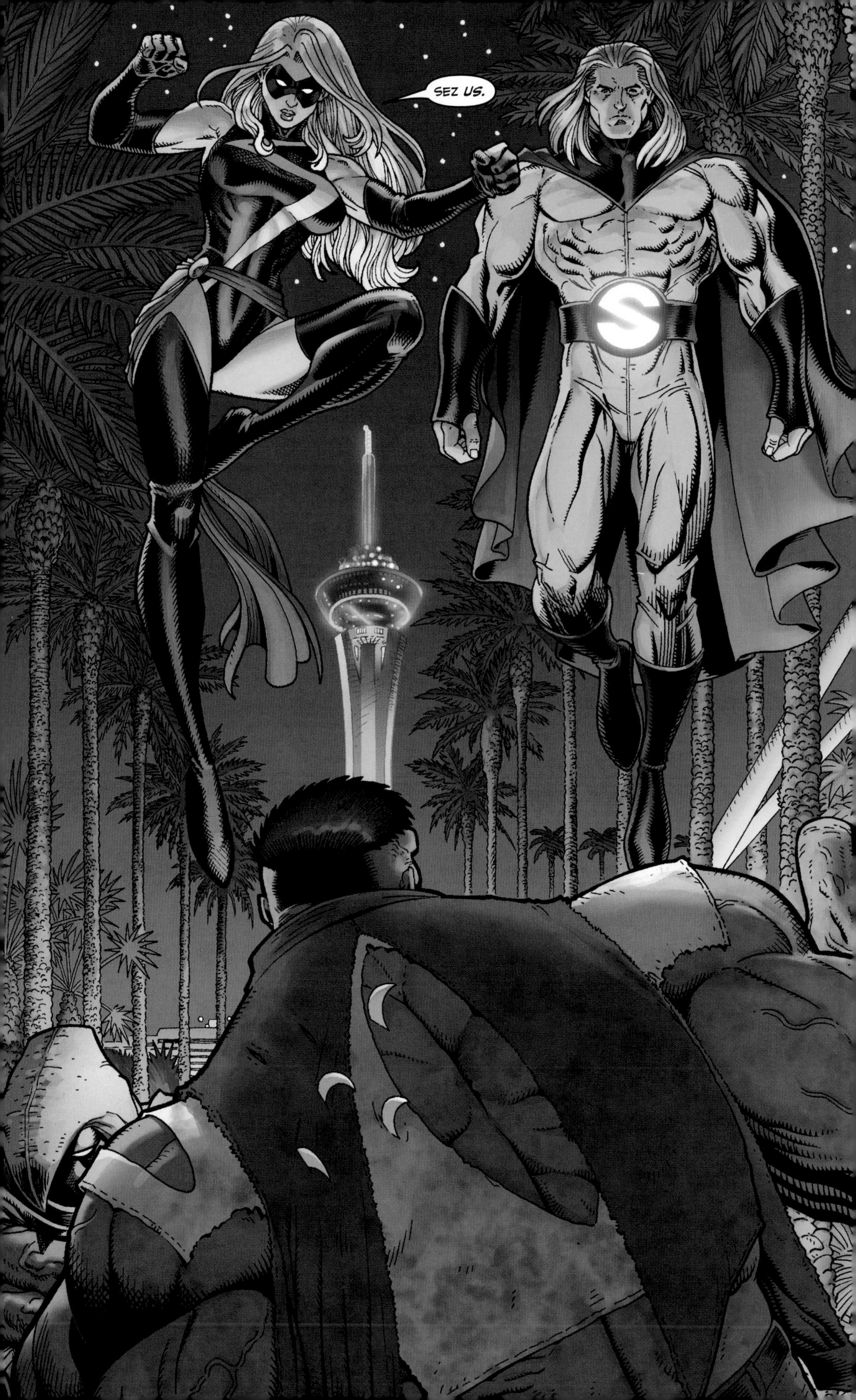
SEZ US.

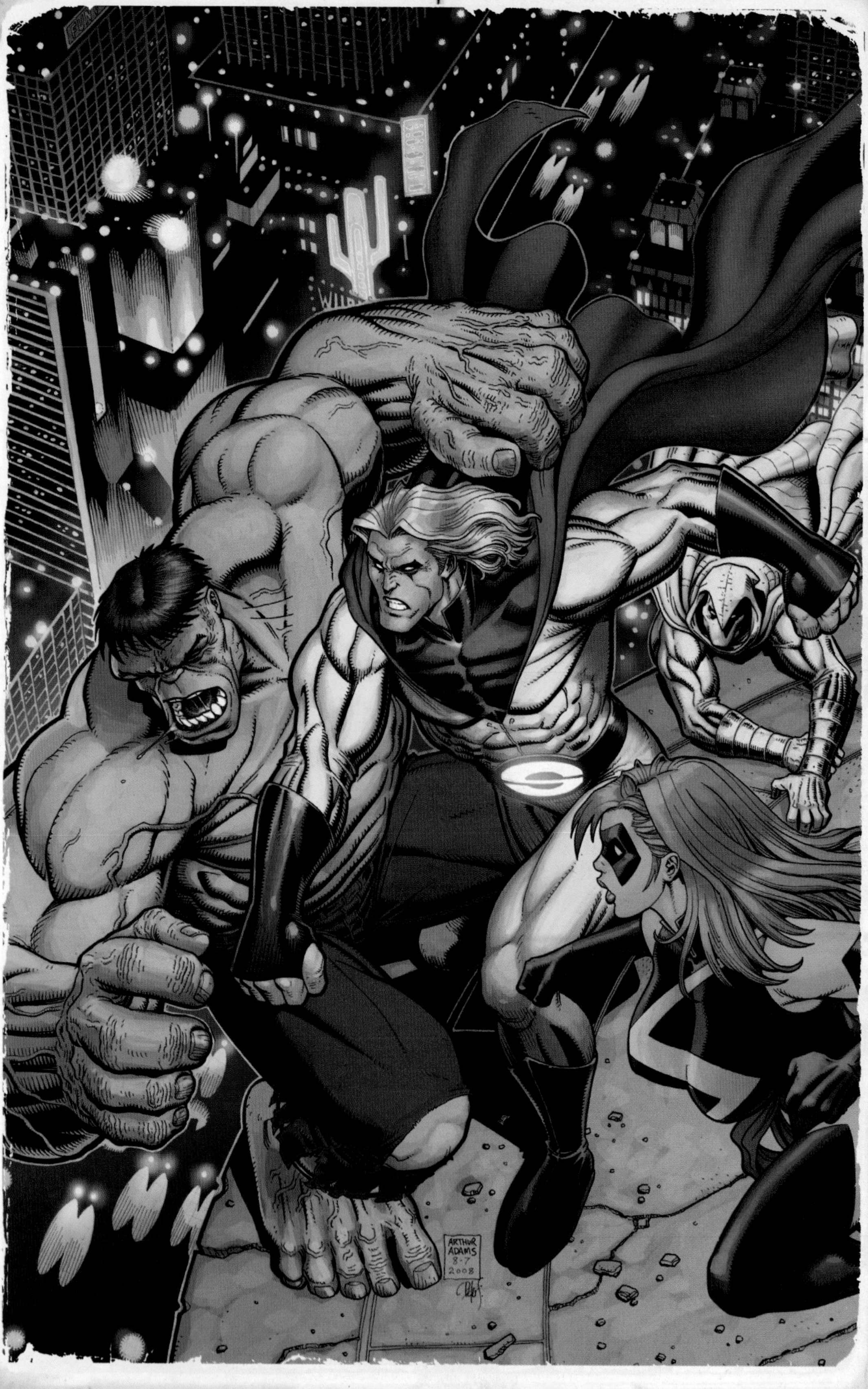
ARTHUR ADAMS
8-7
2008

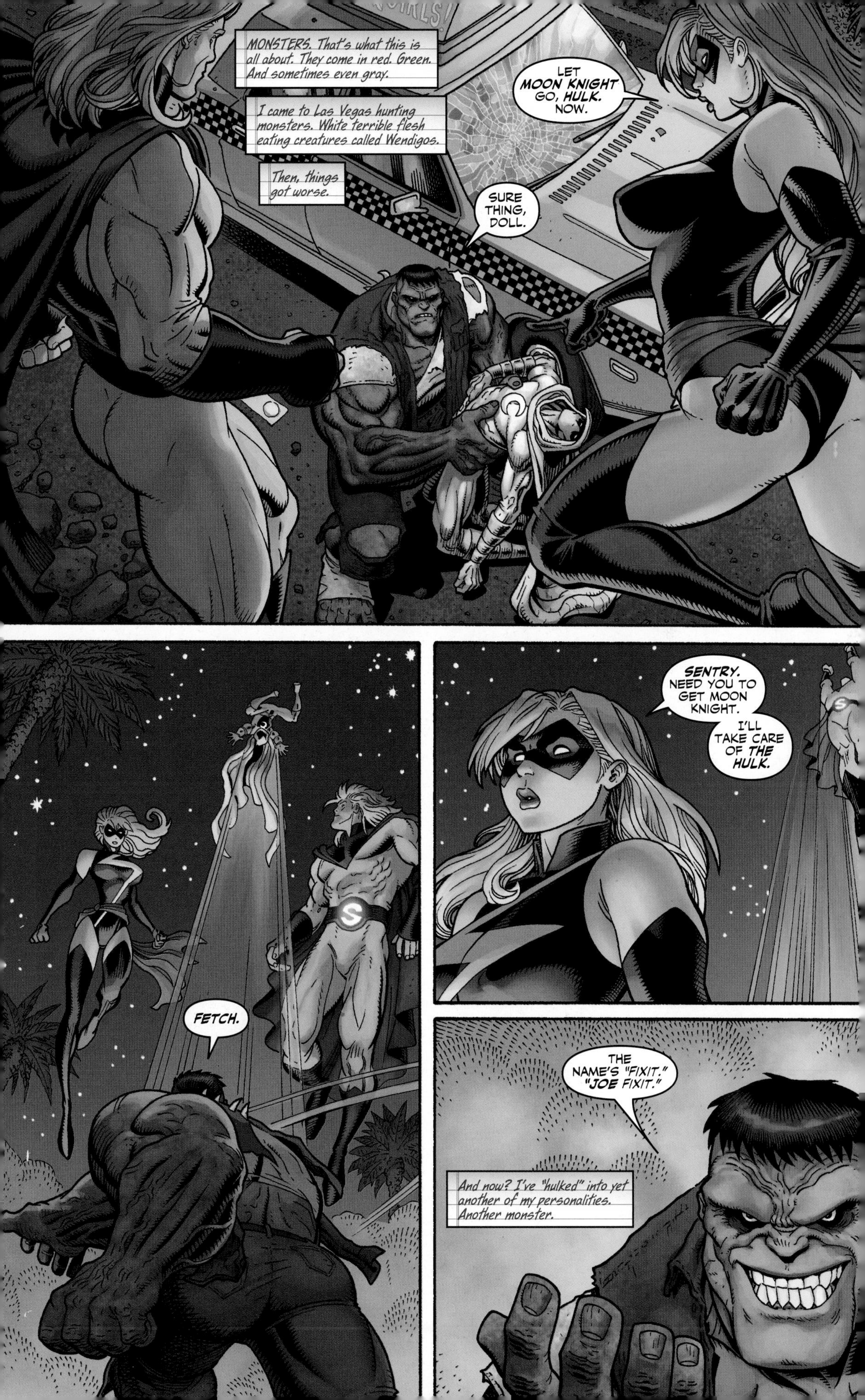

MONSTERS. That's what this is all about. They come in red. Green. And sometimes even gray.
I came to Las Vegas hunting monsters. White terrible flesh eating creatures called Wendigos.
Then, things got worse.
LET MOON KNIGHT GO, HULK. NOW.
SURE THING, DOLL.
FETCH.
SENTRY. NEED YOU TO GET MOON KNIGHT.
I'LL TAKE CARE OF THE HULK.
THE NAME'S "FIXIT." "JOE FIXIT."
And now? I've "hulked" into yet another of my personalities. Another monster.

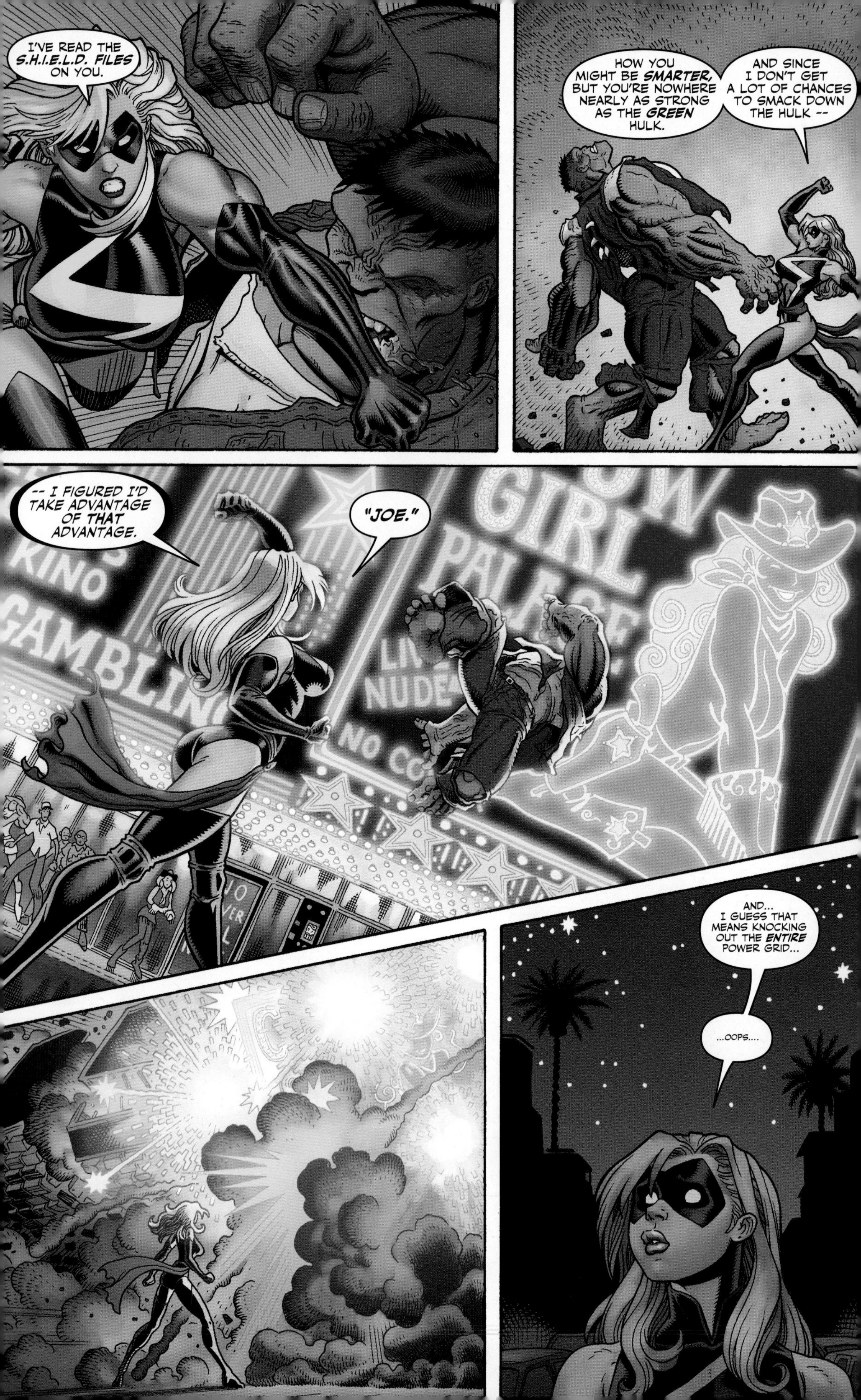

I'VE READ THE S.H.I.E.L.D. FILES ON YOU.
HOW YOU MIGHT BE SMARTER, BUT YOU'RE NOWHERE NEARLY AS STRONG AS THE GREEN HULK.
AND SINCE I DON'T GET A LOT OF CHANCES TO SMACK DOWN THE HULK --
-- I FIGURED I'D TAKE ADVANTAGE OF THAT ADVANTAGE.
"JOE."
GIRL
PALACE
KINO
GAMBLING
NUDE
NO CO
AND... I GUESS THAT MEANS KNOCKING OUT THE ENTIRE POWER GRID...
...OOPS....

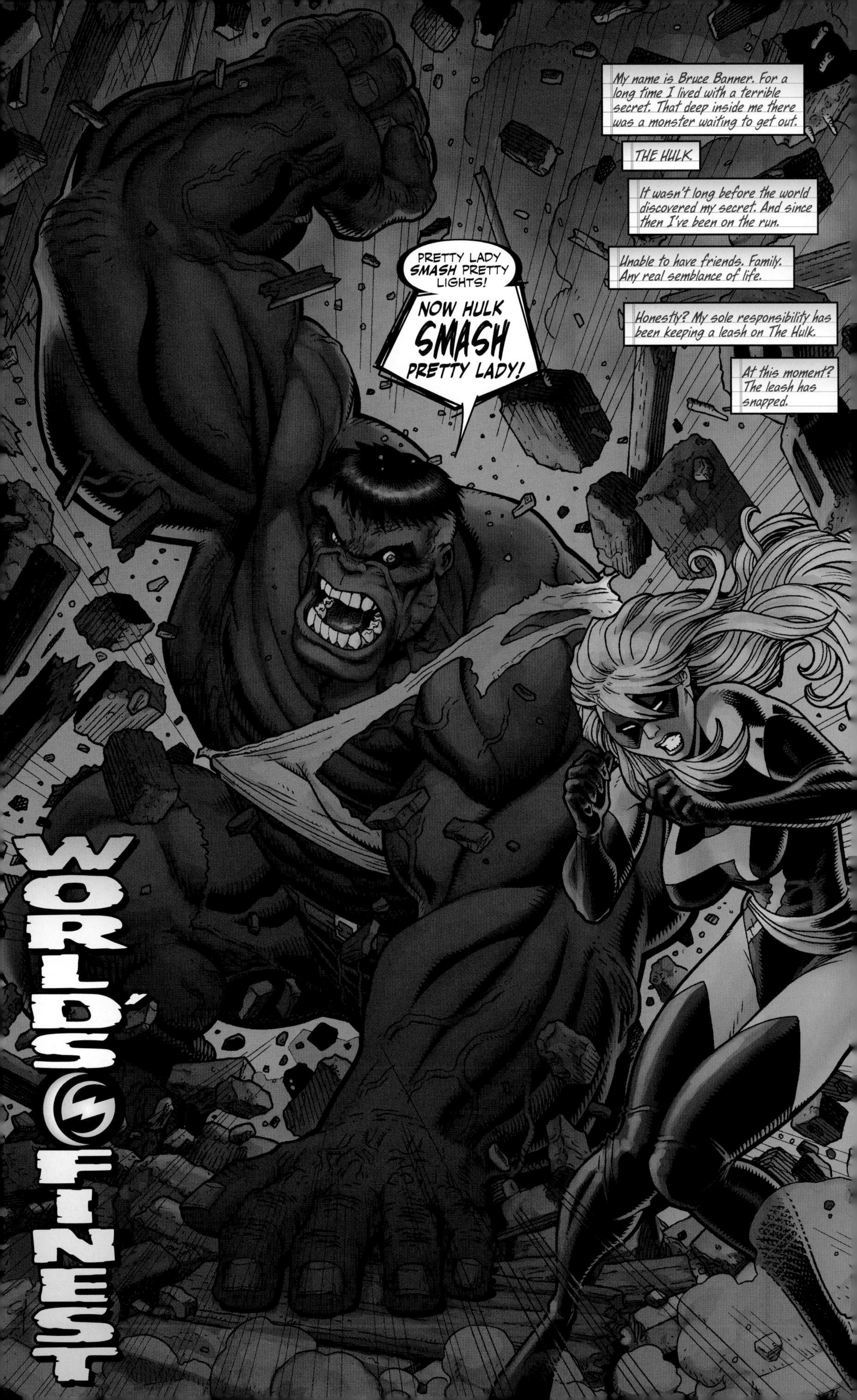
My name is Bruce Banner. For a long time I lived with a terrible secret. That deep inside me there was a monster waiting to get out.
THE HULK.
It wasn't long before the world discovered my secret. And since then I've been on the run.
Unable to have friends. Family. Any real semblance of life.
Honestly? My sole responsibility has been keeping a leash on The Hulk.
At this moment? The leash has snapped.
PRETTY LADY SMASH PRETTY LIGHTS!
NOW HULK SMASH PRETTY LADY!
WORLDS' FINEST

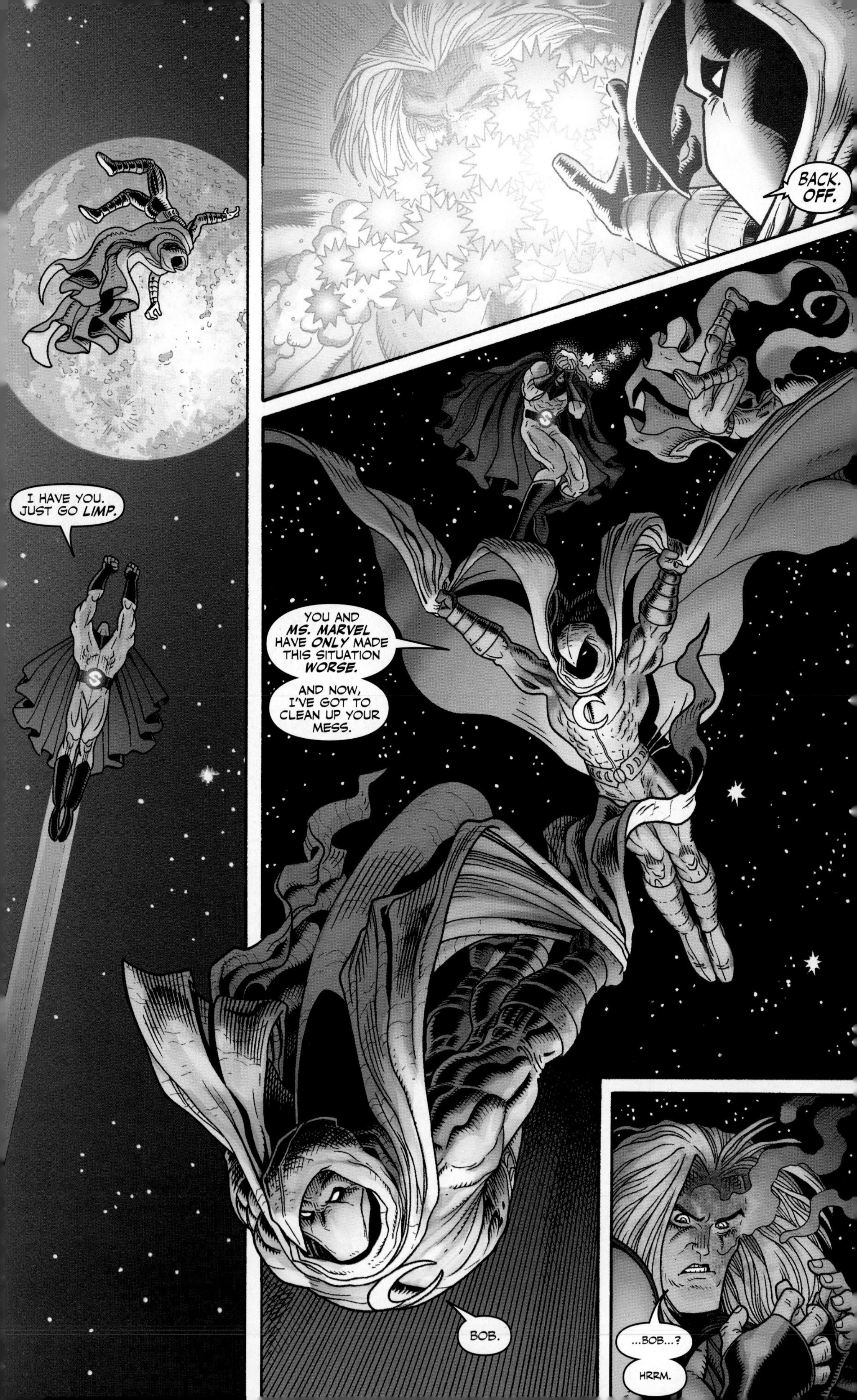
I HAVE YOU.
JUST GO LIMP.
BACK.
OFF.
YOU AND
MS. MARVEL
HAVE ONLY MADE
THIS SITUATION
WORSE.
AND NOW,
I'VE GOT TO
CLEAN UP YOUR
MESS.
BOB.
...BOB...?
HRRM.

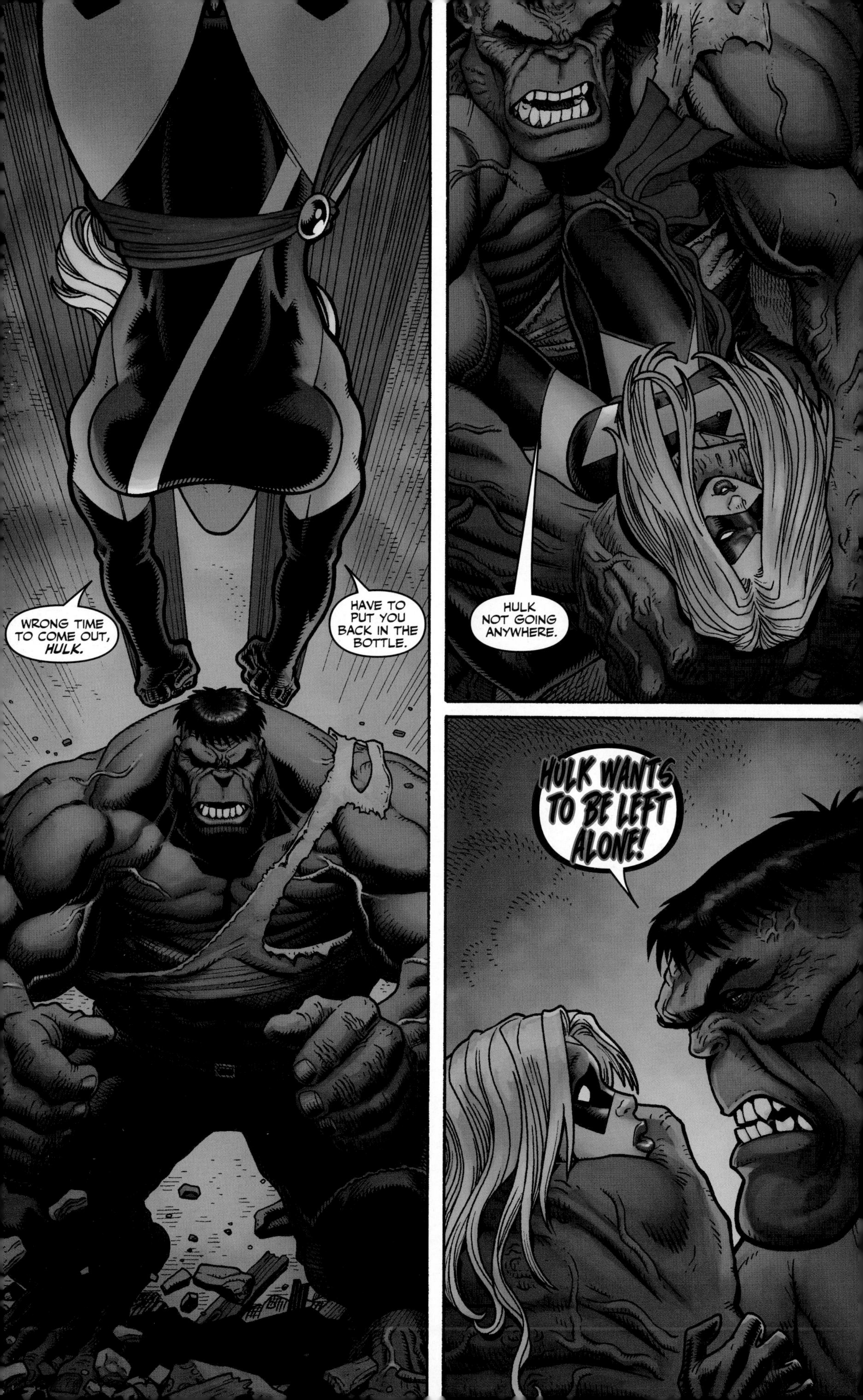
WRONG TIME TO COME OUT, HULK.
HAVE TO PUT YOU BACK IN THE BOTTLE.
HULK NOT GOING ANYWHERE.
HULK WANTS TO BE LEFT ALONE!

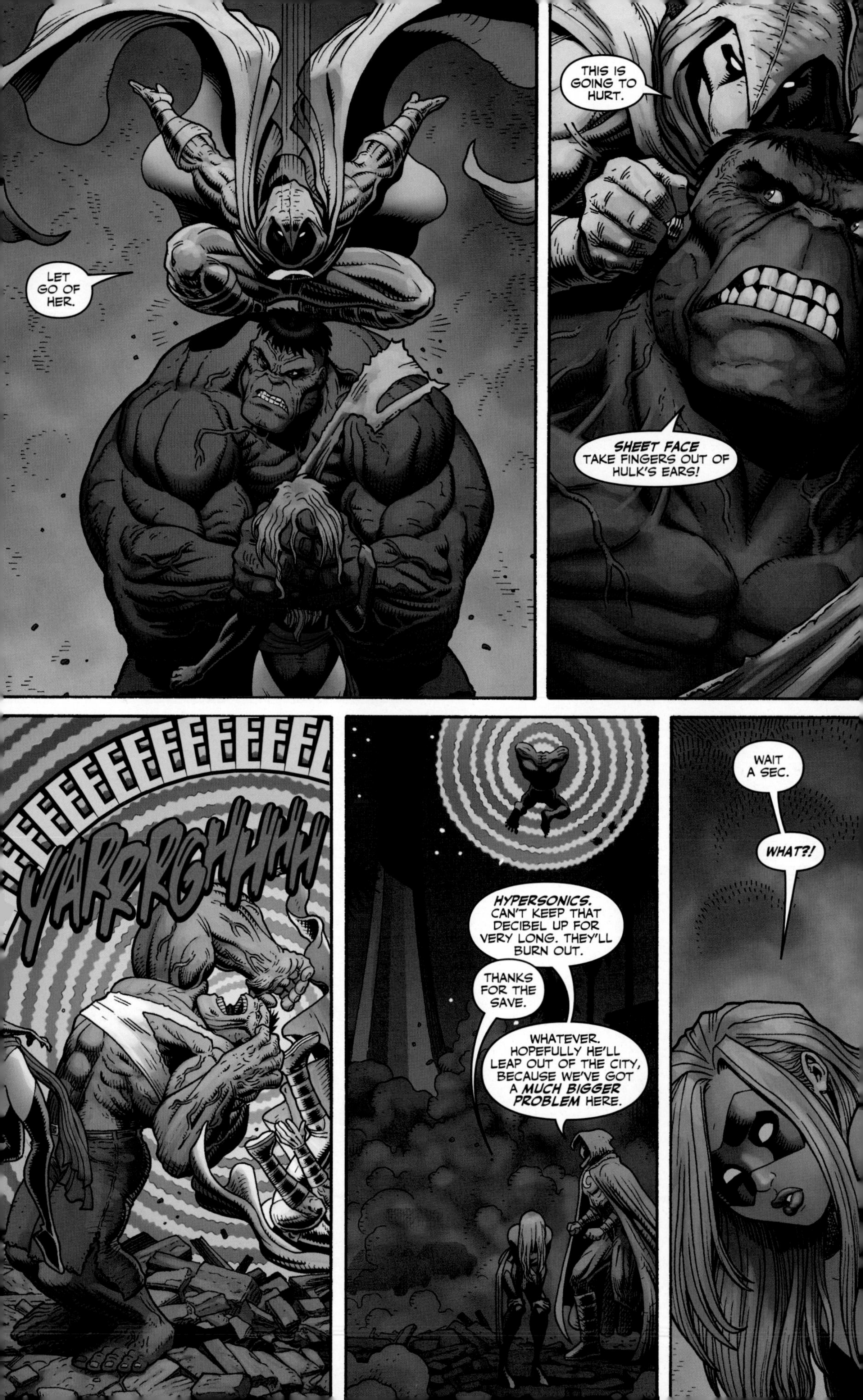
LET GO OF HER.
THIS IS GOING TO HURT.
SHEET FACE TAKE FINGERS OUT OF HULK'S EARS!
EEEEEEEEEEEEEEEEEE
YARRRGHHHH
HYPERSONICS. CAN'T KEEP THAT DECIBEL UP FOR VERY LONG. THEY'LL BURN OUT.
THANKS FOR THE SAVE.
WHATEVER. HOPEFULLY HE'LL LEAP OUT OF THE CITY, BECAUSE WE'VE GOT A MUCH BIGGER PROBLEM HERE.
WAIT A SEC.
WHAT?!

GRRRRR

HULK. YOU HAVE TO LISTEN TO ME.

WE NEED YOU TO GET OUT OF ANY *POPULATED* AREA.

WE USED TO BE FRIENDS --

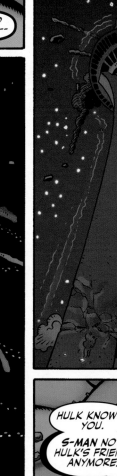

HULK KNOWS YOU.

S-MAN NOT HULK'S FRIEND ANYMORE!

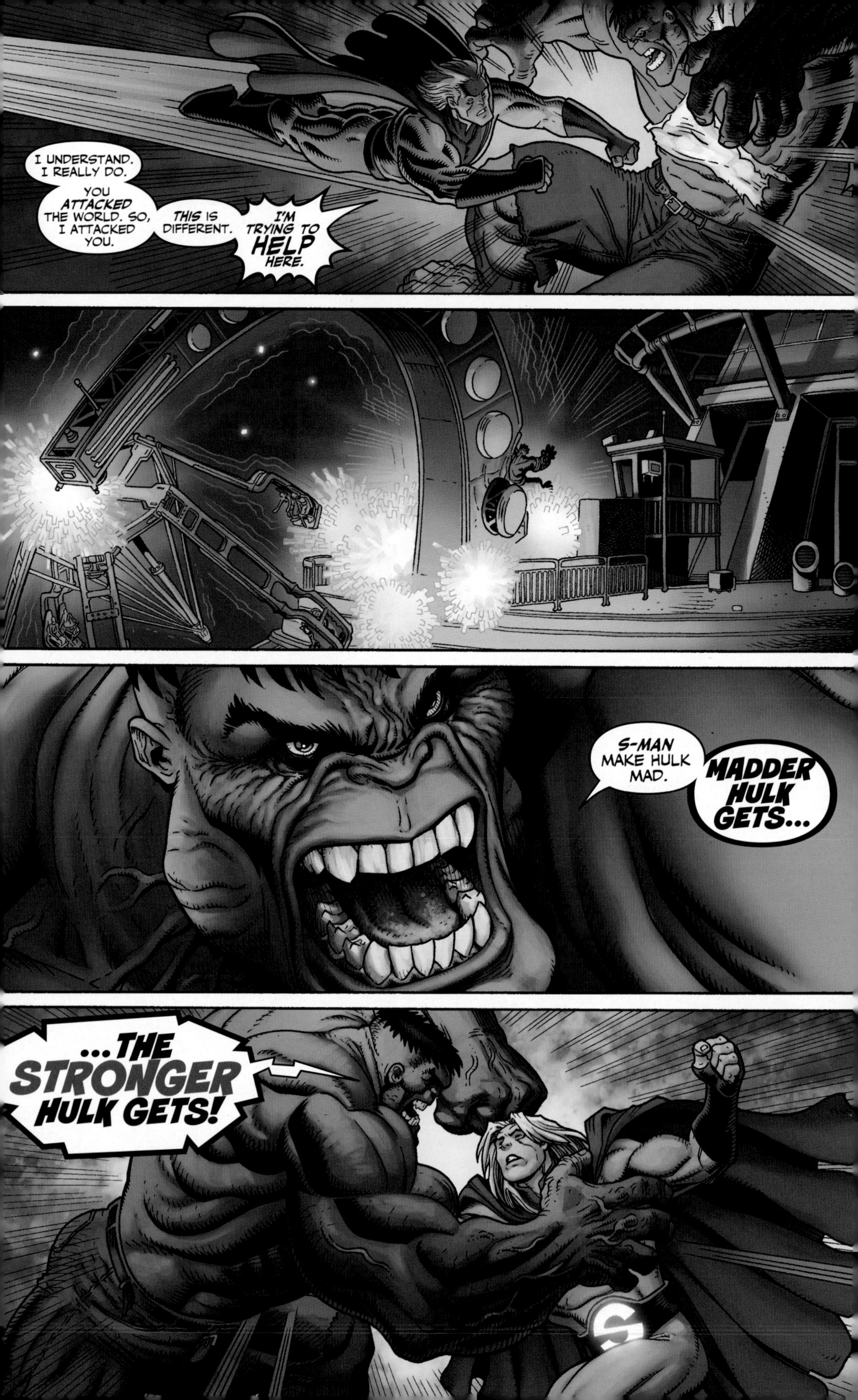
I UNDERSTAND. I REALLY DO.
YOU ATTACKED THE WORLD. SO, I ATTACKED YOU.
THIS IS DIFFERENT.
I'M TRYING TO HELP HERE.
S-MAN MAKE HULK MAD.
MADDER HULK GETS...
...THE STRONGER HULK GETS!

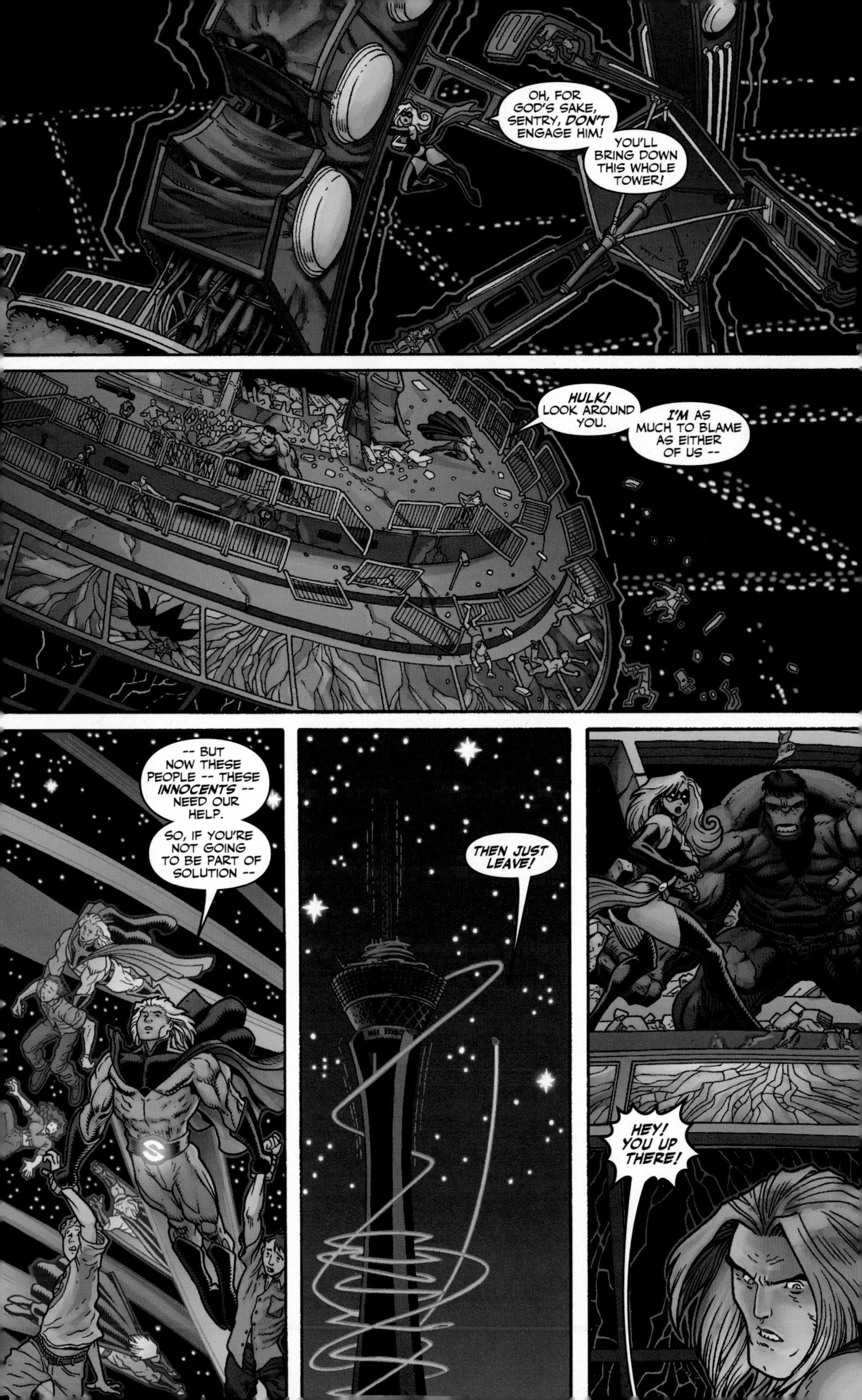
OH, FOR GOD'S SAKE, SENTRY, DON'T ENGAGE HIM!
YOU'LL BRING DOWN THIS WHOLE TOWER!
HULK! LOOK AROUND YOU.
I'M AS MUCH TO BLAME AS EITHER OF US --
-- BUT NOW THESE PEOPLE -- THESE INNOCENTS -- NEED OUR HELP.
SO, IF YOU'RE NOT GOING TO BE PART OF SOLUTION --
THEN JUST LEAVE!
HEY! YOU UP THERE!

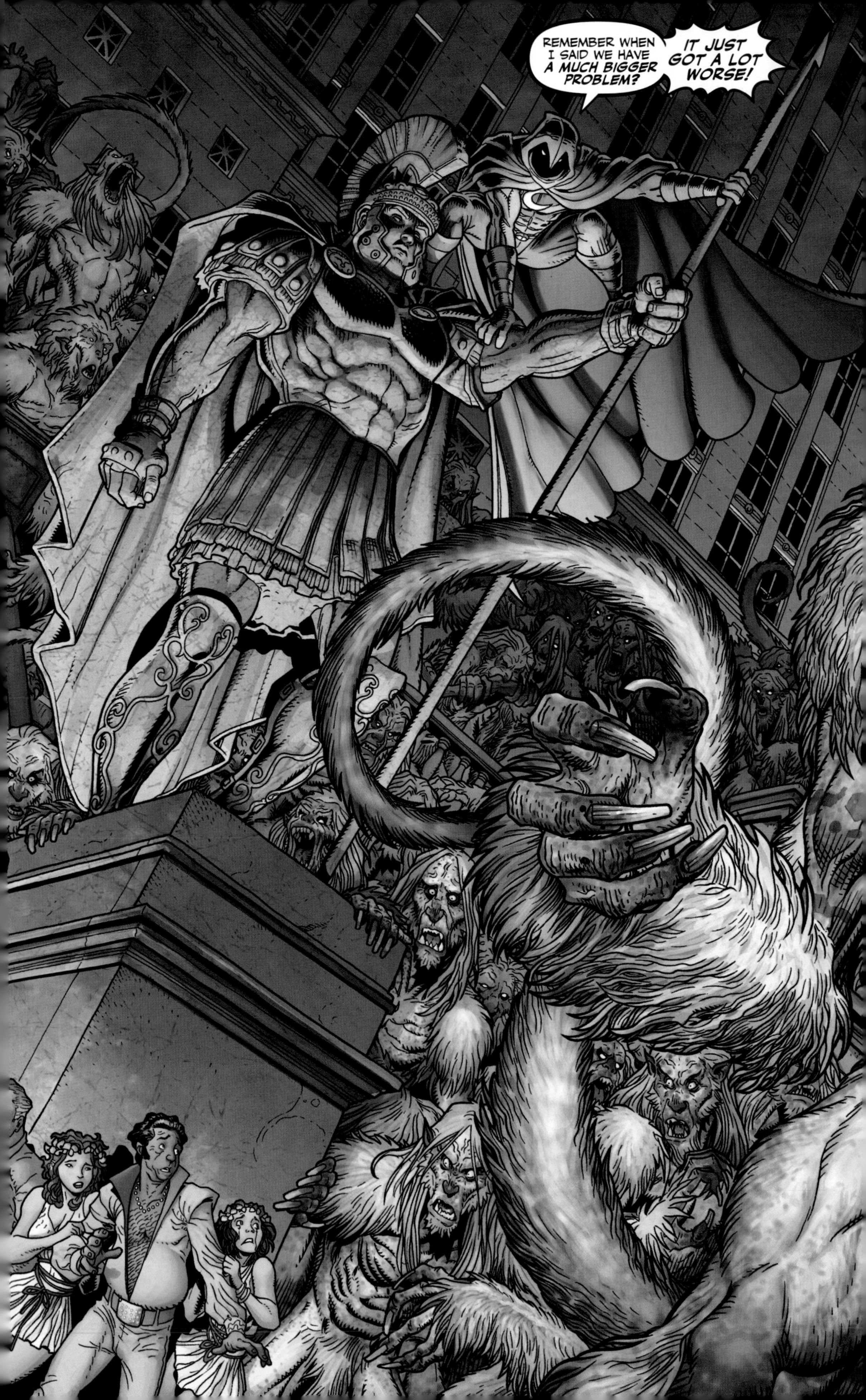
REMEMBER WHEN I SAID WE HAVE A MUCH BIGGER PROBLEM?
IT JUST GOT A LOT WORSE!

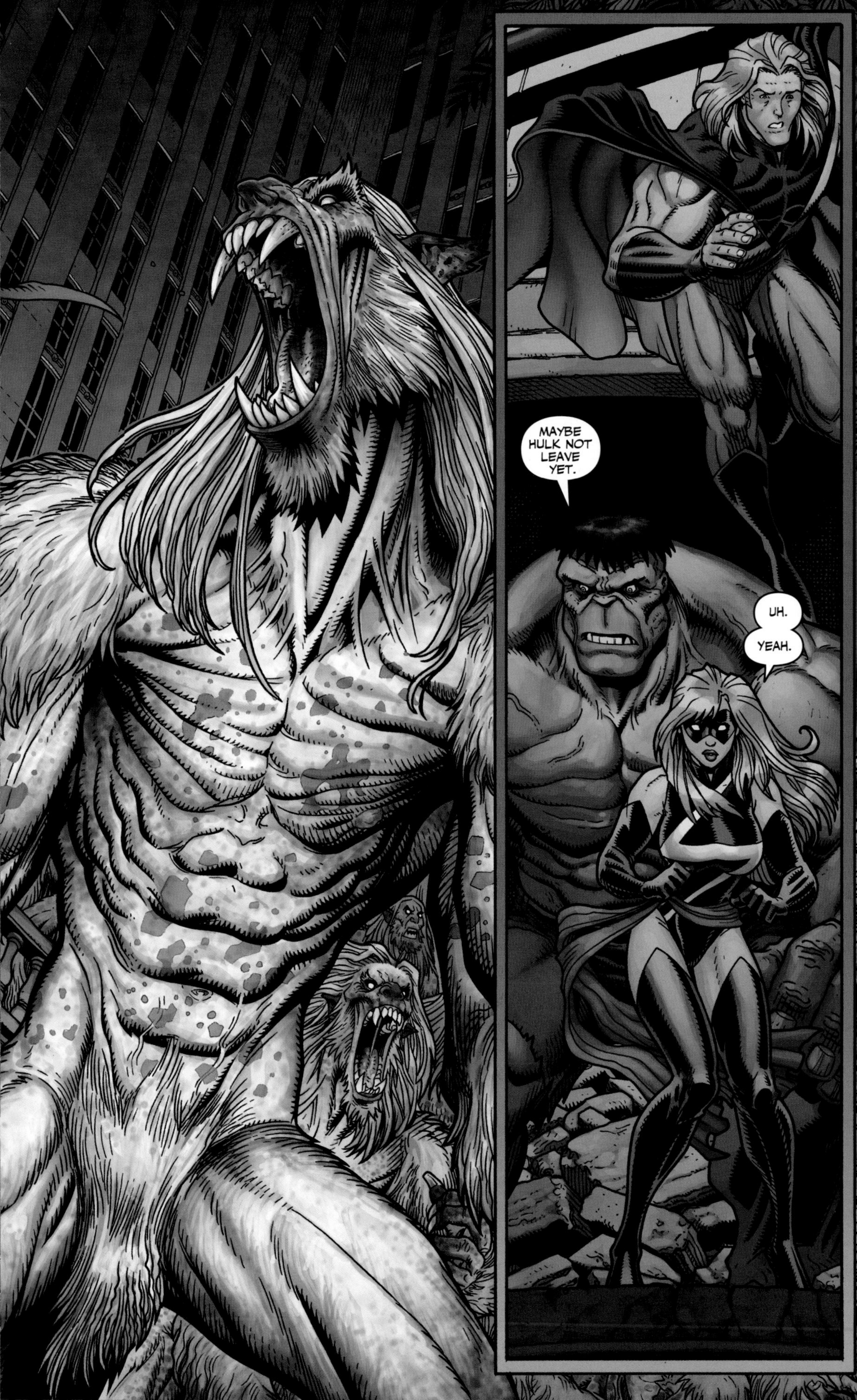
MAYBE HULK NOT LEAVE YET.
UH.
YEAH.

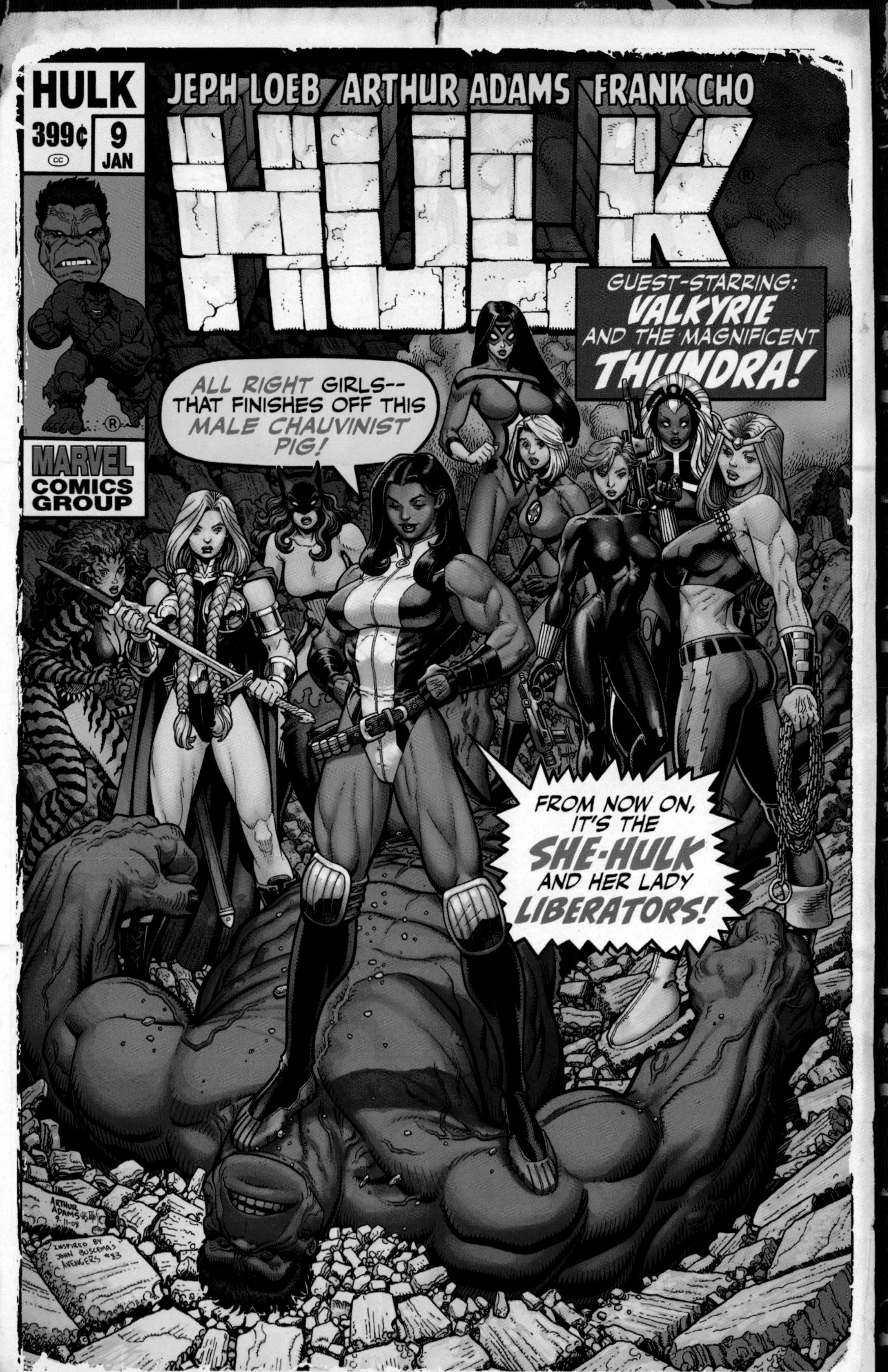

HULK
399¢
9
JAN
JEPH LOEB ARTHUR ADAMS FRANK CHO
HULK
MARVEL COMICS GROUP
GUEST-STARRING: VALKYRIE AND THE MAGNIFICENT THUNDRA!
ALL RIGHT GIRLS-- THAT FINISHES OFF THIS MALE CHAUVINIST PIG!
FROM NOW ON, IT'S THE SHE-HULK AND HER LADY LIBERATORS!
ARTHUR ADAMS 9-11-08
INSPIRED BY JOHN BUSCEMA'S AVENGERS #83

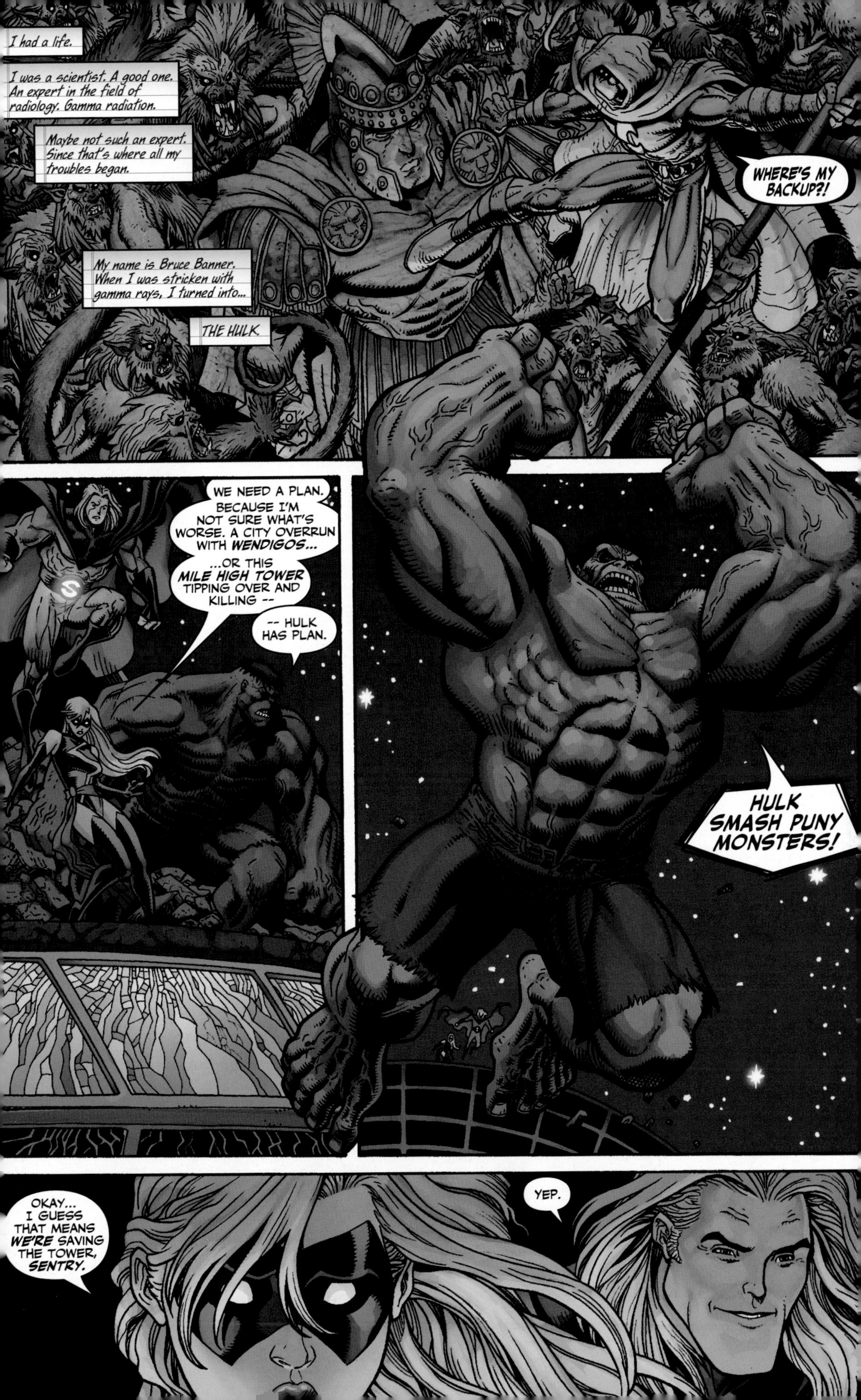
I had a life.
I was a scientist. A good one. An expert in the field of radiology. Gamma radiation.
Maybe not such an expert. Since that's where all my troubles began.
WHERE'S MY BACKUP?!
My name is Bruce Banner. When I was stricken with gamma rays, I turned into...
THE HULK.
WE NEED A PLAN. BECAUSE I'M NOT SURE WHAT'S WORSE. A CITY OVERRUN WITH WENDIGOS...
...OR THIS MILE HIGH TOWER TIPPING OVER AND KILLING --
-- HULK HAS PLAN.
HULK SMASH PUNY MONSTERS!
OKAY... I GUESS THAT MEANS WE'RE SAVING THE TOWER, SENTRY.
YEP.

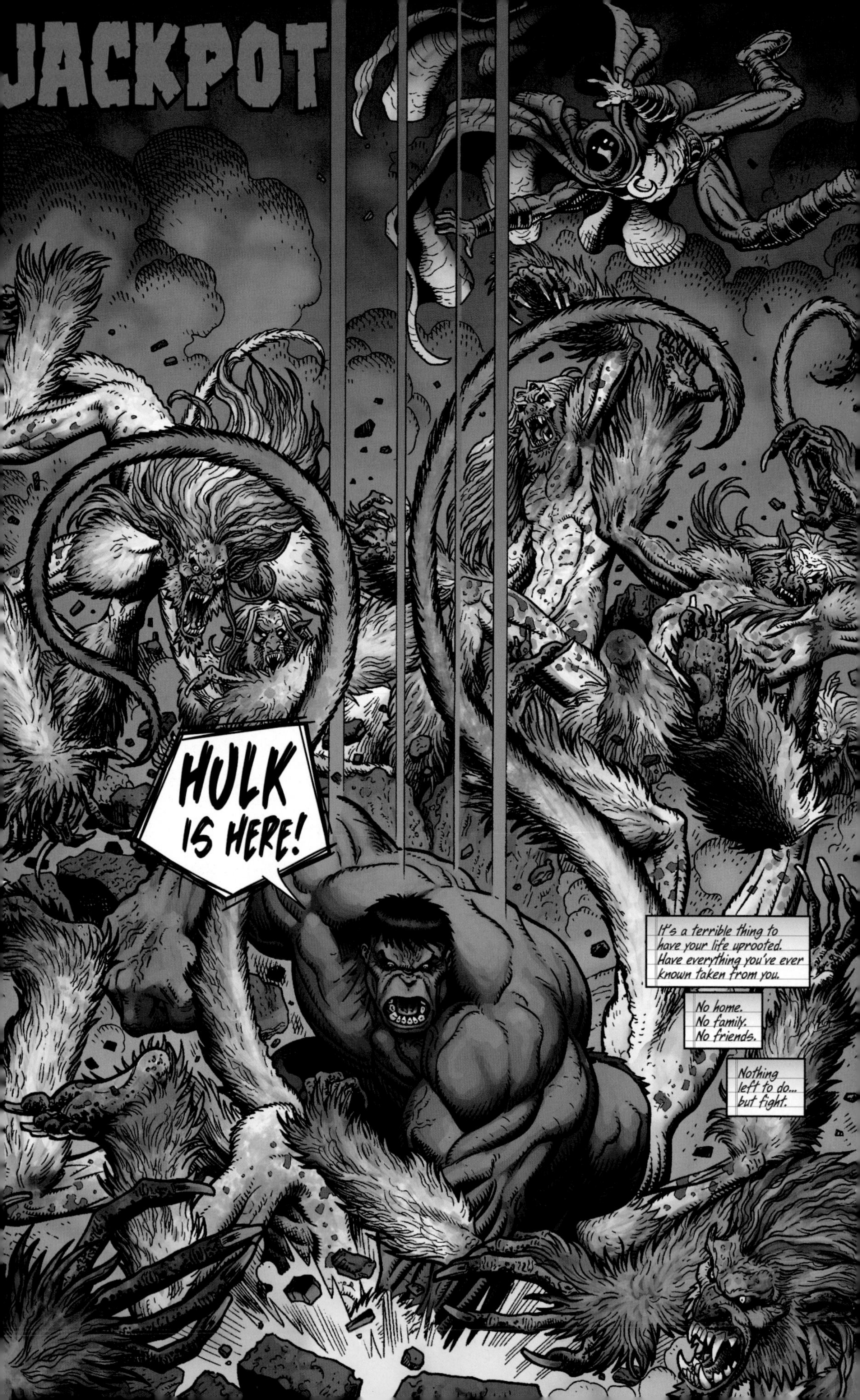
JACKPOT
HULK IS HERE!
It's a terrible thing to have your life uprooted. Have everything you've ever known taken from you.
No home. No family. No friends.
Nothing left to do... but fight.

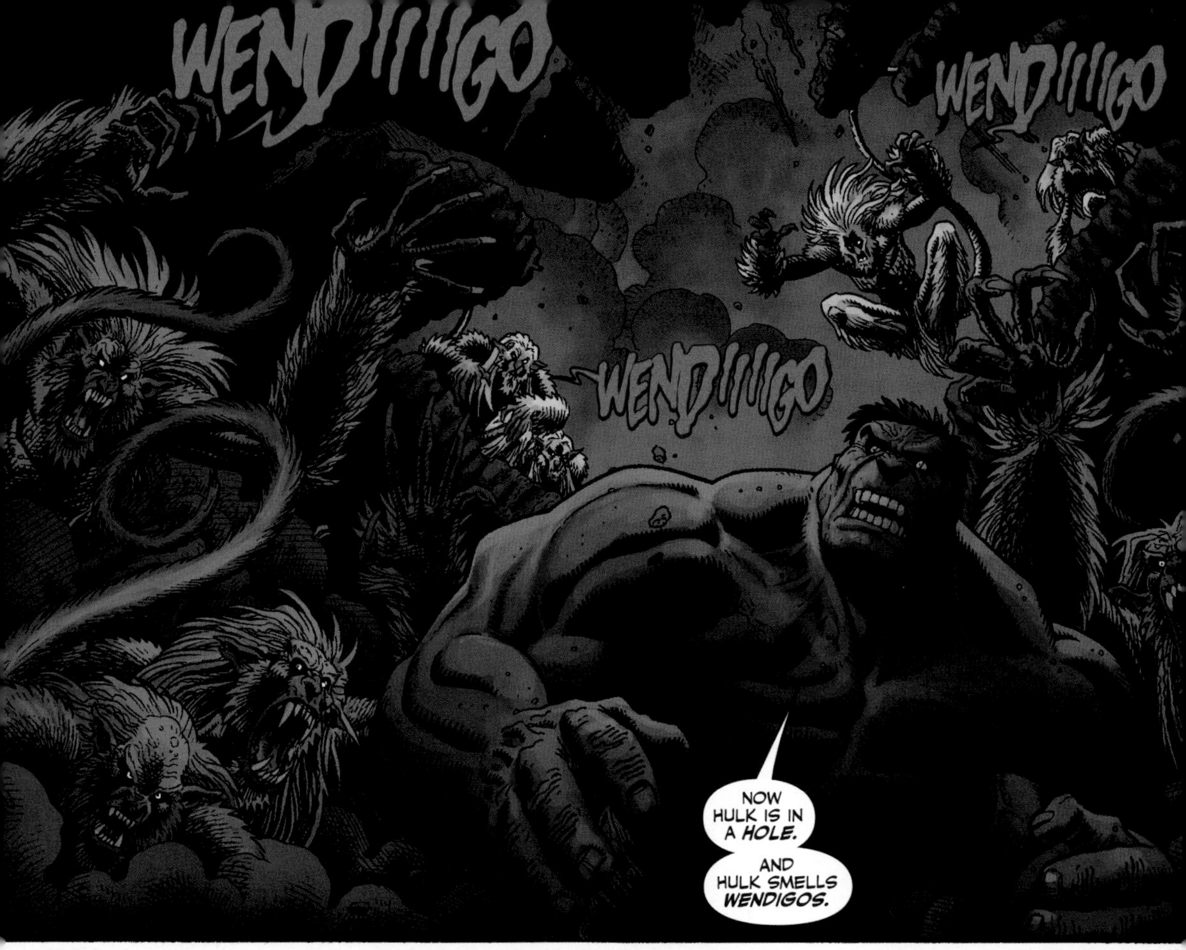
WENDIIIIGO
WENDIIIIGO
WENDIIIIGO
NOW HULK IS IN A HOLE.
AND HULK SMELLS WENDIGOS.

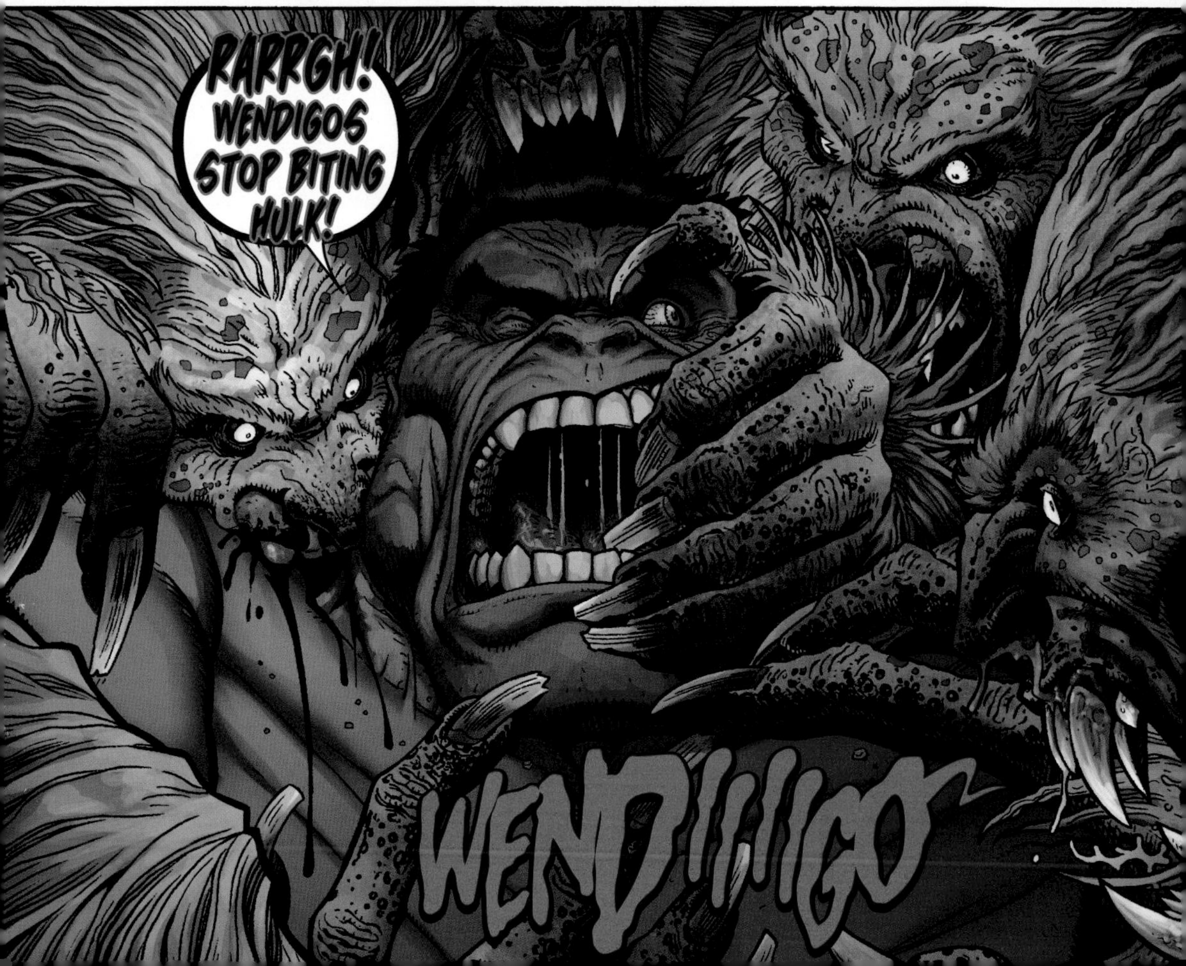
RARRGH! WENDIGOS STOP BITING HULK!
WENDIIIIGO

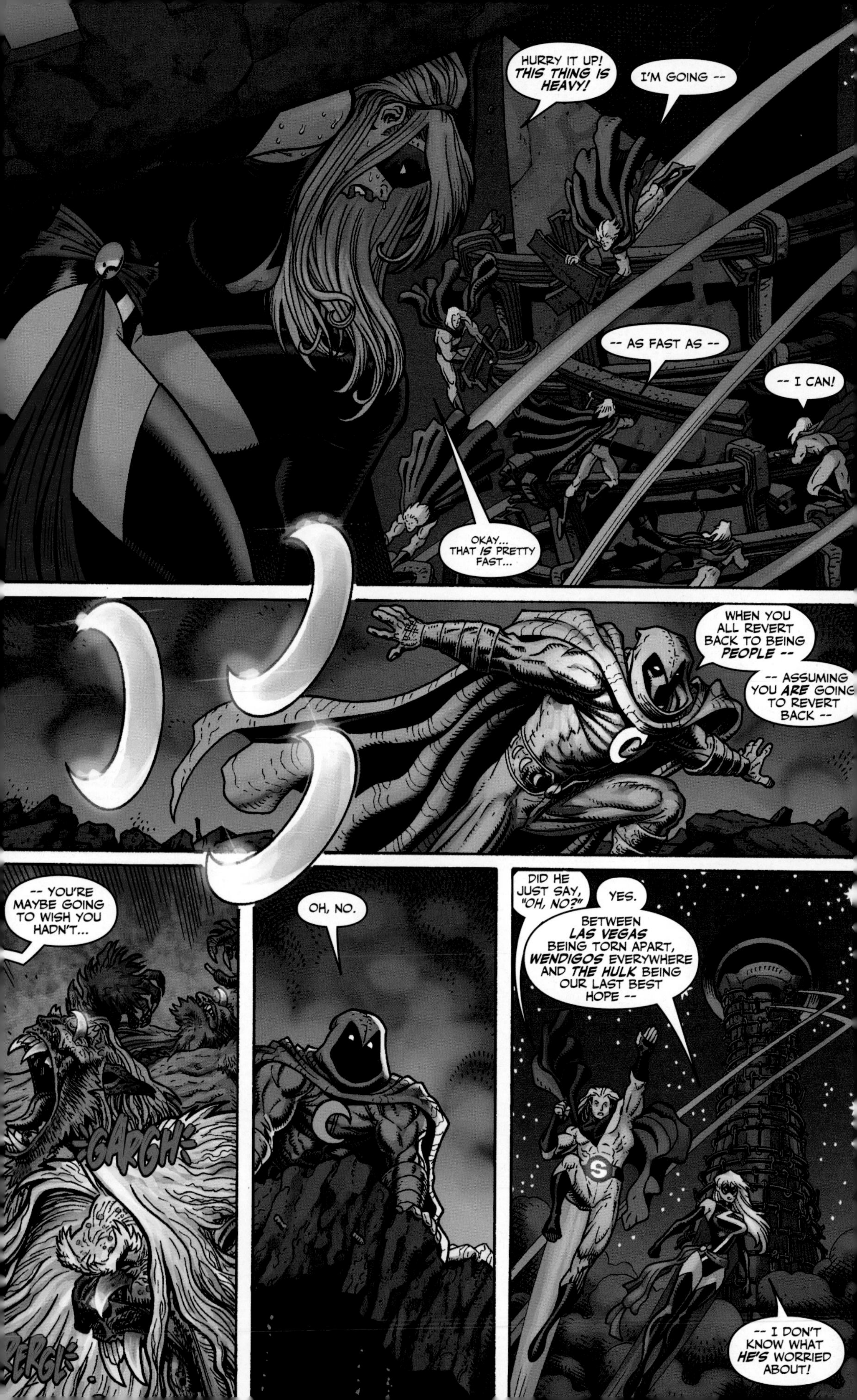
HURRY IT UP! THIS THING IS HEAVY!
I'M GOING --
-- AS FAST AS --
-- I CAN!
OKAY... THAT IS PRETTY FAST...
WHEN YOU ALL REVERT BACK TO BEING PEOPLE --
-- ASSUMING YOU ARE GOING TO REVERT BACK --
-- YOU'RE MAYBE GOING TO WISH YOU HADN'T...
GARGH
OH, NO.
DID HE JUST SAY, "OH, NO?"
YES.
BETWEEN LAS VEGAS BEING TORN APART, WENDIGOS EVERYWHERE AND THE HULK BEING OUR LAST BEST HOPE --
-- I DON'T KNOW WHAT HE'S WORRIED ABOUT!

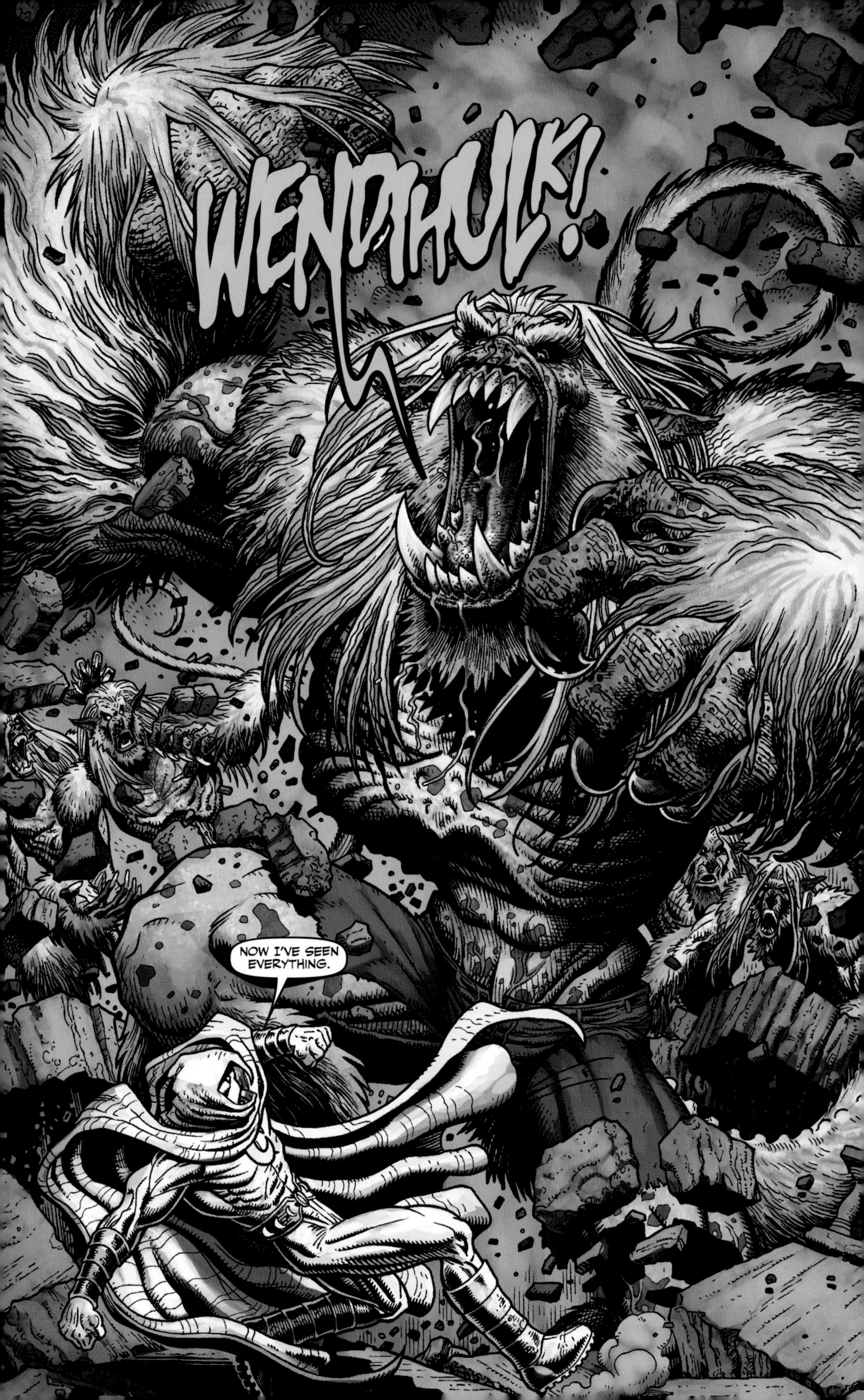
WENDHULK!
NOW I'VE SEEN EVERYTHING.

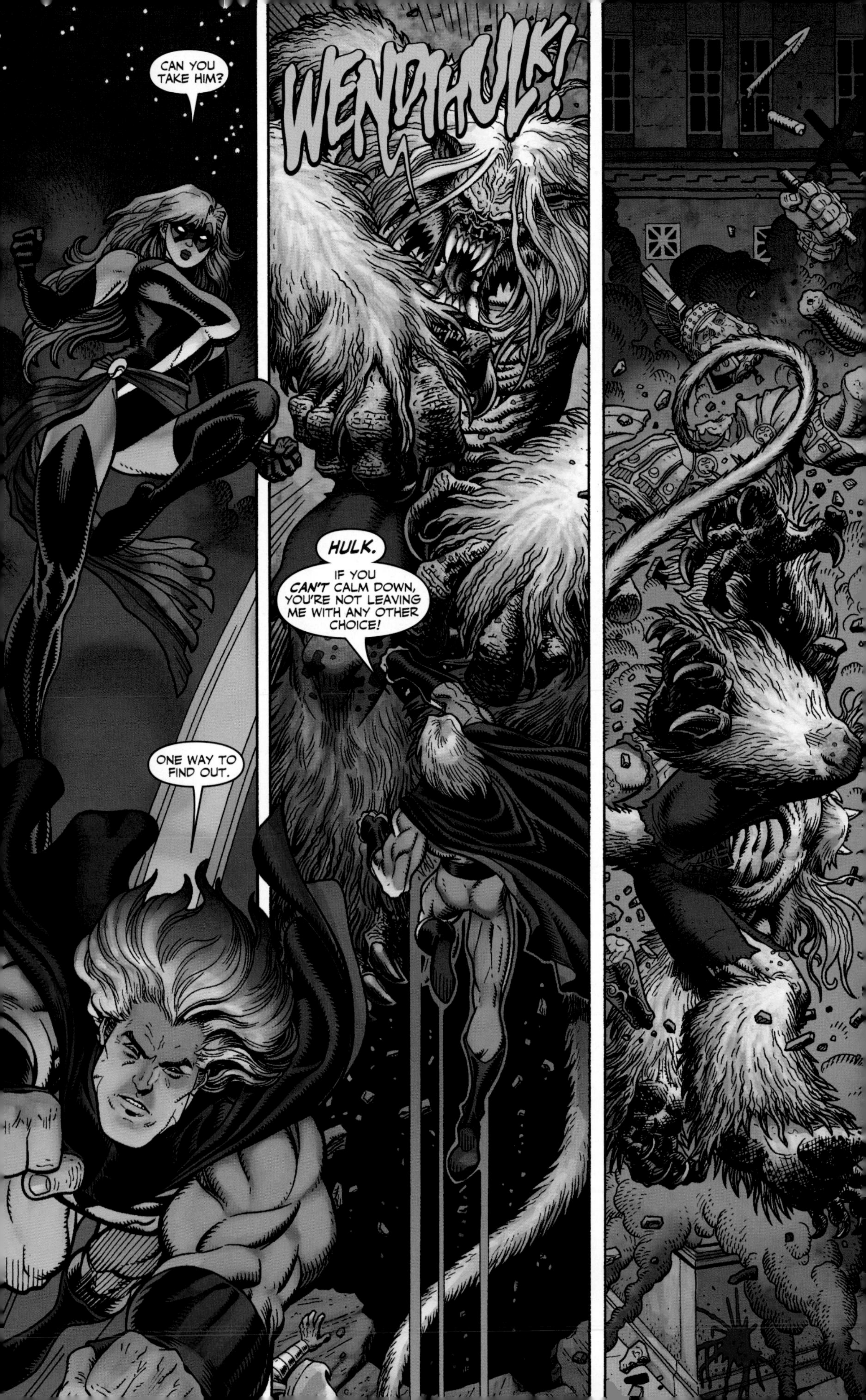
CAN YOU TAKE HIM?
ONE WAY TO FIND OUT.
WENDIHULK!
HULK.
IF YOU *CAN'T* CALM DOWN, YOU'RE NOT LEAVING ME WITH ANY OTHER CHOICE!

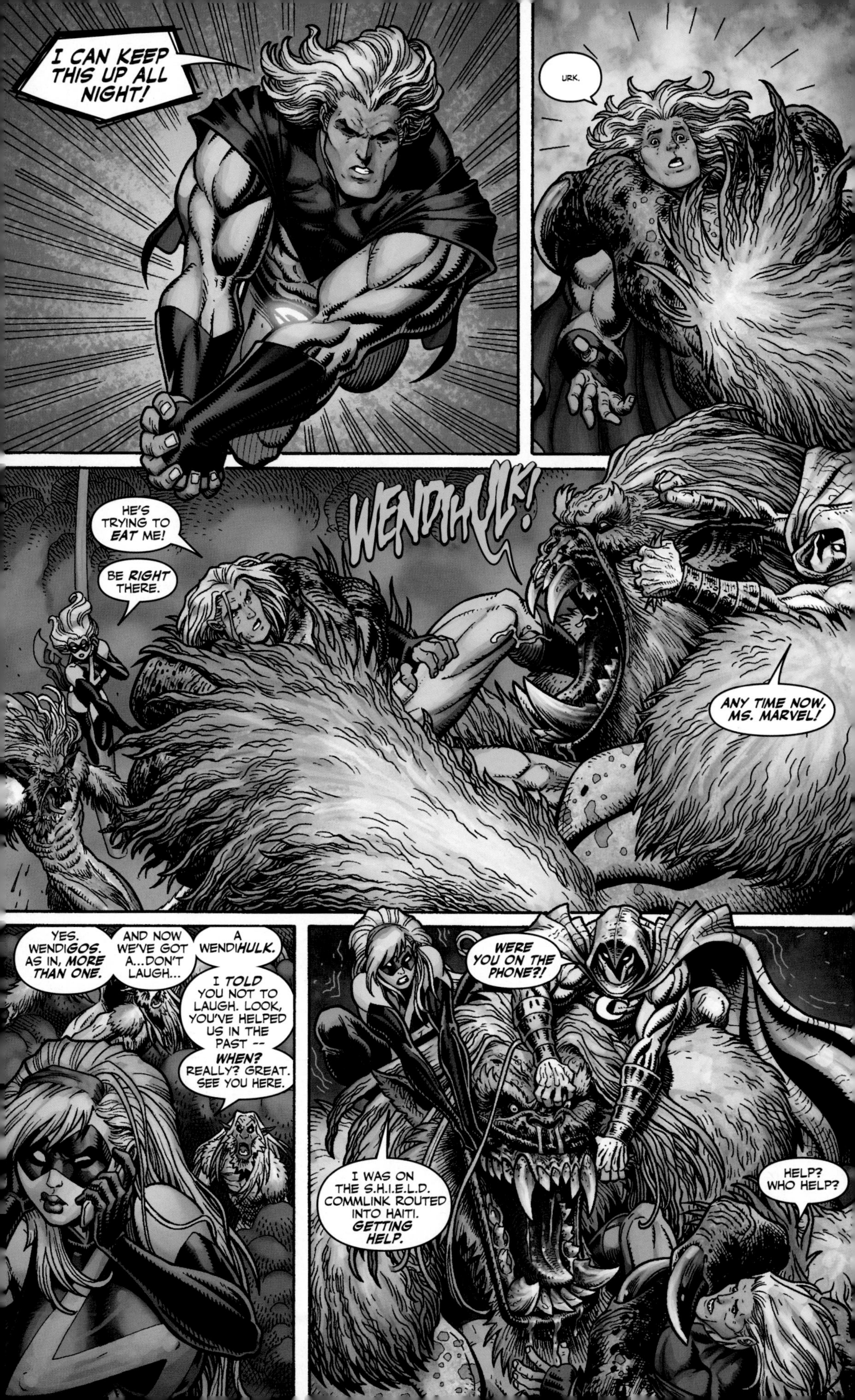
I CAN KEEP THIS UP ALL NIGHT!
URK.
HE'S TRYING TO EAT ME!
BE RIGHT THERE.
WENDIHULK!
ANY TIME NOW, MS. MARVEL!
YES. WENDIGOS. AS IN, MORE THAN ONE.
AND NOW WE'VE GOT A...DON'T LAUGH...
A WENDIHULK.
I TOLD YOU NOT TO LAUGH. LOOK, YOU'VE HELPED US IN THE PAST -- WHEN? REALLY? GREAT. SEE YOU HERE.
WERE YOU ON THE PHONE?!
I WAS ON THE S.H.I.E.L.D. COMMLINK ROUTED INTO HAITI. GETTING HELP.
HELP? WHO HELP?

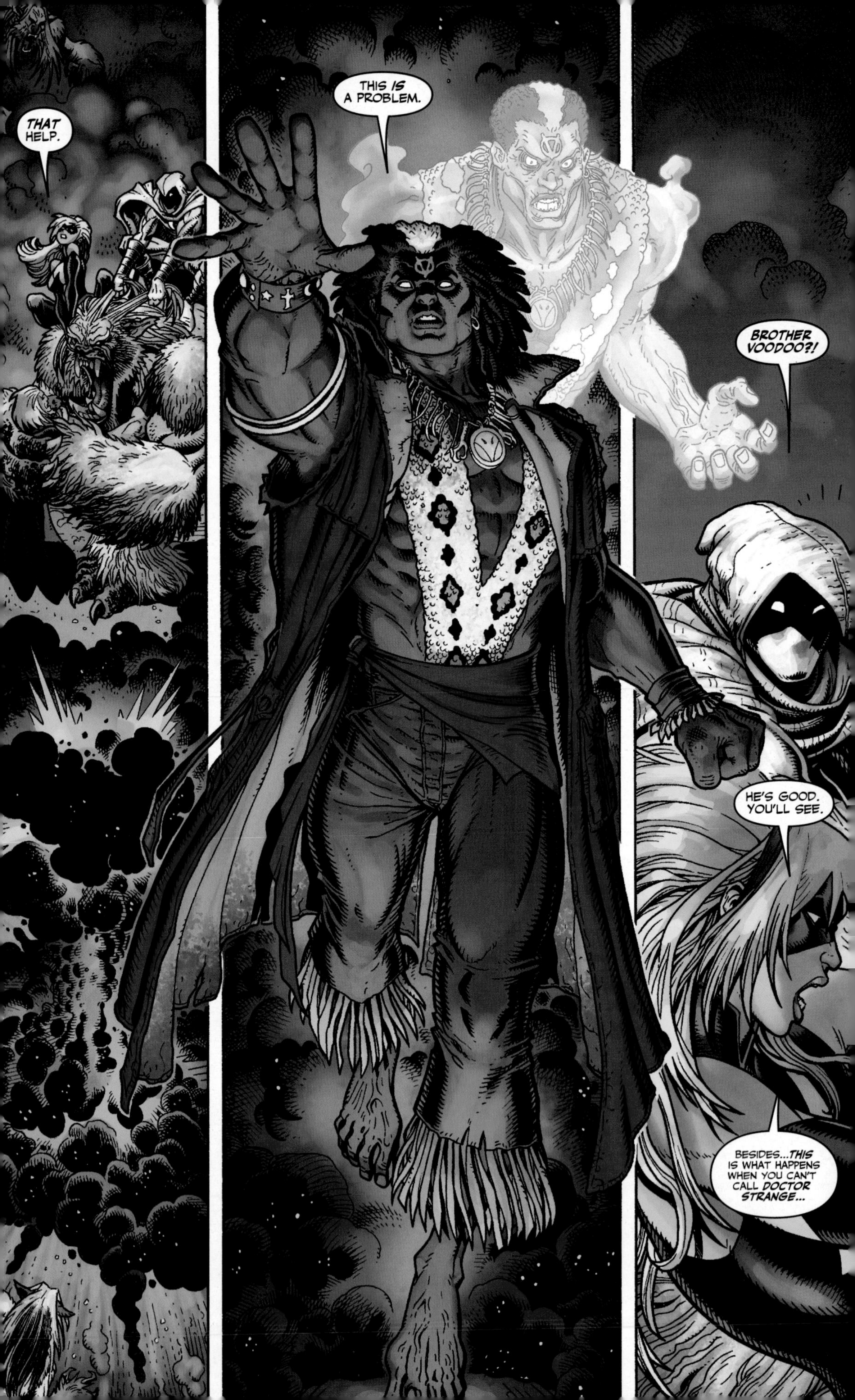
THAT HELP.
THIS IS A PROBLEM.
BROTHER VOODOO?!
HE'S GOOD. YOU'LL SEE.
BESIDES...THIS IS WHAT HAPPENS WHEN YOU CAN'T CALL DOCTOR STRANGE...

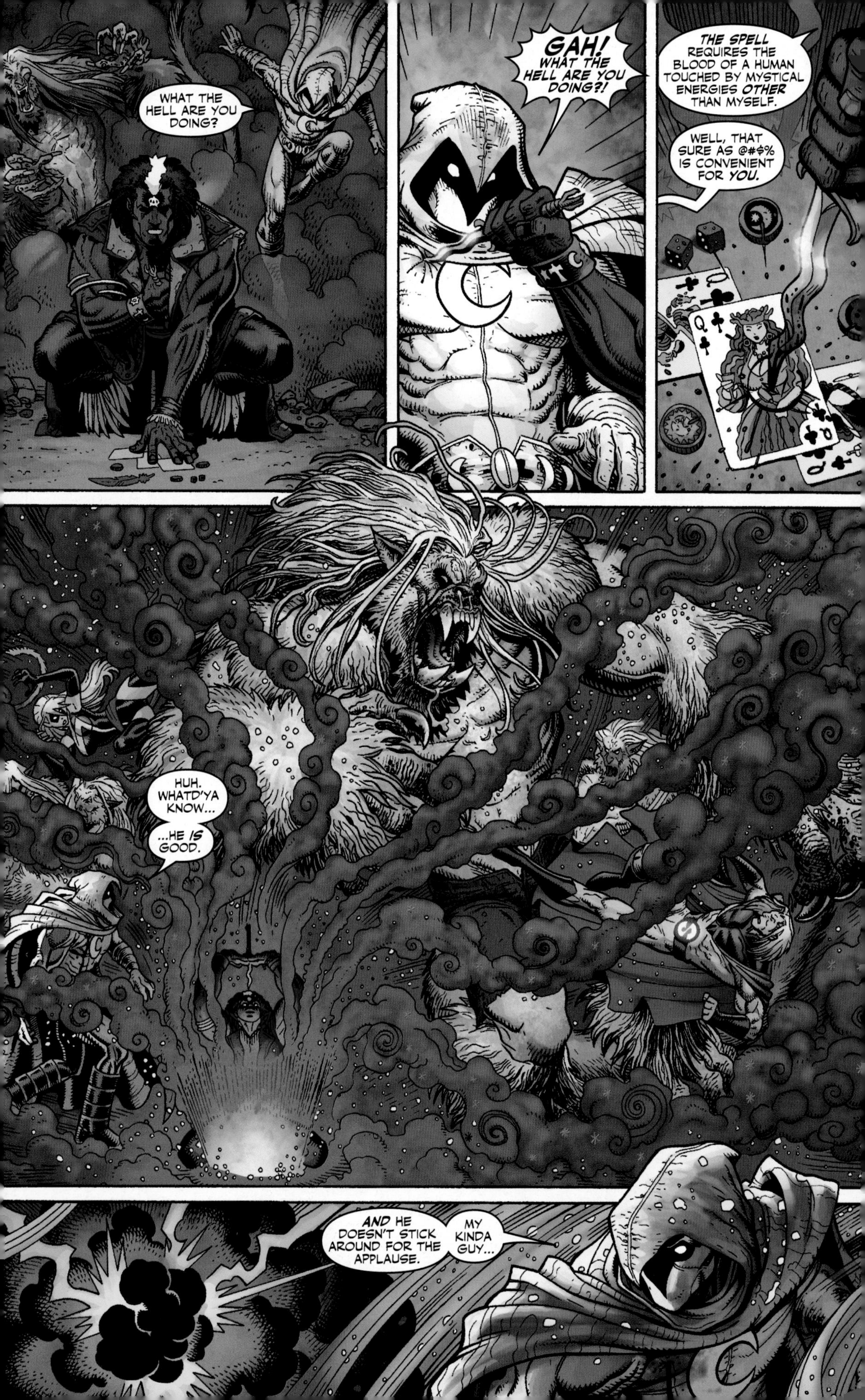
WHAT THE HELL ARE YOU DOING?
GAH! WHAT THE HELL ARE YOU DOING?!
THE SPELL REQUIRES THE BLOOD OF A HUMAN TOUCHED BY MYSTICAL ENERGIES OTHER THAN MYSELF.
WELL, THAT SURE AS @#$% IS CONVENIENT FOR YOU.
HUH. WHATD'YA KNOW...
...HE IS GOOD.
AND HE DOESN'T STICK AROUND FOR THE APPLAUSE.
MY KINDA GUY...

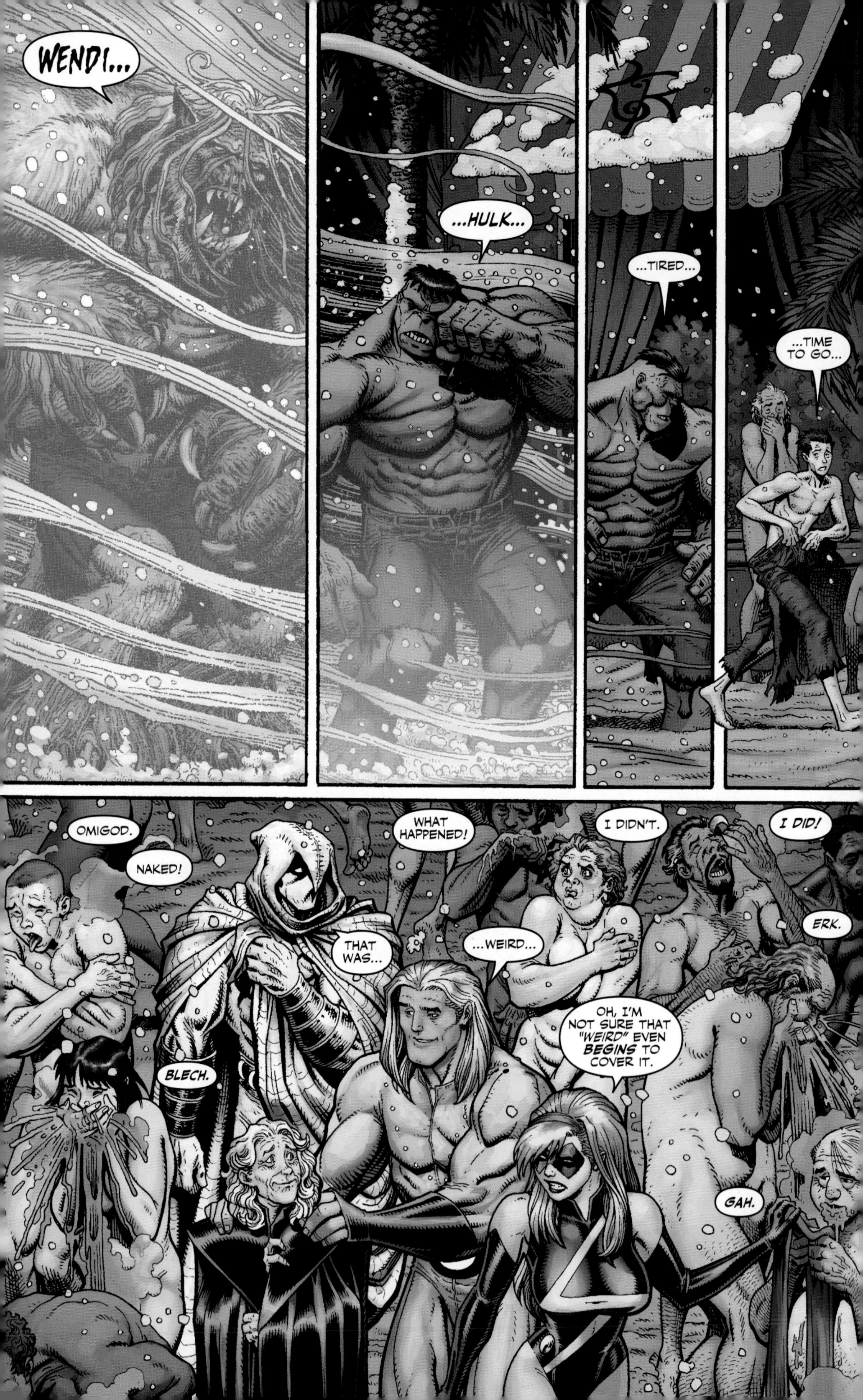
WENDI...
...HULK...
...TIRED...
...TIME TO GO...
OMIGOD.
NAKED!
WHAT HAPPENED!
I DIDN'T.
I DID!
THAT WAS...
...WEIRD...
ERK.
OH, I'M NOT SURE THAT "WEIRD" EVEN BEGINS TO COVER IT.
BLECH.
GAH.

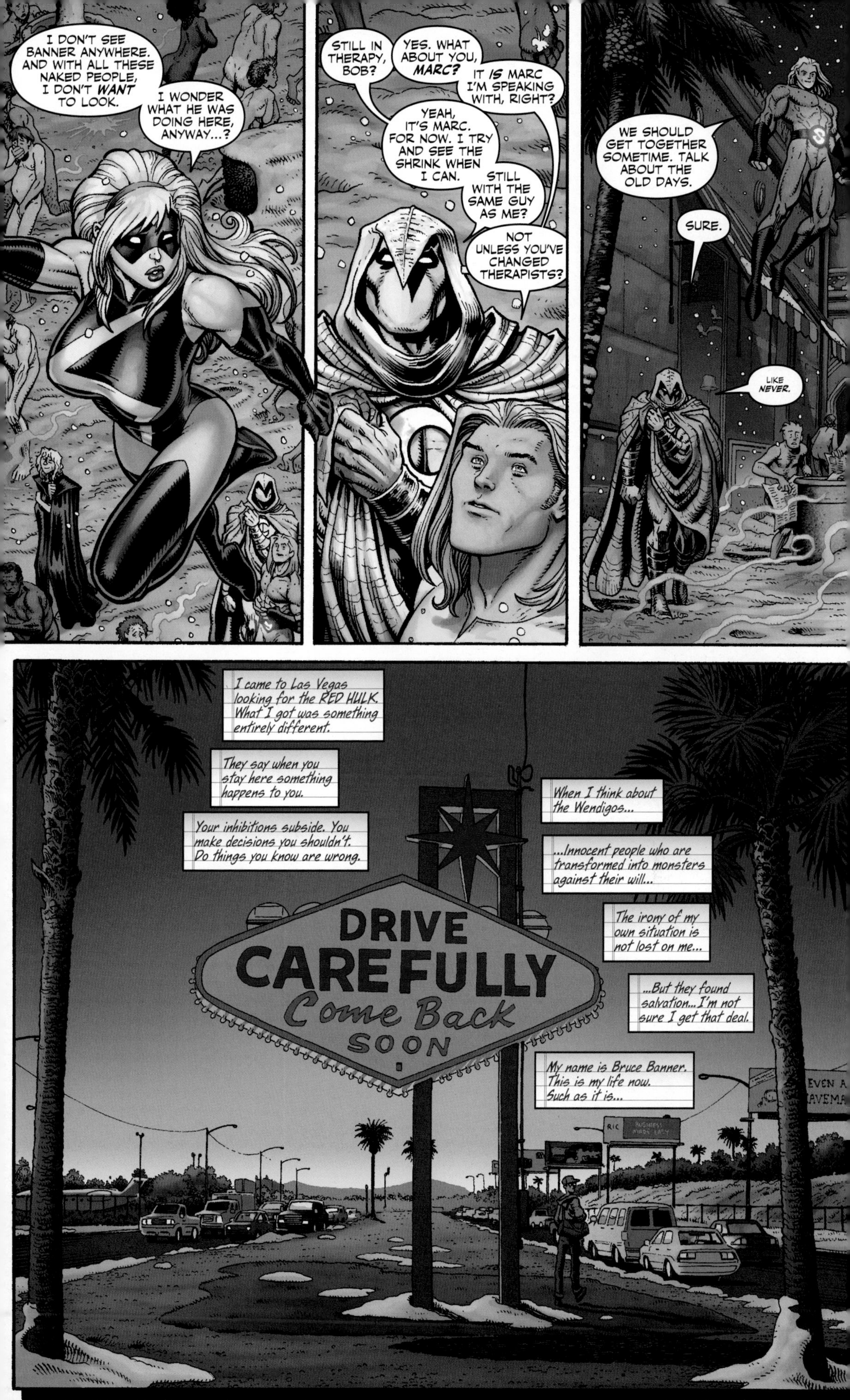
I DON'T SEE BANNER ANYWHERE. AND WITH ALL THESE NAKED PEOPLE, I DON'T *WANT* TO LOOK.
I WONDER WHAT HE WAS DOING HERE, ANYWAY...?
STILL IN THERAPY, BOB?
YES. WHAT ABOUT YOU, *MARC?*
IT *IS* MARC I'M SPEAKING WITH, RIGHT?
YEAH, IT'S MARC. FOR NOW. I TRY AND SEE THE SHRINK WHEN I CAN.
STILL WITH THE SAME GUY AS ME?
NOT UNLESS YOU'VE CHANGED THERAPISTS?
WE SHOULD GET TOGETHER SOMETIME. TALK ABOUT THE OLD DAYS.
SURE.
LIKE *NEVER.*
I came to Las Vegas looking for the RED HULK. What I got was something entirely different.
They say when you stay here something happens to you.
Your inhibitions subside. You make decisions you shouldn't. Do things you know are wrong.
When I think about the Wendigos...
...Innocent people who are transformed into monsters against their will...
The irony of my own situation is not lost on me...
...But they found salvation...I'm not sure I get that deal.
My name is Bruce Banner. This is my life now. Such as it is...
DRIVE CAREFULLY Come Back SOON

ROUND ★ TWO

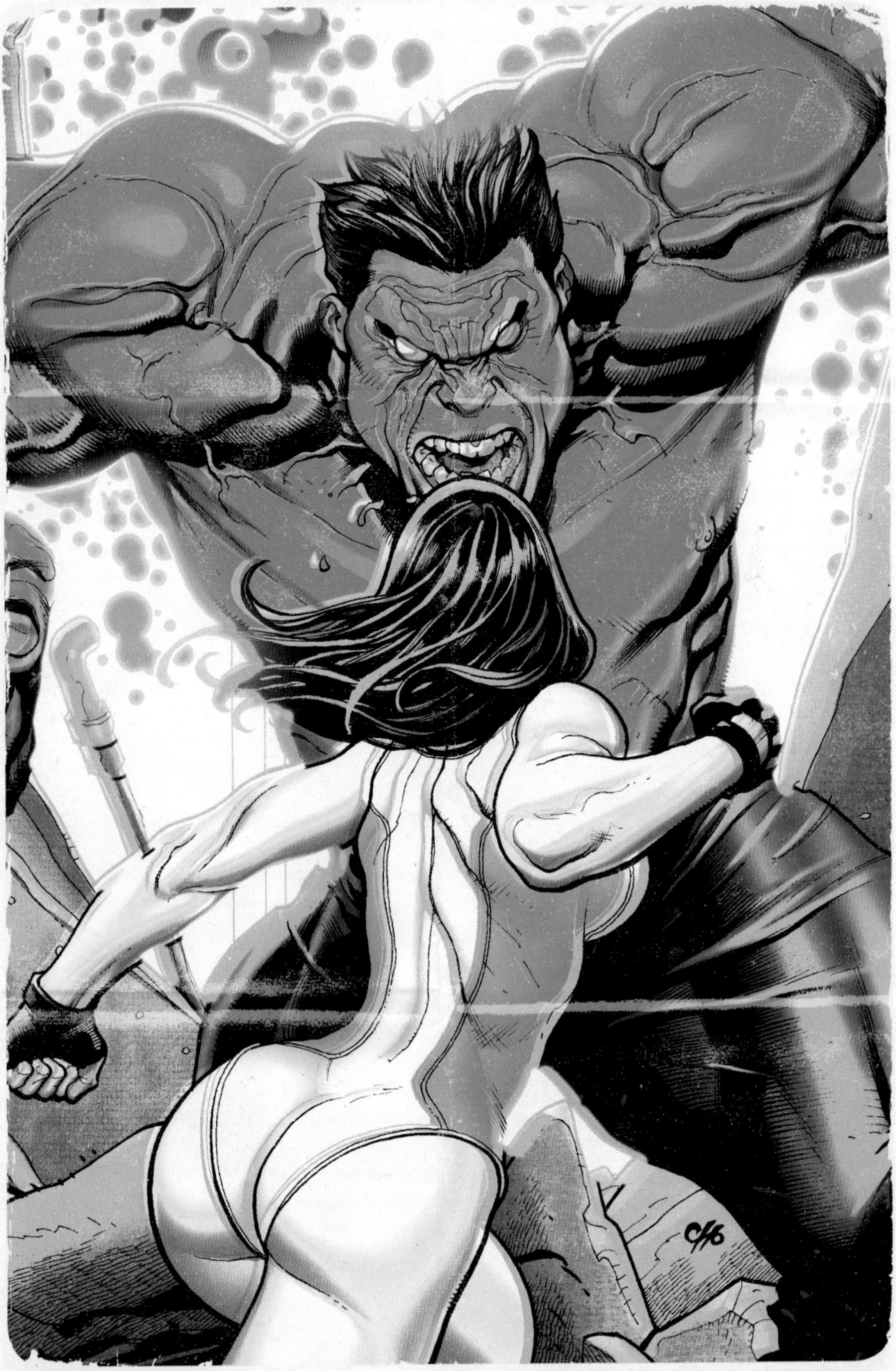

HELL HATH NO FURY

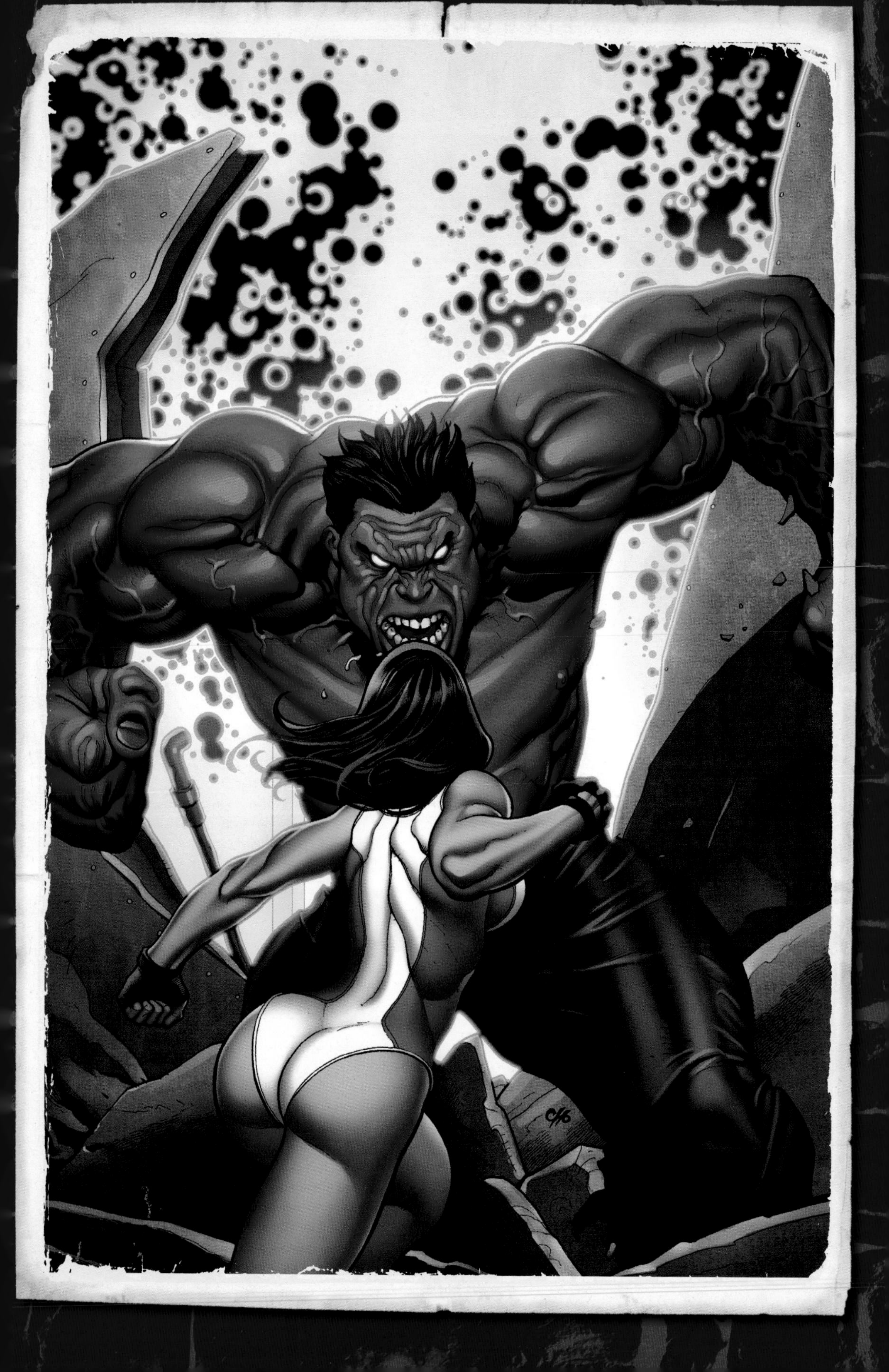

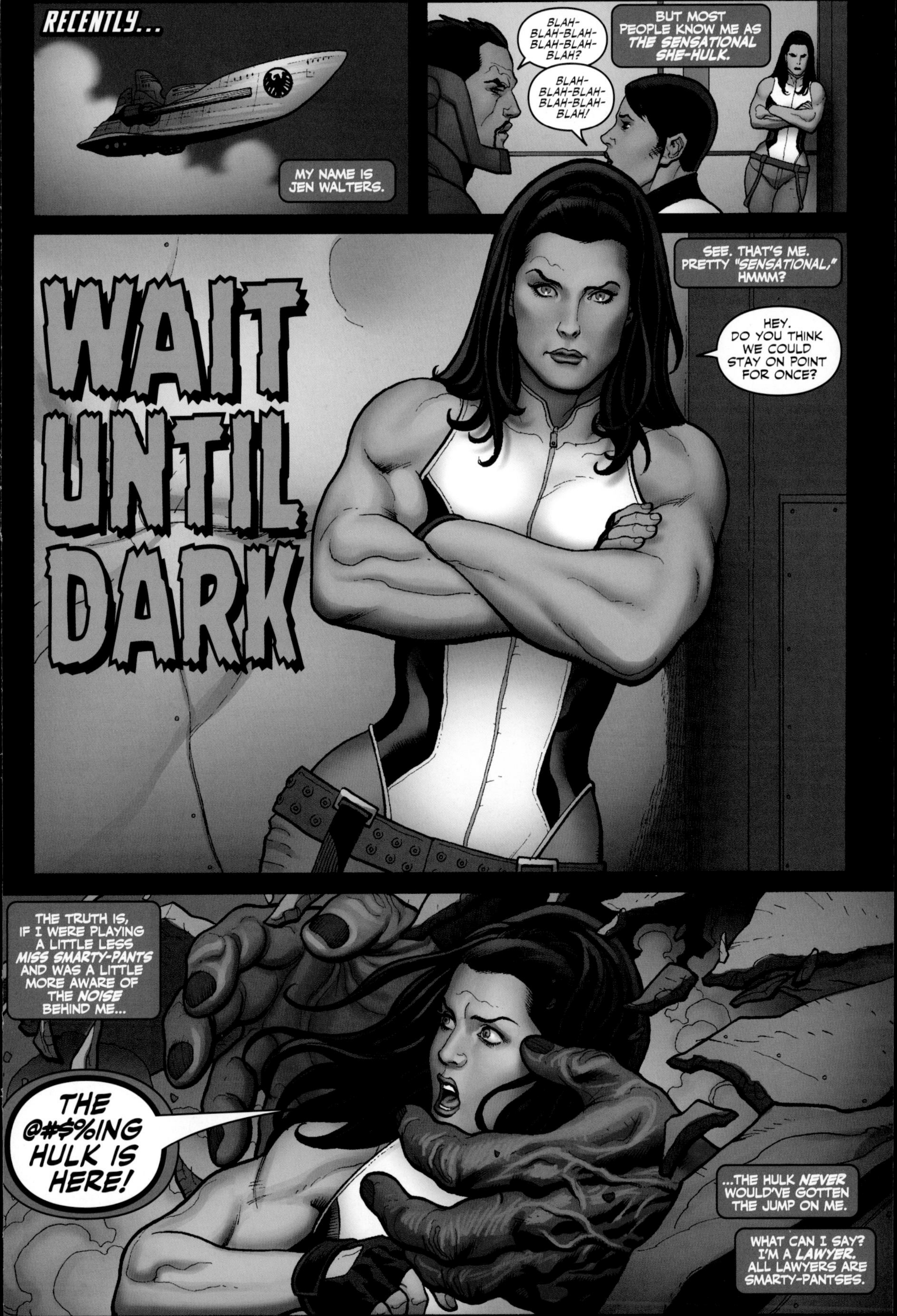
RECENTLY...
MY NAME IS JEN WALTERS.
BLAH-BLAH-BLAH-BLAH-BLAH-BLAH?
BLAH-BLAH-BLAH-BLAH-BLAH-BLAH!
BUT MOST PEOPLE KNOW ME AS THE SENSATIONAL SHE-HULK.
WAIT UNTIL DARK
SEE. THAT'S ME. PRETTY "SENSATIONAL," HMMM?
HEY. DO YOU THINK WE COULD STAY ON POINT FOR ONCE?
THE TRUTH IS, IF I WERE PLAYING A LITTLE LESS MISS SMARTY-PANTS AND WAS A LITTLE MORE AWARE OF THE NOISE BEHIND ME...
THE @#$%ING HULK IS HERE!
...THE HULK NEVER WOULD'VE GOTTEN THE JUMP ON ME.
WHAT CAN I SAY? I'M A LAWYER. ALL LAWYERS ARE SMARTY-PANTSES.

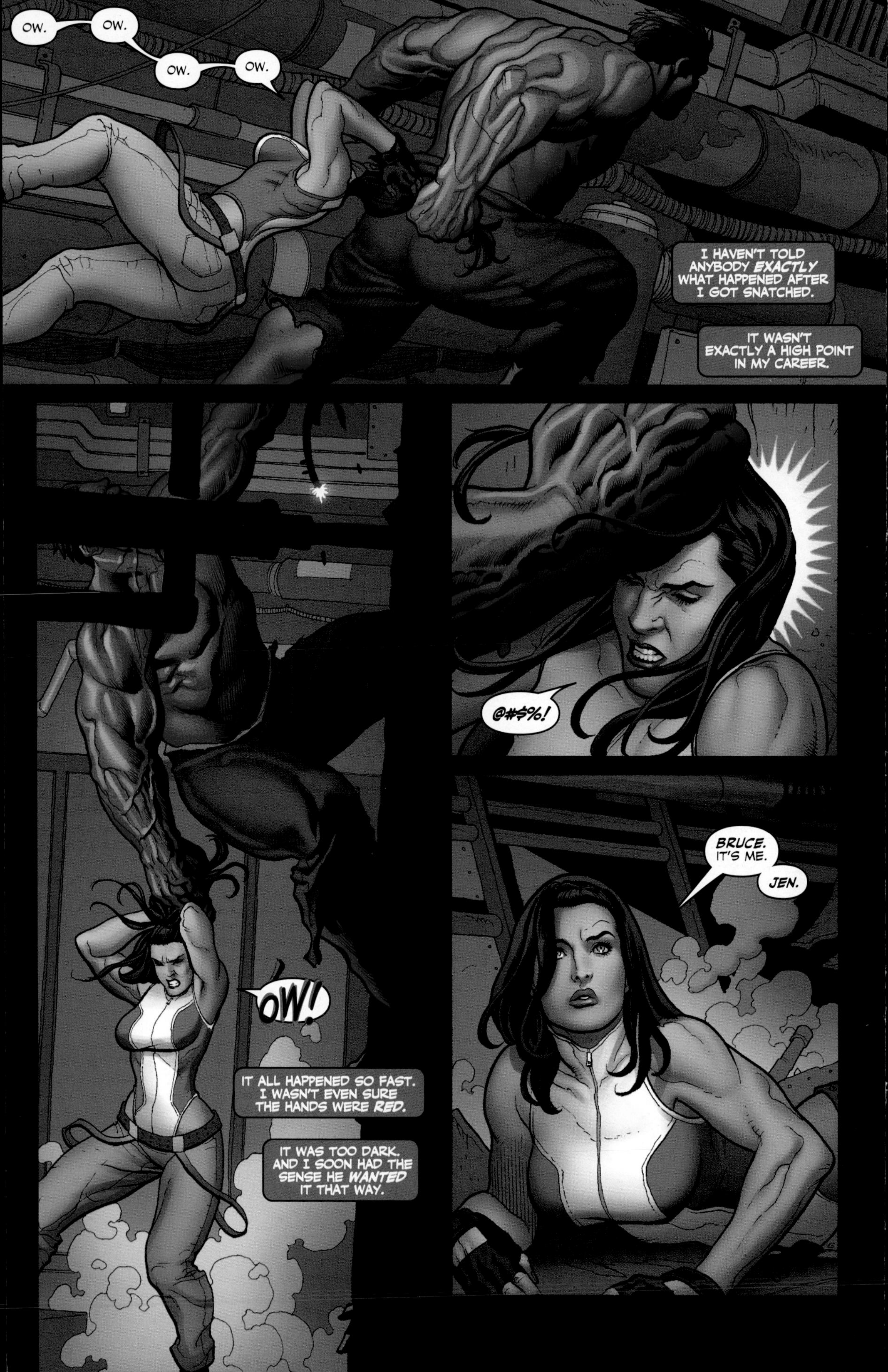
OW.
OW.
OW.
OW.
I HAVEN'T TOLD ANYBODY EXACTLY WHAT HAPPENED AFTER I GOT SNATCHED.
IT WASN'T EXACTLY A HIGH POINT IN MY CAREER.
@#$%!
OW!
IT ALL HAPPENED SO FAST. I WASN'T EVEN SURE THE HANDS WERE RED.
IT WAS TOO DARK. AND I SOON HAD THE SENSE HE WANTED IT THAT WAY.
BRUCE. IT'S ME.
JEN.

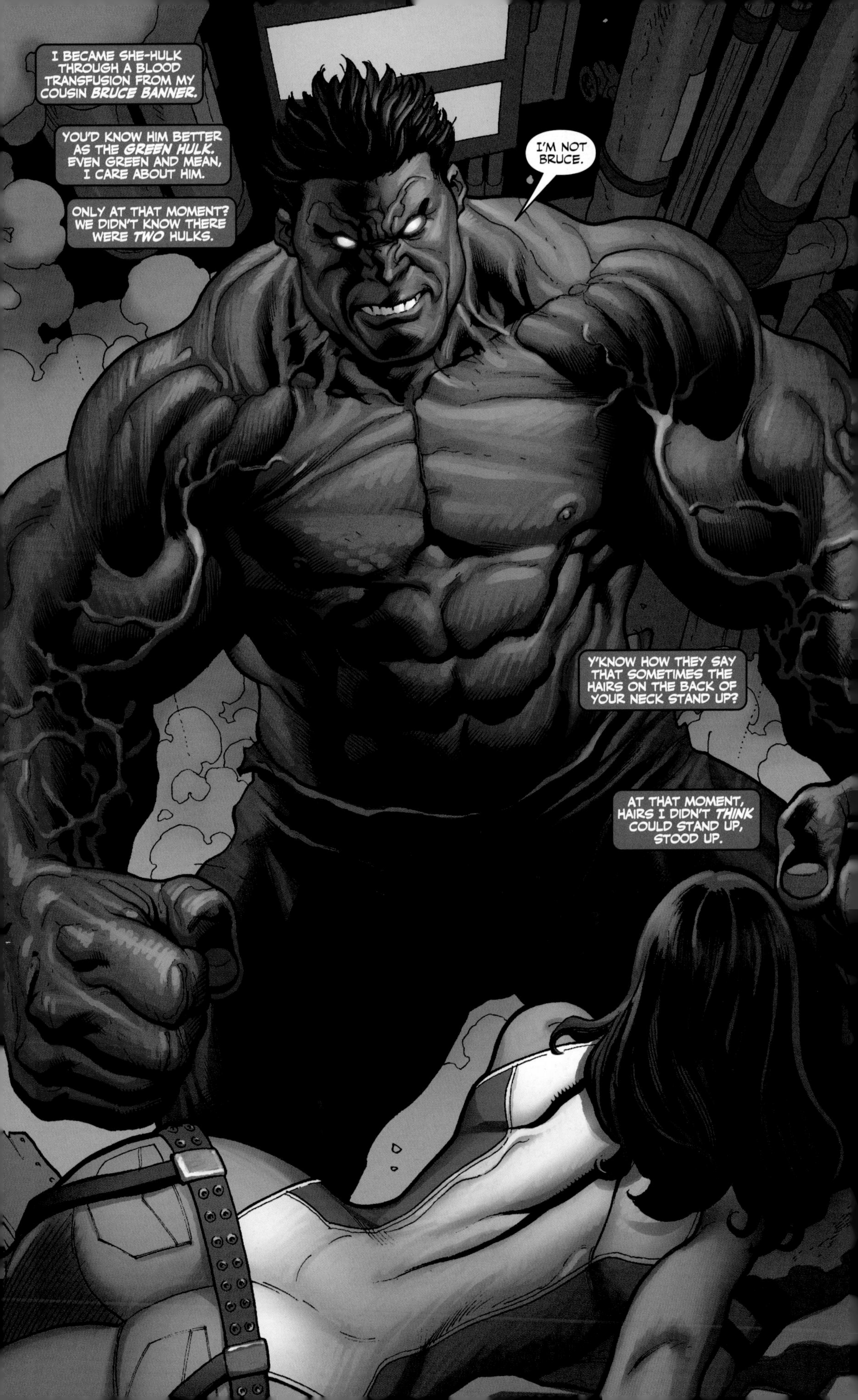
I BECAME SHE-HULK THROUGH A BLOOD TRANSFUSION FROM MY COUSIN BRUCE BANNER.
YOU'D KNOW HIM BETTER AS THE GREEN HULK. EVEN GREEN AND MEAN, I CARE ABOUT HIM.
ONLY AT THAT MOMENT? WE DIDN'T KNOW THERE WERE TWO HULKS.
I'M NOT BRUCE.
Y'KNOW HOW THEY SAY THAT SOMETIMES THE HAIRS ON THE BACK OF YOUR NECK STAND UP?
AT THAT MOMENT, HAIRS I DIDN'T THINK COULD STAND UP, STOOD UP.

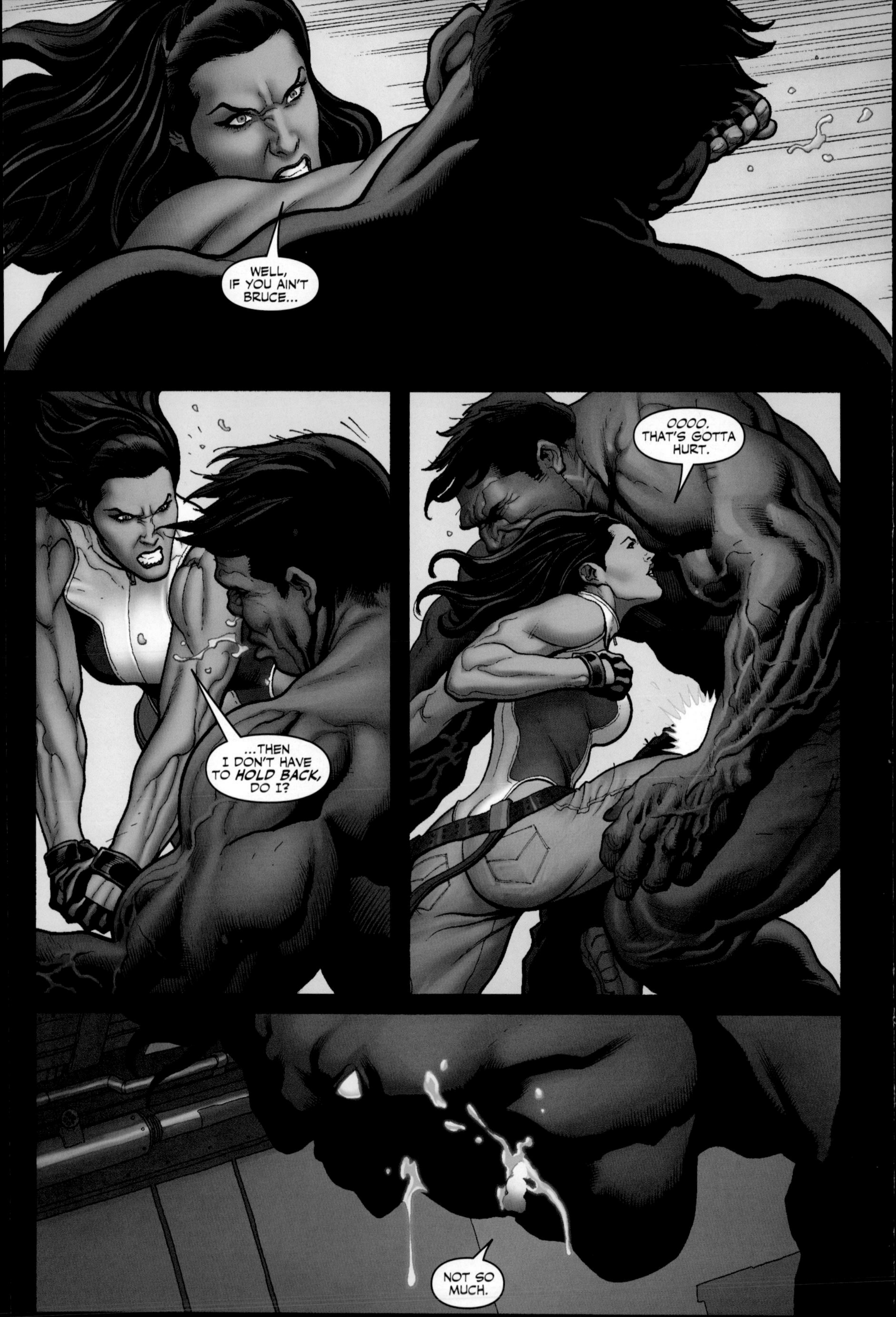
WELL, IF YOU AIN'T BRUCE...
...THEN I DON'T HAVE TO HOLD BACK, DO I?
OOOO. THAT'S GOTTA HURT.
NOT SO MUCH.

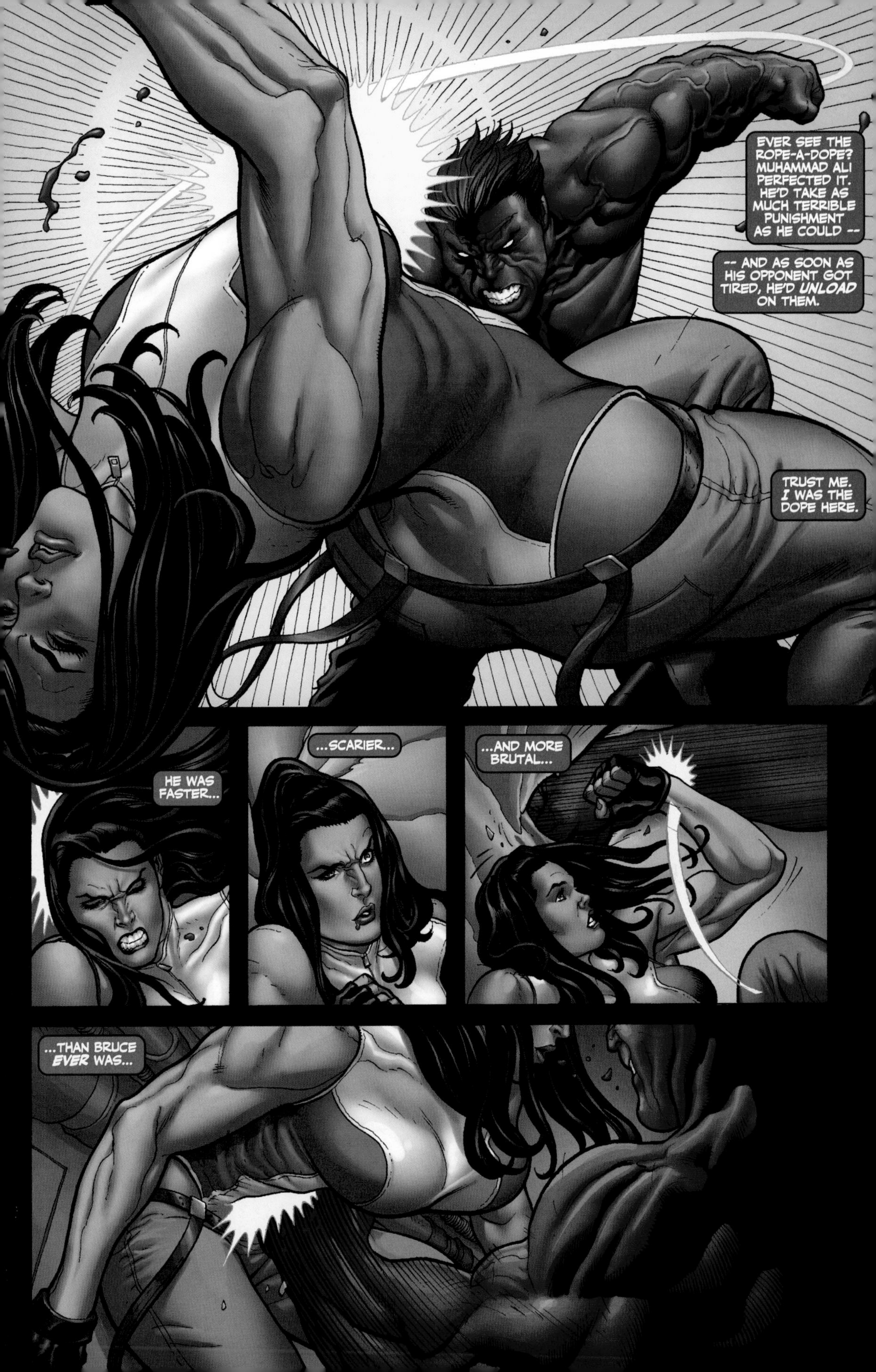
EVER SEE THE ROPE-A-DOPE? MUHAMMAD ALI PERFECTED IT. HE'D TAKE AS MUCH TERRIBLE PUNISHMENT AS HE COULD --
-- AND AS SOON AS HIS OPPONENT GOT TIRED, HE'D UNLOAD ON THEM.
TRUST ME. I WAS THE DOPE HERE.
HE WAS FASTER...
...SCARIER...
...AND MORE BRUTAL...
...THAN BRUCE EVER WAS...

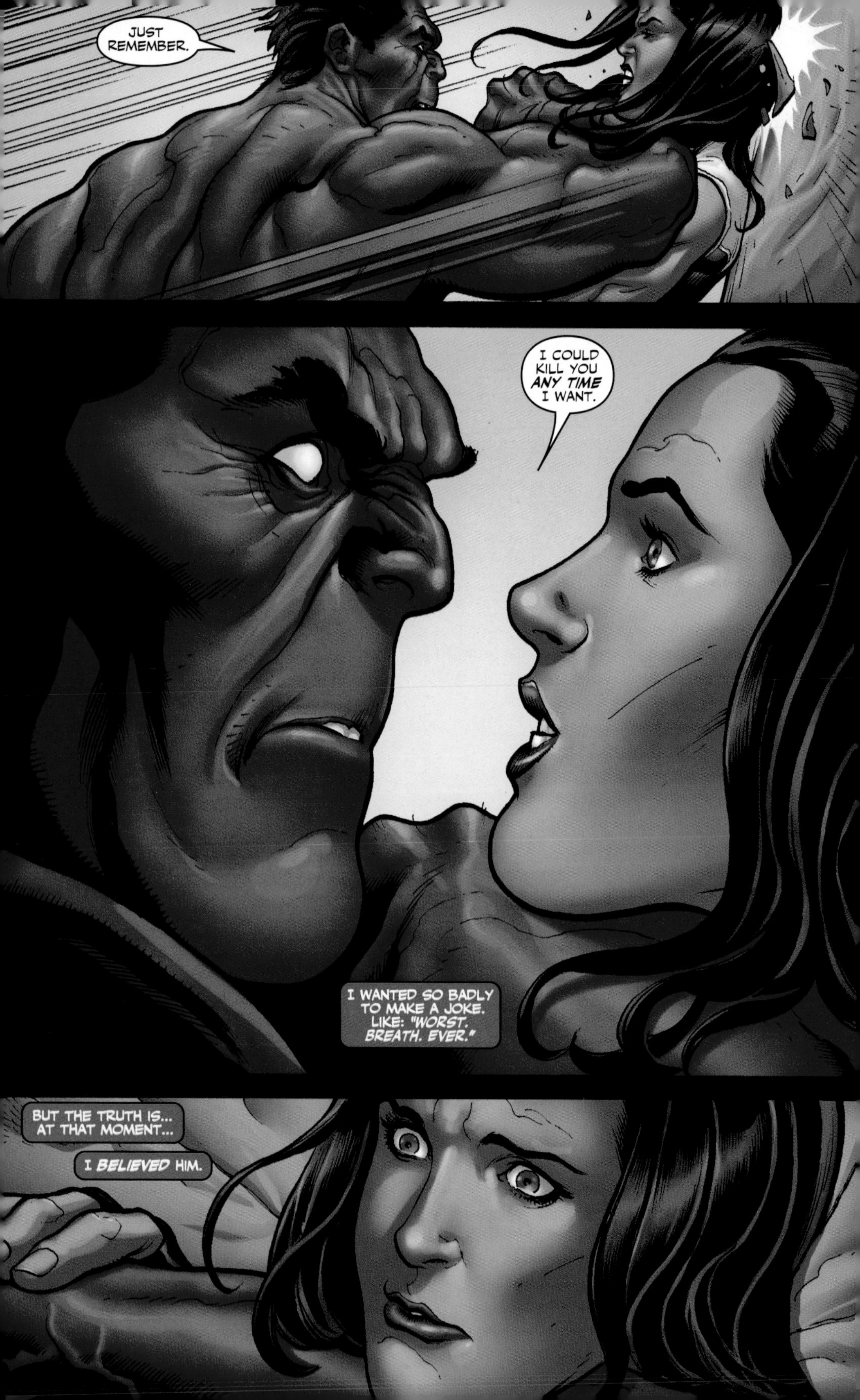
JUST REMEMBER.
I COULD KILL YOU ANY TIME I WANT.
I WANTED SO BADLY TO MAKE A JOKE. LIKE: "WORST. BREATH. EVER."
BUT THE TRUTH IS... AT THAT MOMENT...
I BELIEVED HIM.

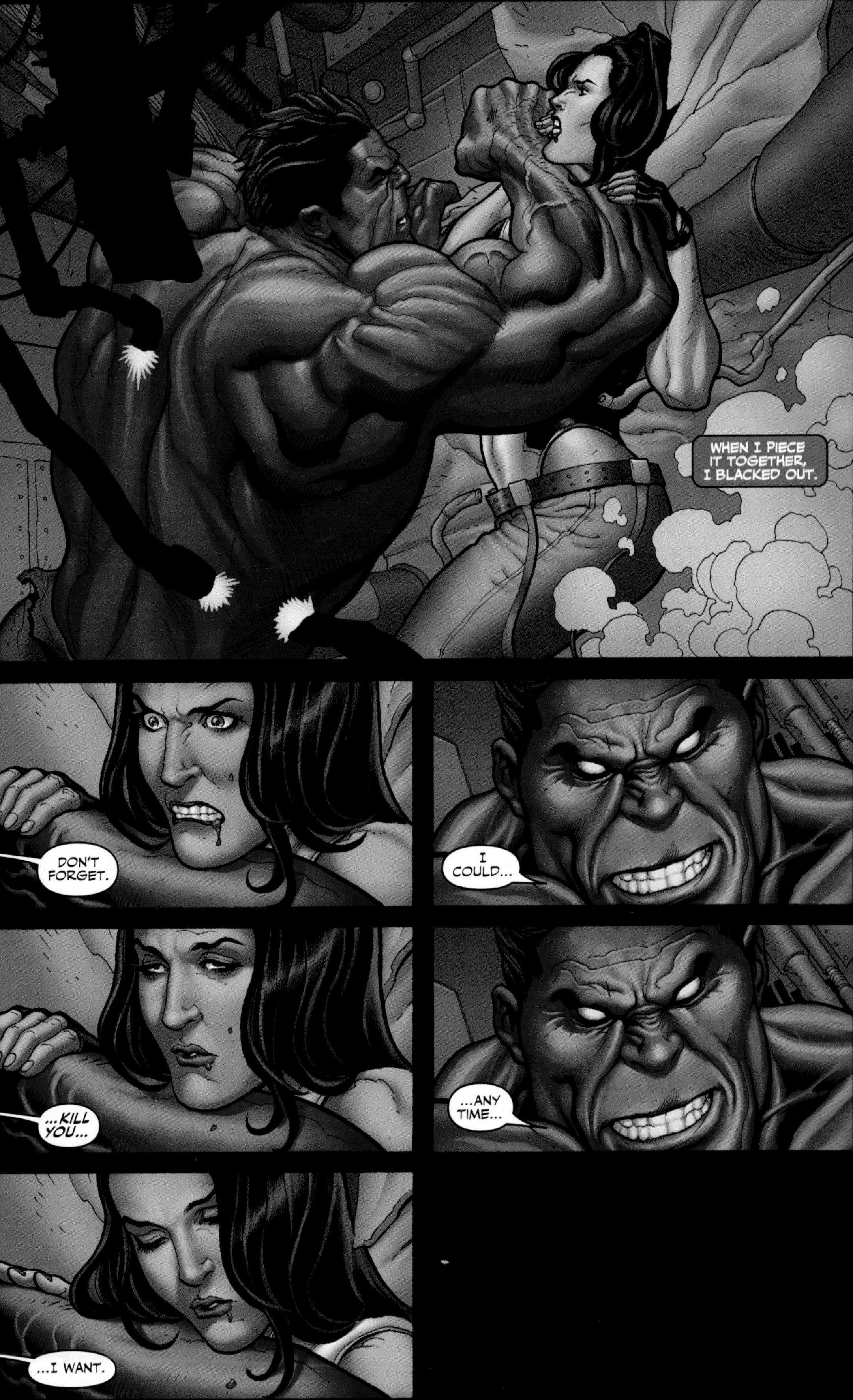
WHEN I PIECE IT TOGETHER, I BLACKED OUT.
DON'T FORGET.
I COULD...
...KILL YOU...
...ANY TIME...
...I WANT.

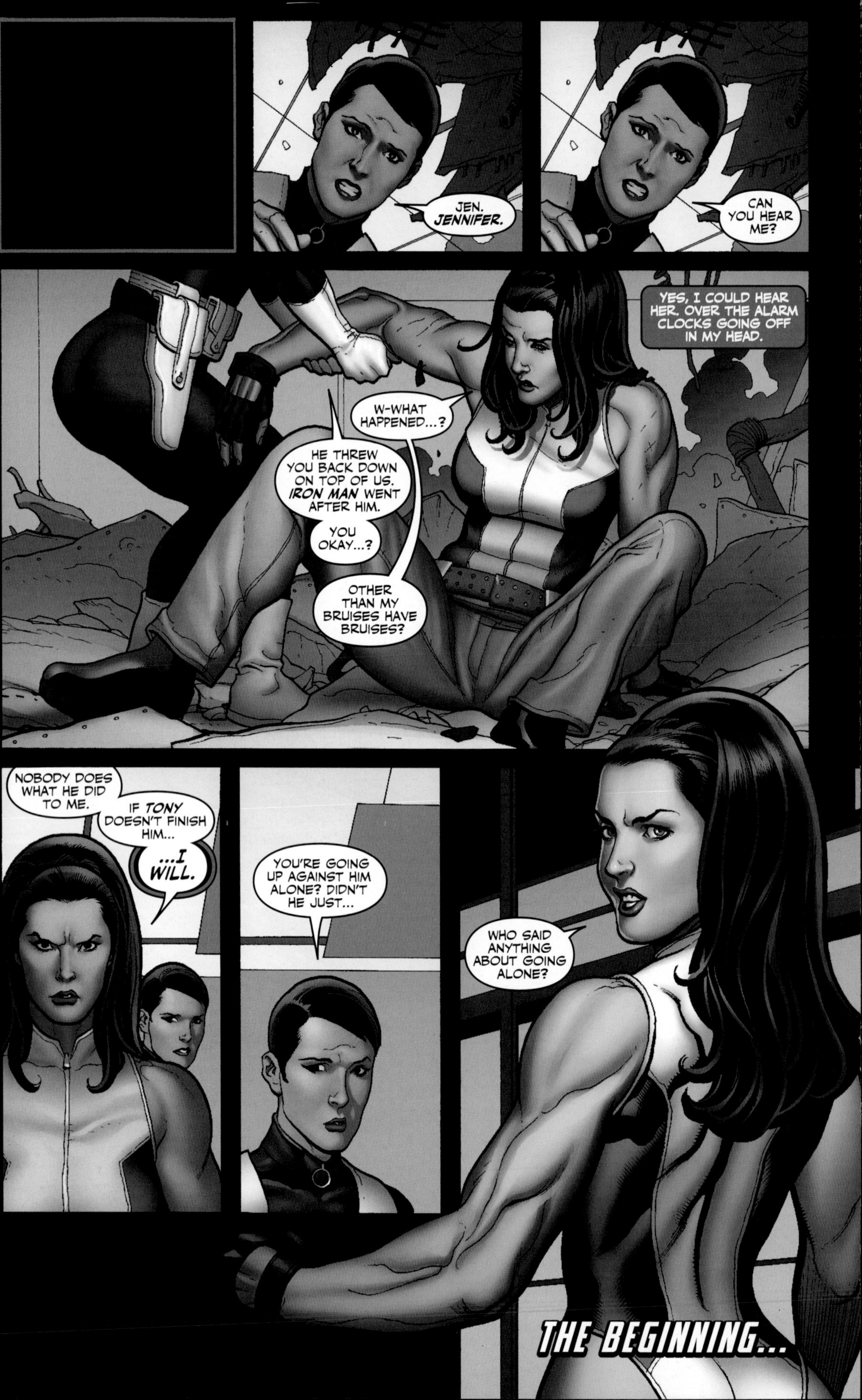
JEN. JENNIFER.
CAN YOU HEAR ME?
YES, I COULD HEAR HER. OVER THE ALARM CLOCKS GOING OFF IN MY HEAD.
W-WHAT HAPPENED...?
HE THREW YOU BACK DOWN ON TOP OF US. IRON MAN WENT AFTER HIM.
YOU OKAY...?
OTHER THAN MY BRUISES HAVE BRUISES?
NOBODY DOES WHAT HE DID TO ME.
IF TONY DOESN'T FINISH HIM...
...I WILL.
YOU'RE GOING UP AGAINST HIM ALONE? DIDN'T HE JUST...
WHO SAID ANYTHING ABOUT GOING ALONE?
THE BEGINNING...

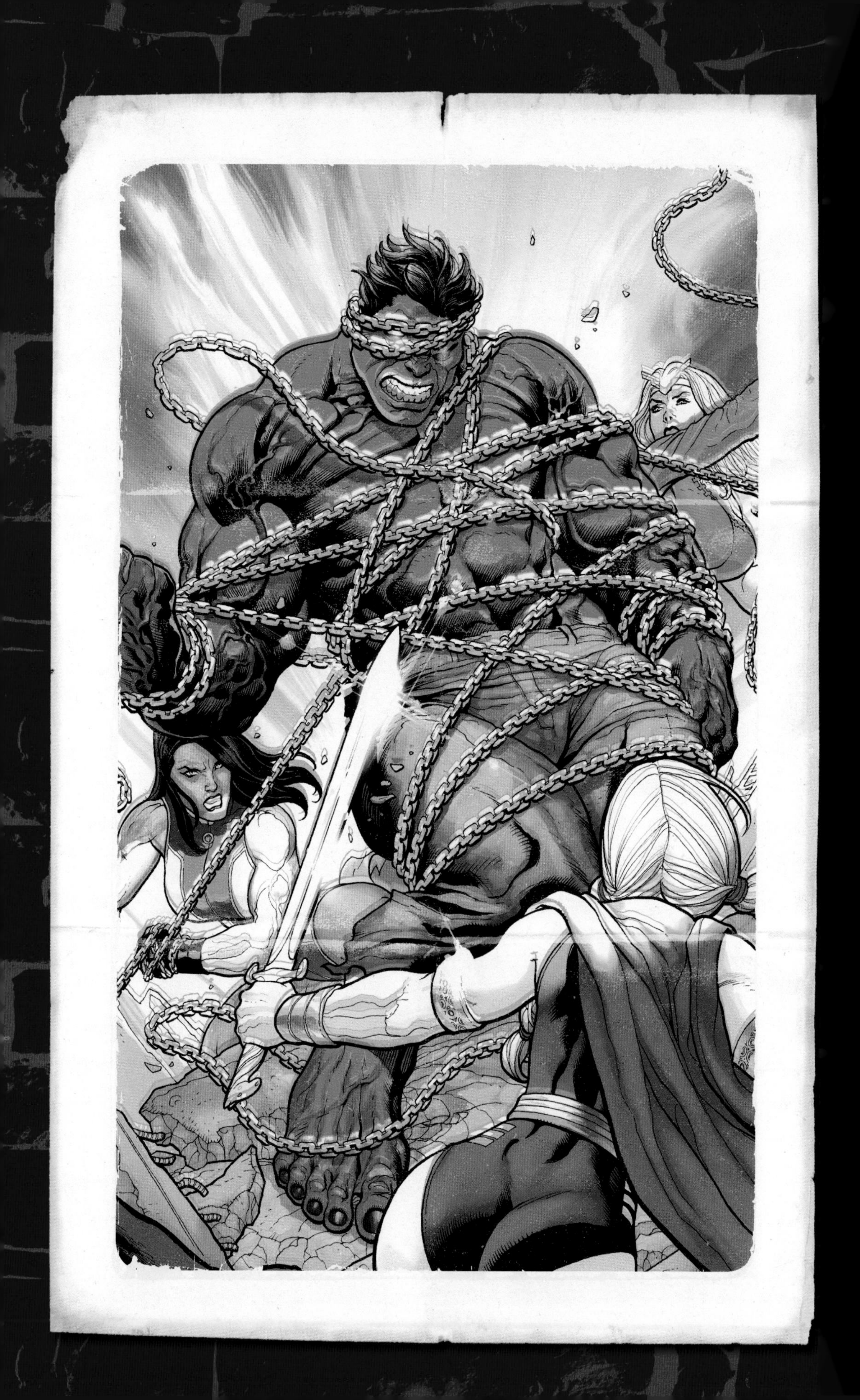

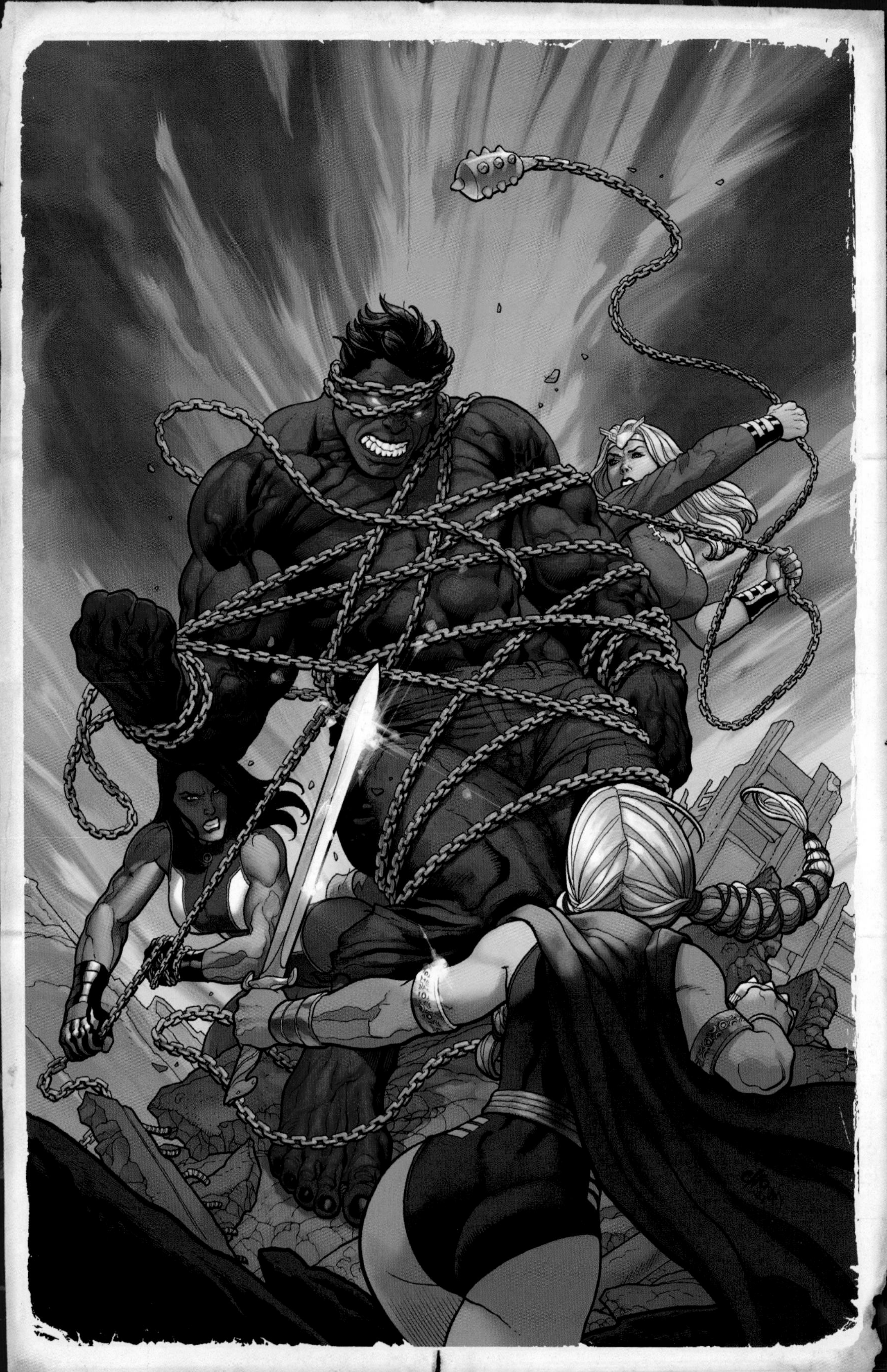

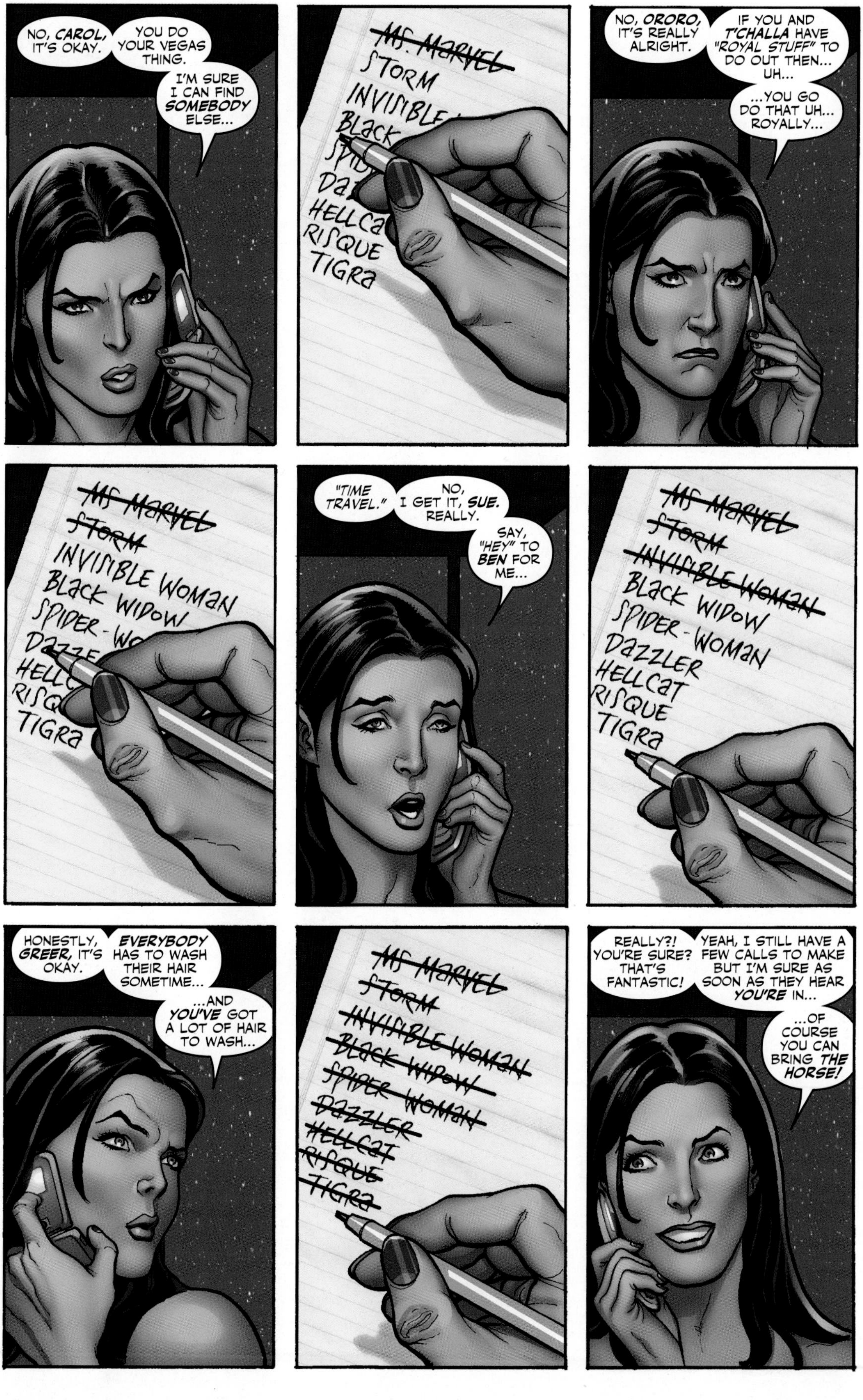
NO, CAROL, IT'S OKAY.
YOU DO YOUR VEGAS THING.
I'M SURE I CAN FIND SOMEBODY ELSE...
MS. MARVEL
STORM
RISQUE
TIGRA
NO, ORORO, IT'S REALLY ALRIGHT.
IF YOU AND T'CHALLA HAVE "ROYAL STUFF" TO DO OUT THEN... UH...
...YOU GO DO THAT UH... ROYALLY...
MS MARVEL
STORM
INVISIBLE WOMAN
BLACK WIDOW
TIGRA
"TIME TRAVEL."
NO, I GET IT, SUE. REALLY.
SAY, "HEY" TO BEN FOR ME...
MS MARVEL
STORM
INVISIBLE WOMAN
BLACK WIDOW
SPIDER-WOMAN
DAZZLER
HELLCAT
RISQUE
TIGRA
HONESTLY, GREER, IT'S OKAY.
EVERYBODY HAS TO WASH THEIR HAIR SOMETIME...
...AND YOU'VE GOT A LOT OF HAIR TO WASH...
MS MARVEL
STORM
INVISIBLE WOMAN
BLACK WIDOW
SPIDER WOMAN
DAZZLER
HELLCAT
RISQUE
TIGRA
REALLY?! YOU'RE SURE? THAT'S FANTASTIC!
YEAH, I STILL HAVE A FEW CALLS TO MAKE BUT I'M SURE AS SOON AS THEY HEAR YOU'RE IN...
...OF COURSE YOU CAN BRING THE HORSE!

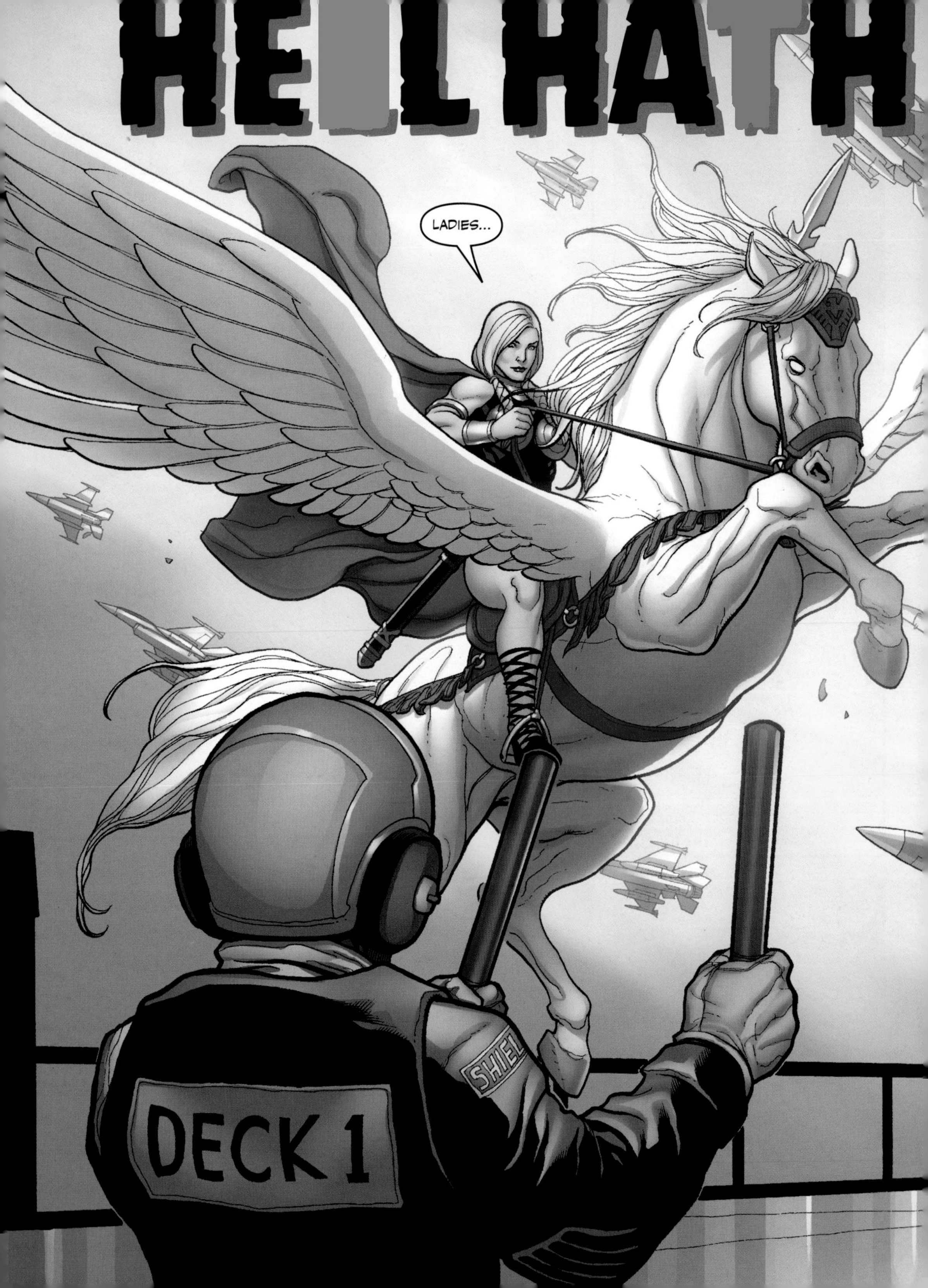
LADIES...
SHIEL
DECK 1

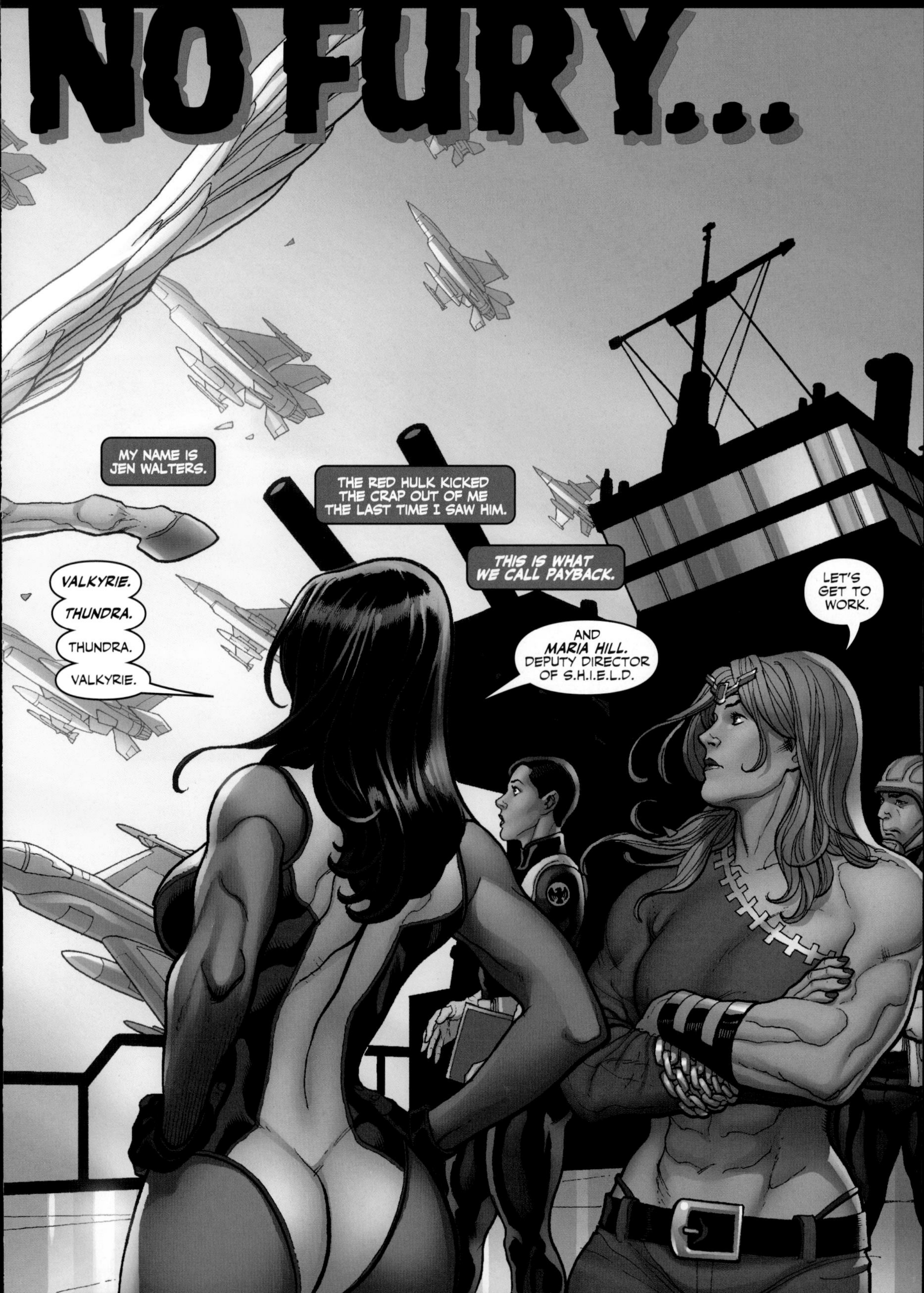
NO FURY...
MY NAME IS JEN WALTERS.
THE RED HULK KICKED THE CRAP OUT OF ME THE LAST TIME I SAW HIM.
THIS IS WHAT WE CALL PAYBACK.
VALKYRIE.
THUNDRA.
THUNDRA.
VALKYRIE.
AND MARIA HILL. DEPUTY DIRECTOR OF S.H.I.E.L.D.
LET'S GET TO WORK.

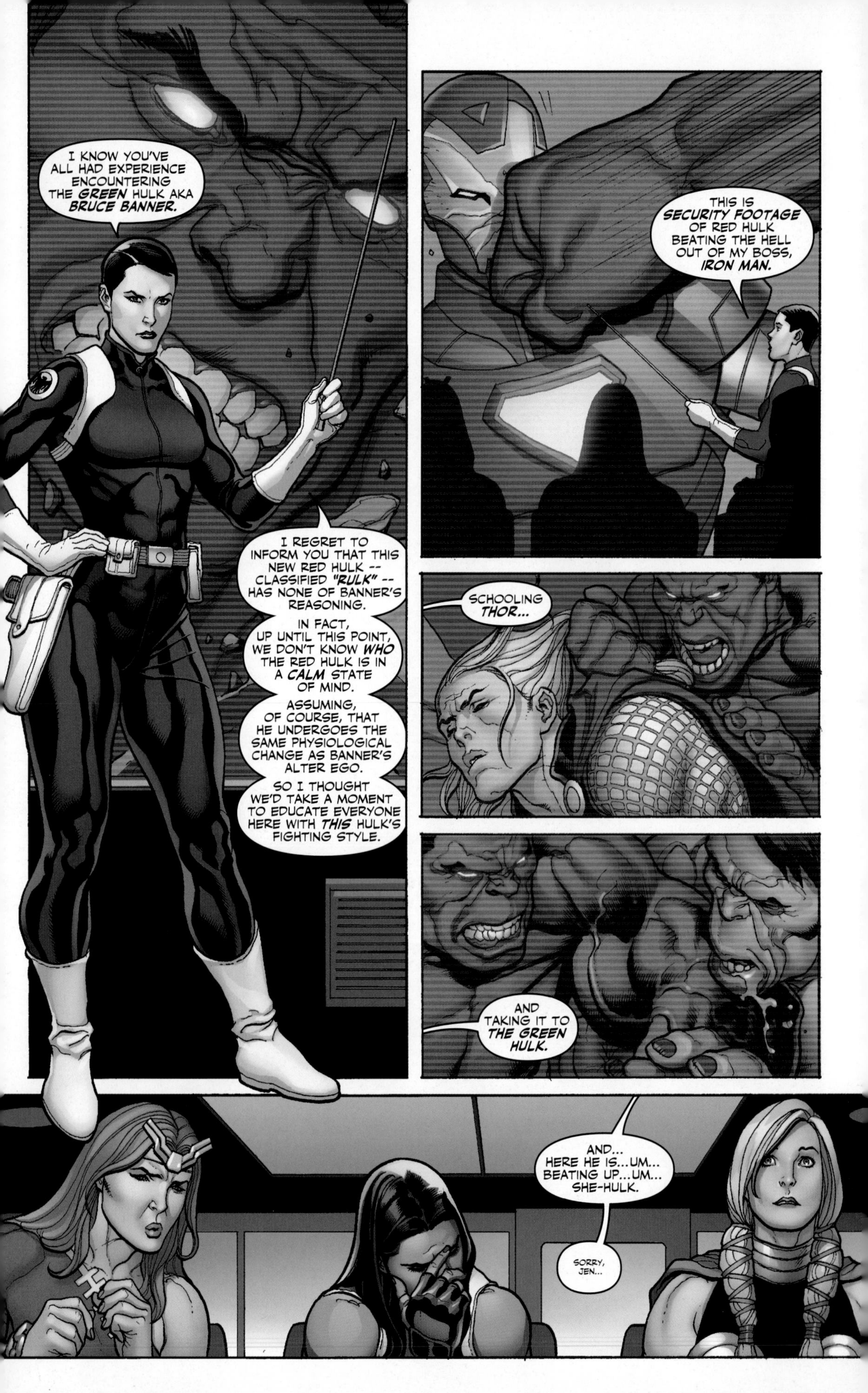
I KNOW YOU'VE ALL HAD EXPERIENCE ENCOUNTERING THE GREEN HULK AKA BRUCE BANNER.
THIS IS SECURITY FOOTAGE OF RED HULK BEATING THE HELL OUT OF MY BOSS, IRON MAN.
I REGRET TO INFORM YOU THAT THIS NEW RED HULK -- CLASSIFIED "RULK" -- HAS NONE OF BANNER'S REASONING.
IN FACT, UP UNTIL THIS POINT, WE DON'T KNOW WHO THE RED HULK IS IN A CALM STATE OF MIND.
ASSUMING, OF COURSE, THAT HE UNDERGOES THE SAME PHYSIOLOGICAL CHANGE AS BANNER'S ALTER EGO.
SO I THOUGHT WE'D TAKE A MOMENT TO EDUCATE EVERYONE HERE WITH THIS HULK'S FIGHTING STYLE.
SCHOOLING THOR...
AND TAKING IT TO THE GREEN HULK.
AND... HERE HE IS...UM... BEATING UP...UM... SHE-HULK.
SORRY, JEN...

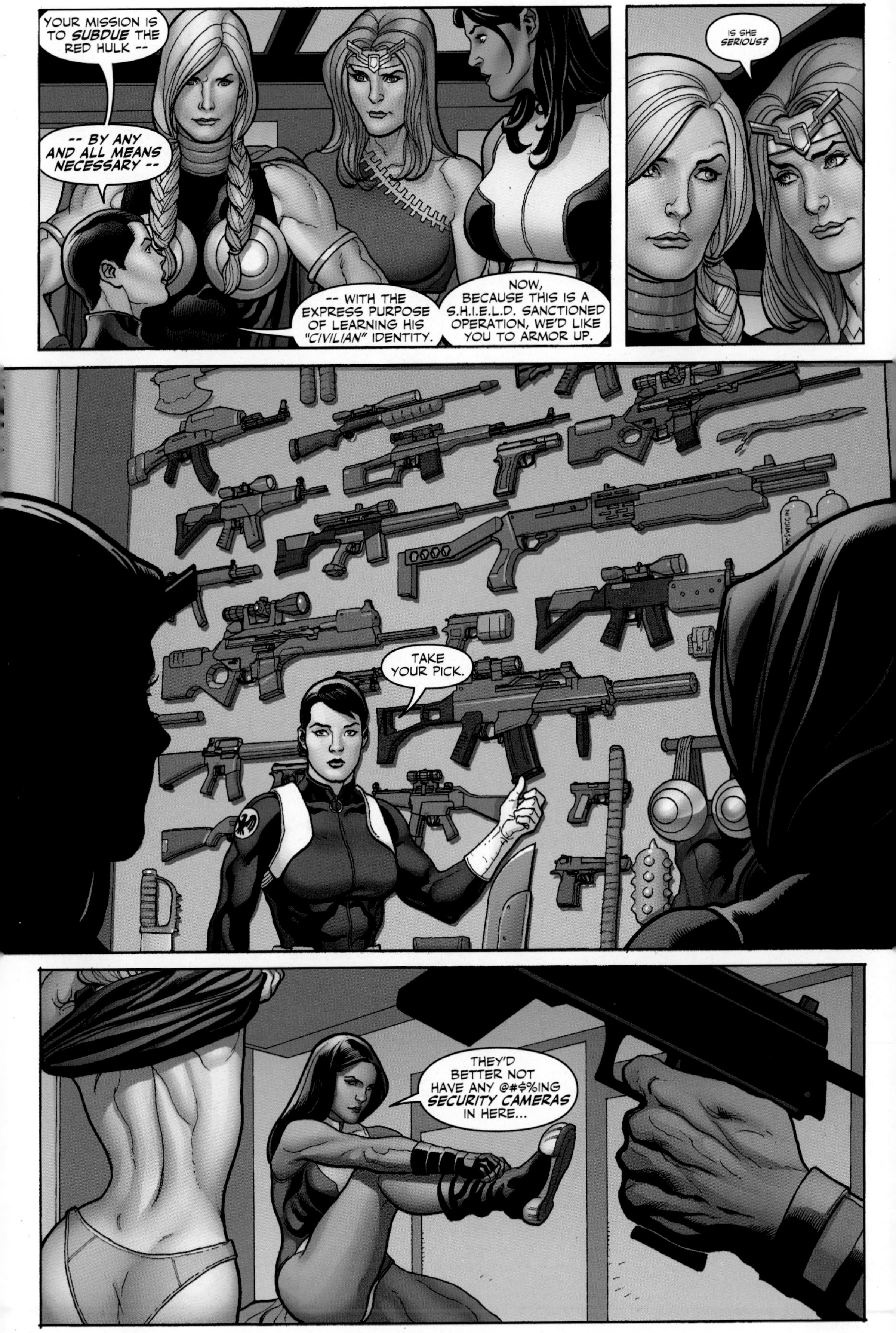
YOUR MISSION IS TO SUBDUE THE RED HULK --
-- BY ANY AND ALL MEANS NECESSARY --
-- WITH THE EXPRESS PURPOSE OF LEARNING HIS "CIVILIAN" IDENTITY.
NOW, BECAUSE THIS IS A S.H.I.E.L.D. SANCTIONED OPERATION, WE'D LIKE YOU TO ARMOR UP.
IS SHE SERIOUS?
TAKE YOUR PICK.
THEY'D BETTER NOT HAVE ANY @#$%ING SECURITY CAMERAS IN HERE...

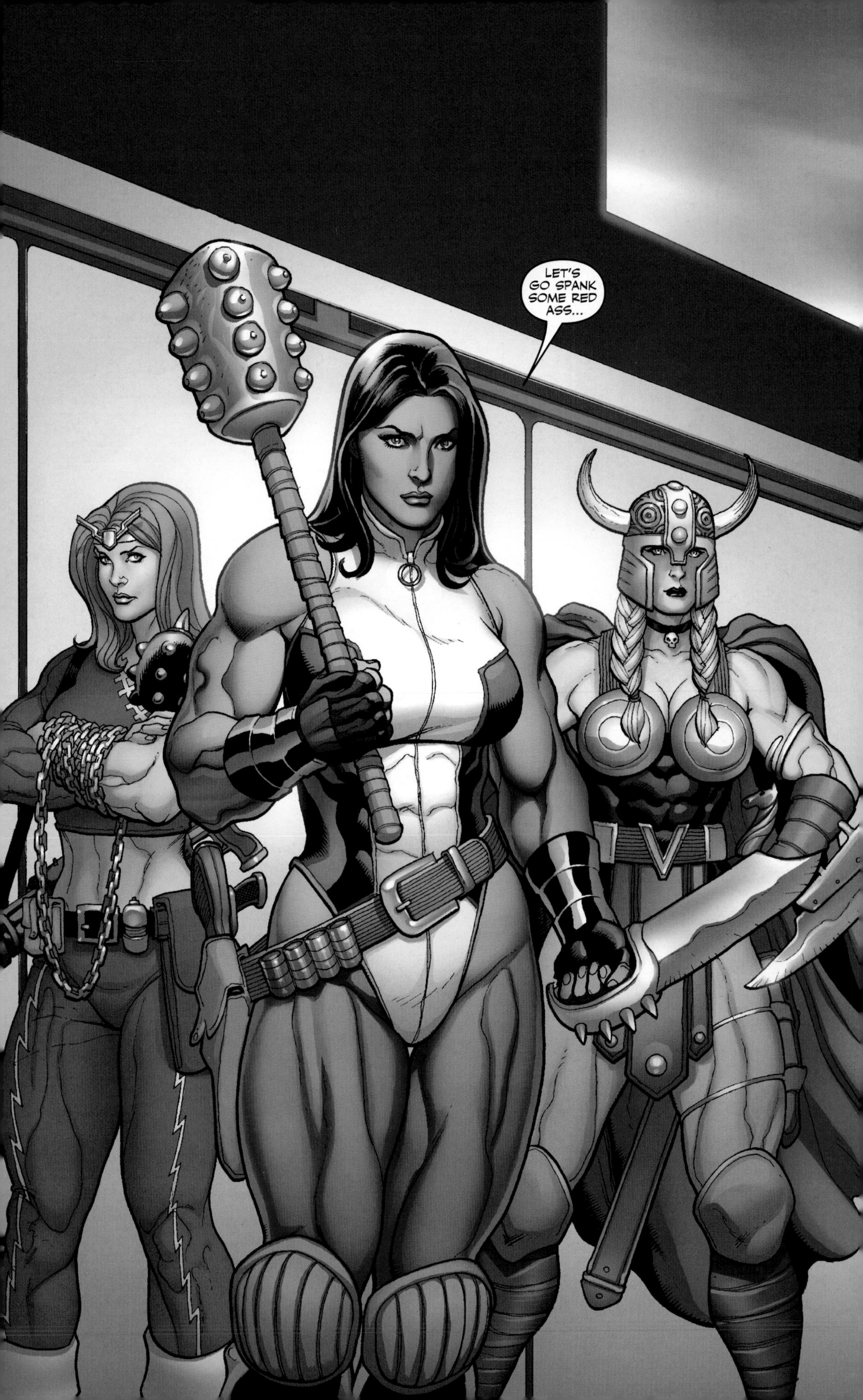
LET'S GO SPANK SOME RED ASS...

IT TOOK A FEW DAYS TO LOCATE HIM.

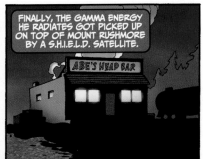

FINALLY, THE GAMMA ENERGY HE RADIATES GOT PICKED UP ON TOP OF MOUNT RUSHMORE BY A S.H.I.E.L.D. SATELLITE.

ABE'S HEAD BAR

WE WERE THERE WITHIN THE HOUR.

I'D ASK YOU TO SURRENDER...

...BUT, WE'RE *REALLY* HOPING YOU'LL PUT UP A FIGHT...

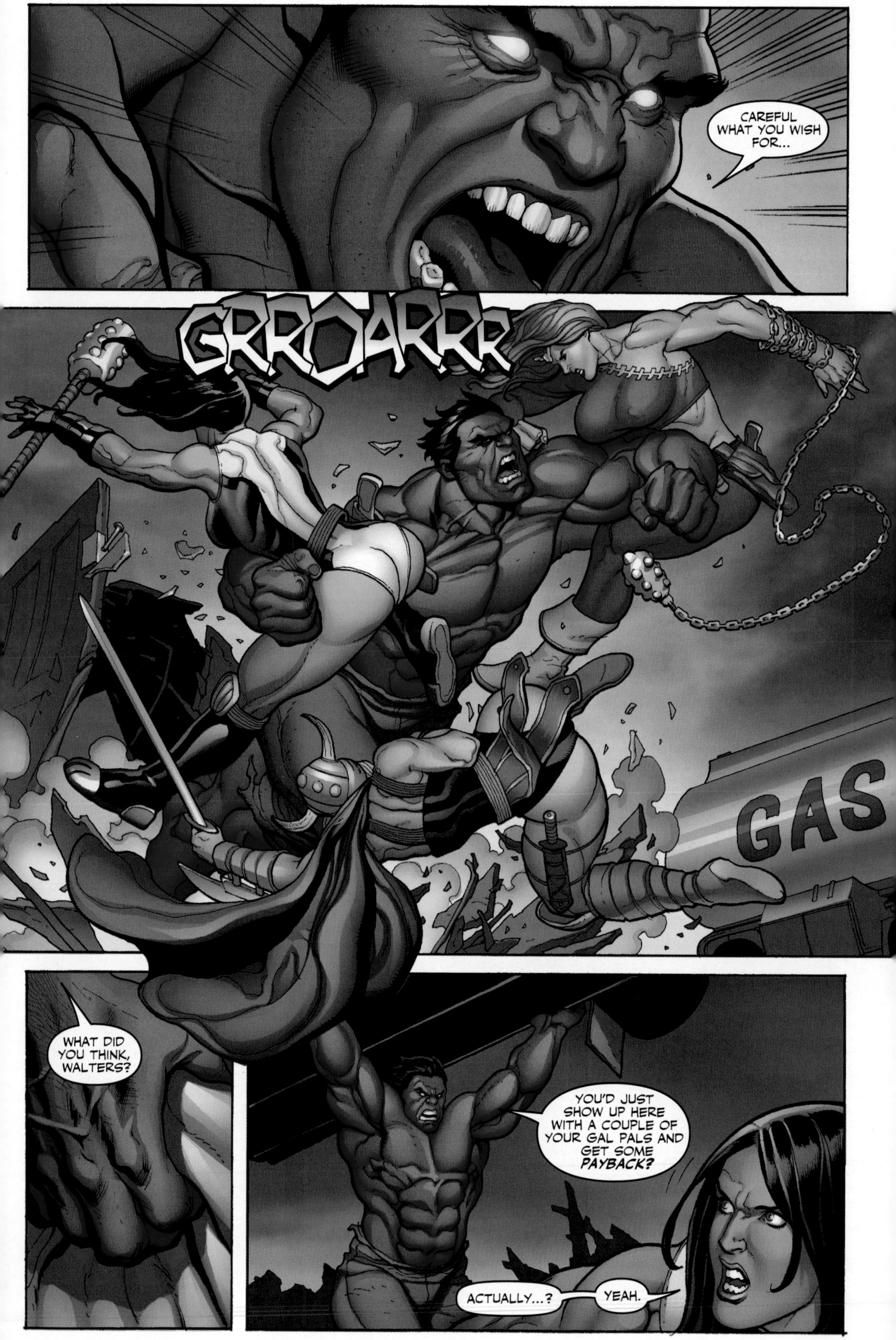
CAREFUL WHAT YOU WISH FOR...
GRROARRR
GAS
WHAT DID YOU THINK, WALTERS?
YOU'D JUST SHOW UP HERE WITH A COUPLE OF YOUR GAL PALS AND GET SOME PAYBACK?
ACTUALLY...?
YEAH.

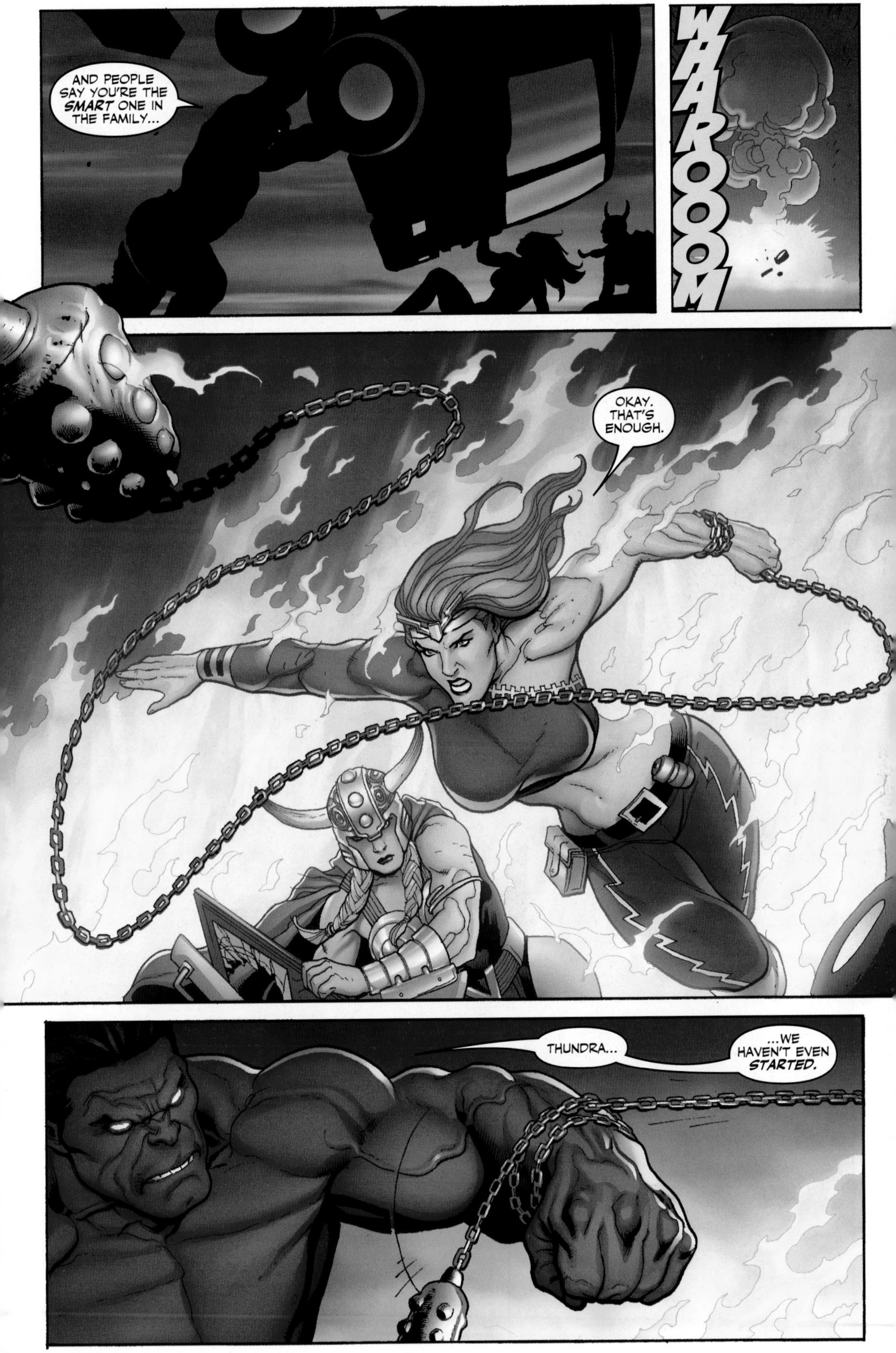
AND PEOPLE SAY YOU'RE THE *SMART* ONE IN THE FAMILY...
WHAROOOOM
OKAY. THAT'S ENOUGH.
THUNDRA...
...WE HAVEN'T EVEN *STARTED.*

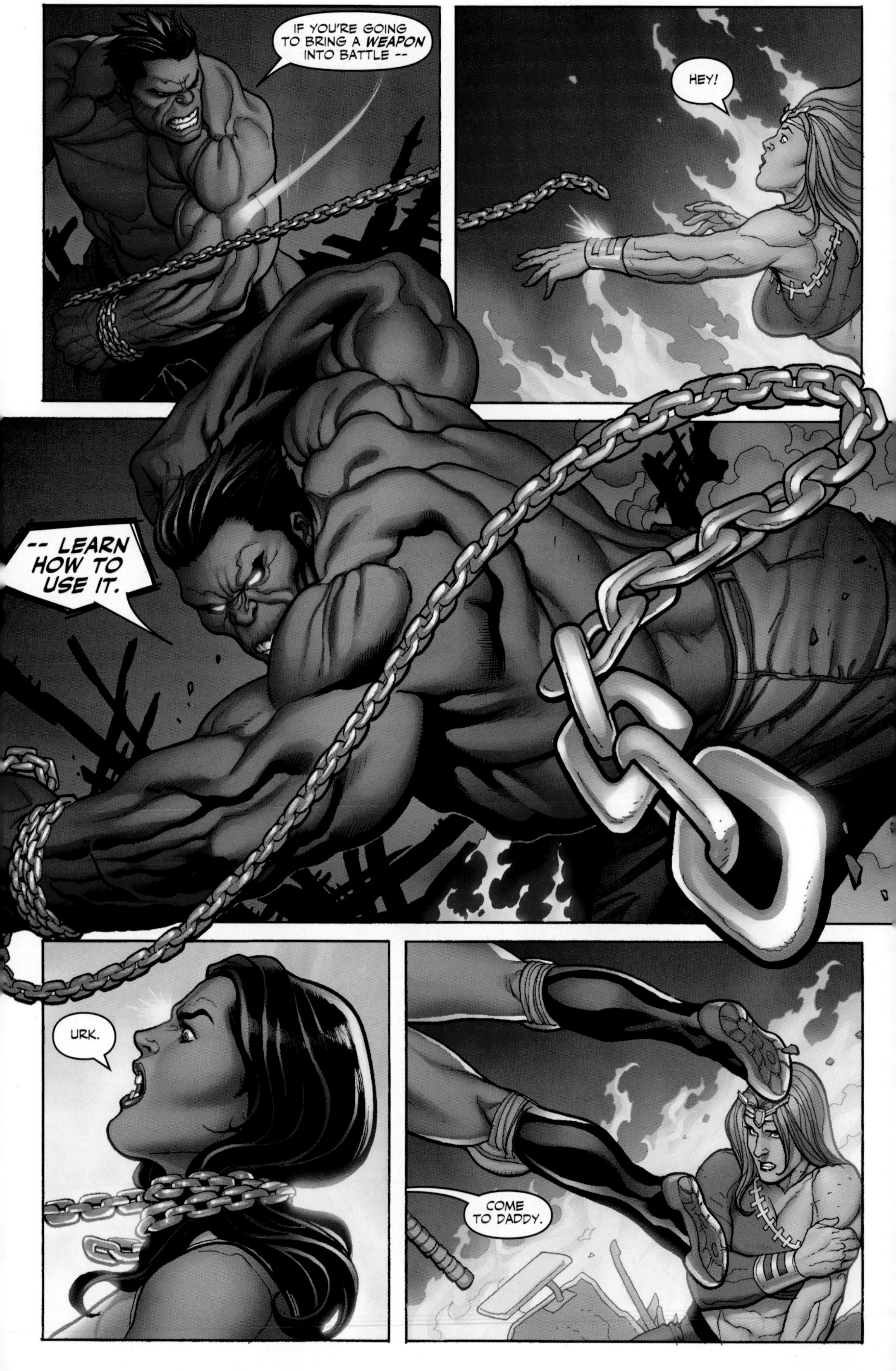
IF YOU'RE GOING TO BRING A WEAPON INTO BATTLE --
HEY!
-- LEARN HOW TO USE IT.
URK.
COME TO DADDY.

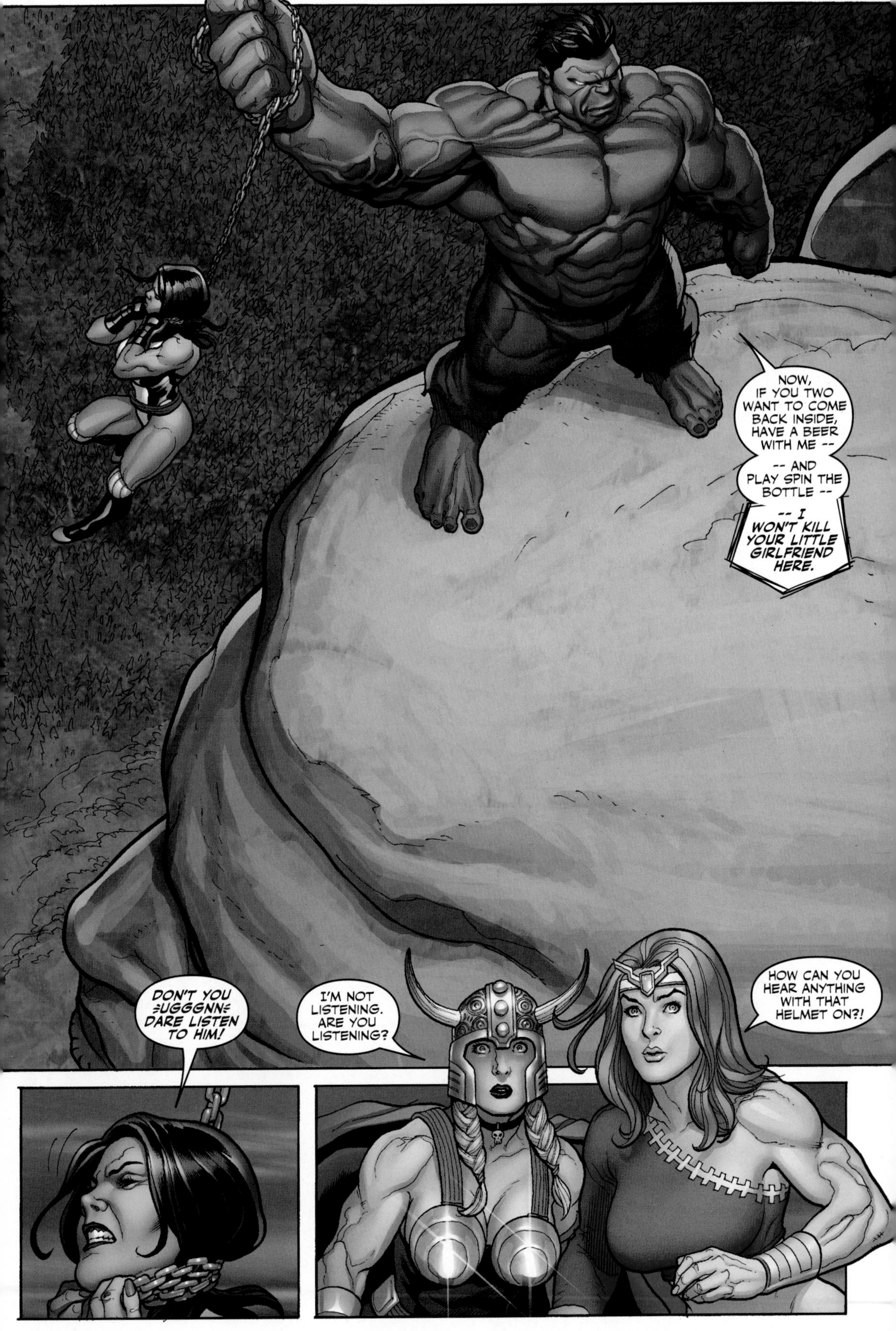
NOW, IF YOU TWO WANT TO COME BACK INSIDE, HAVE A BEER WITH ME --
-- AND PLAY SPIN THE BOTTLE --
-- I WON'T KILL YOUR LITTLE GIRLFRIEND HERE.
HOW CAN YOU HEAR ANYTHING WITH THAT HELMET ON?!
I'M NOT LISTENING. ARE YOU LISTENING?
DON'T YOU =UGGGNN= DARE LISTEN TO HIM!

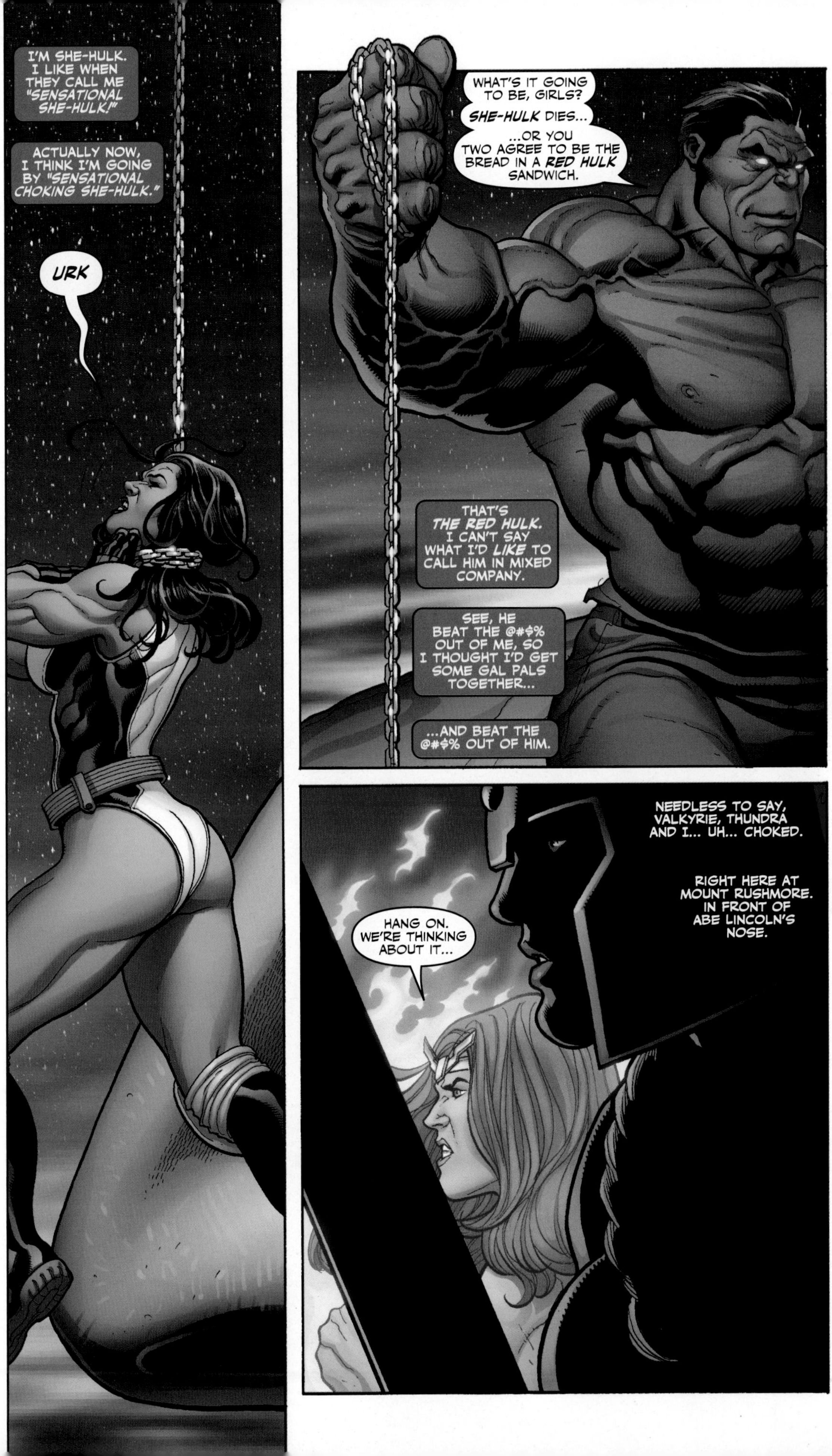
I'M SHE-HULK. I LIKE WHEN THEY CALL ME "SENSATIONAL SHE-HULK!"
ACTUALLY NOW, I THINK I'M GOING BY "SENSATIONAL CHOKING SHE-HULK."
URK
WHAT'S IT GOING TO BE, GIRLS? SHE-HULK DIES...
...OR YOU TWO AGREE TO BE THE BREAD IN A RED HULK SANDWICH.
THAT'S THE RED HULK. I CAN'T SAY WHAT I'D LIKE TO CALL HIM IN MIXED COMPANY.
SEE, HE BEAT THE @#$% OUT OF ME, SO I THOUGHT I'D GET SOME GAL PALS TOGETHER...
...AND BEAT THE @#$% OUT OF HIM.
NEEDLESS TO SAY, VALKYRIE, THUNDRA AND I... UH... CHOKED.
RIGHT HERE AT MOUNT RUSHMORE. IN FRONT OF ABE LINCOLN'S NOSE.
HANG ON. WE'RE THINKING ABOUT IT...

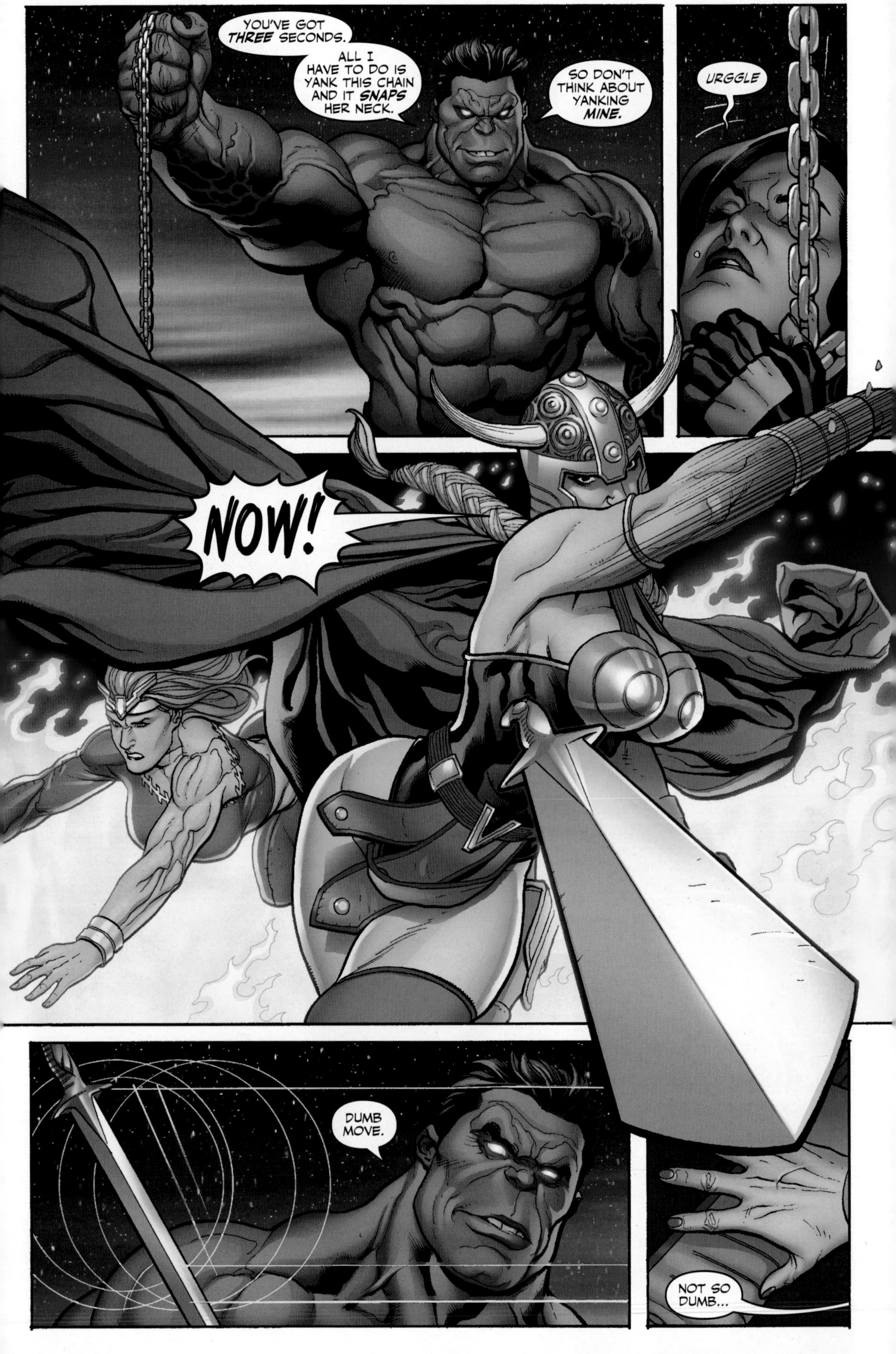
YOU'VE GOT THREE SECONDS.
ALL I HAVE TO DO IS YANK THIS CHAIN AND IT SNAPS HER NECK.
SO DON'T THINK ABOUT YANKING MINE.
URGGLE
NOW!
DUMB MOVE.
NOT SO DUMB...

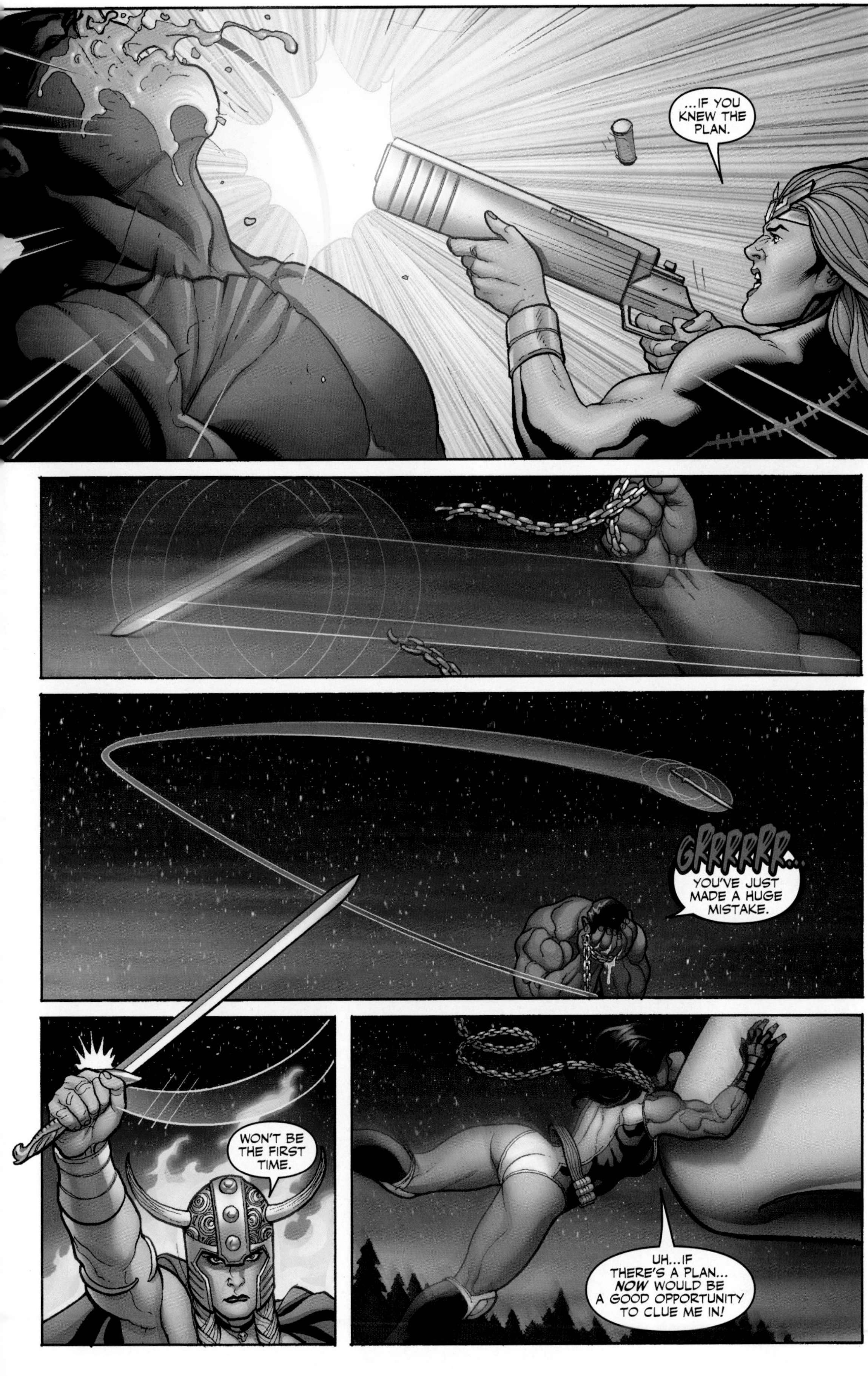
...IF YOU KNEW THE PLAN.
GRRRRRR...
YOU'VE JUST MADE A HUGE MISTAKE.
WON'T BE THE FIRST TIME.
UH...IF THERE'S A PLAN... *NOW* WOULD BE A GOOD OPPORTUNITY TO CLUE ME IN!

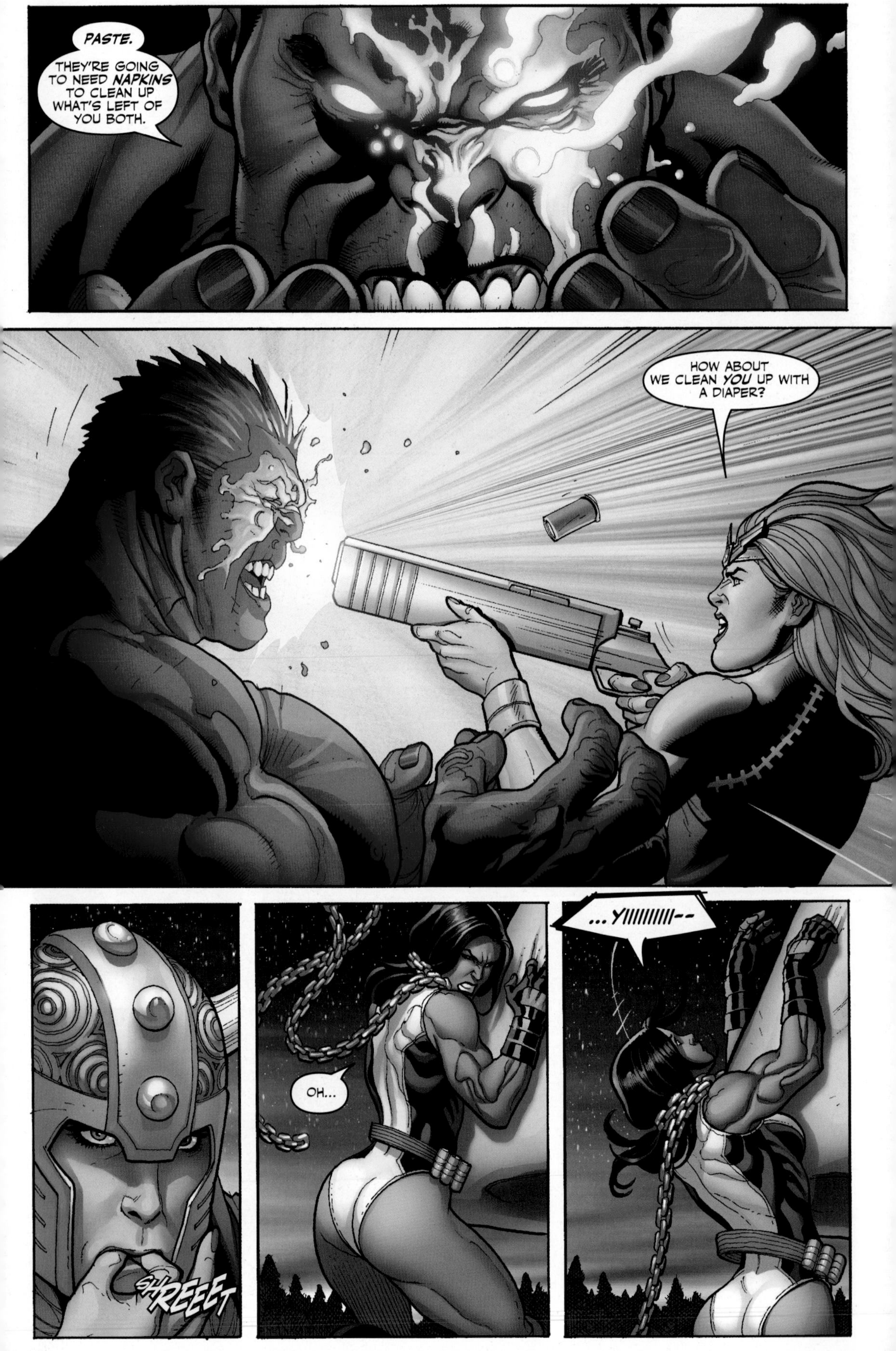
PASTE.
THEY'RE GOING TO NEED NAPKINS TO CLEAN UP WHAT'S LEFT OF YOU BOTH.
HOW ABOUT WE CLEAN YOU UP WITH A DIAPER?
SHREEET
OH...
...YIIIIIIIII--

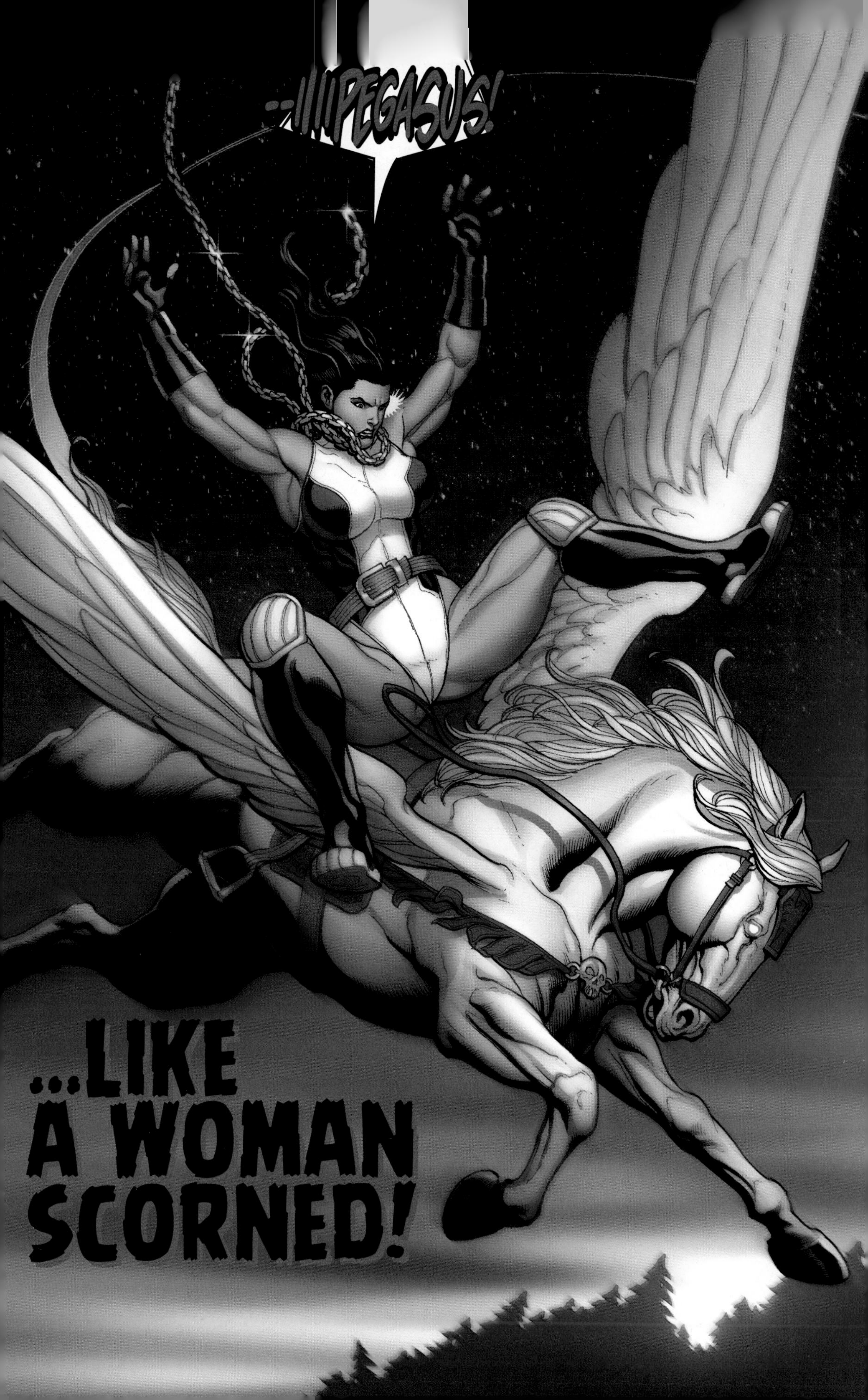
--IIIIPEGASUS!
...LIKE A WOMAN SCORNED!

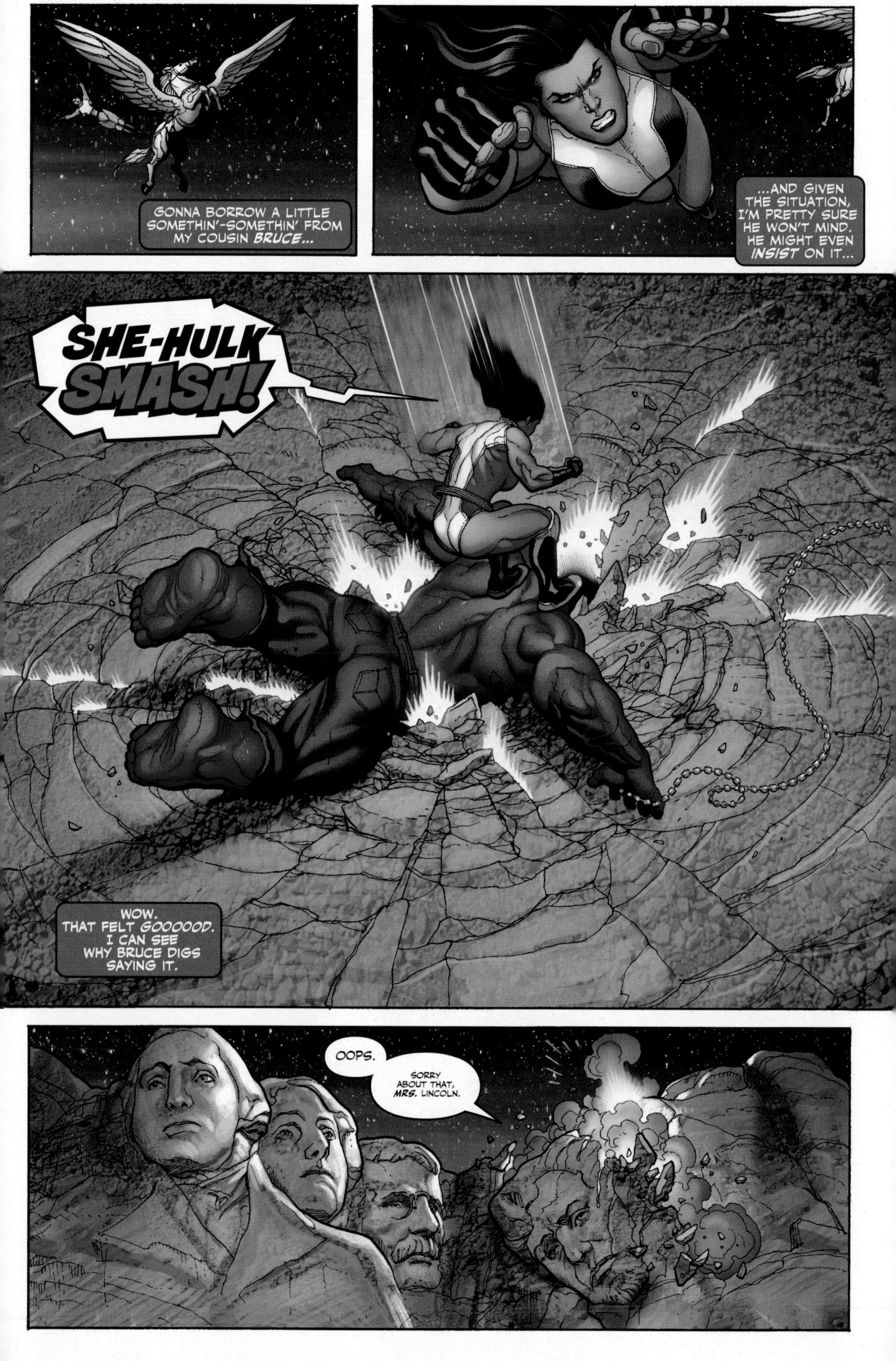
GONNA BORROW A LITTLE SOMETHIN'-SOMETHIN' FROM MY COUSIN BRUCE...
...AND GIVEN THE SITUATION, I'M PRETTY SURE HE WON'T MIND. HE MIGHT EVEN INSIST ON IT...
SHE-HULK SMASH!
WOW. THAT FELT GOOOOOD. I CAN SEE WHY BRUCE DIGS SAYING IT.
OOPS.
SORRY ABOUT THAT, MRS. LINCOLN.

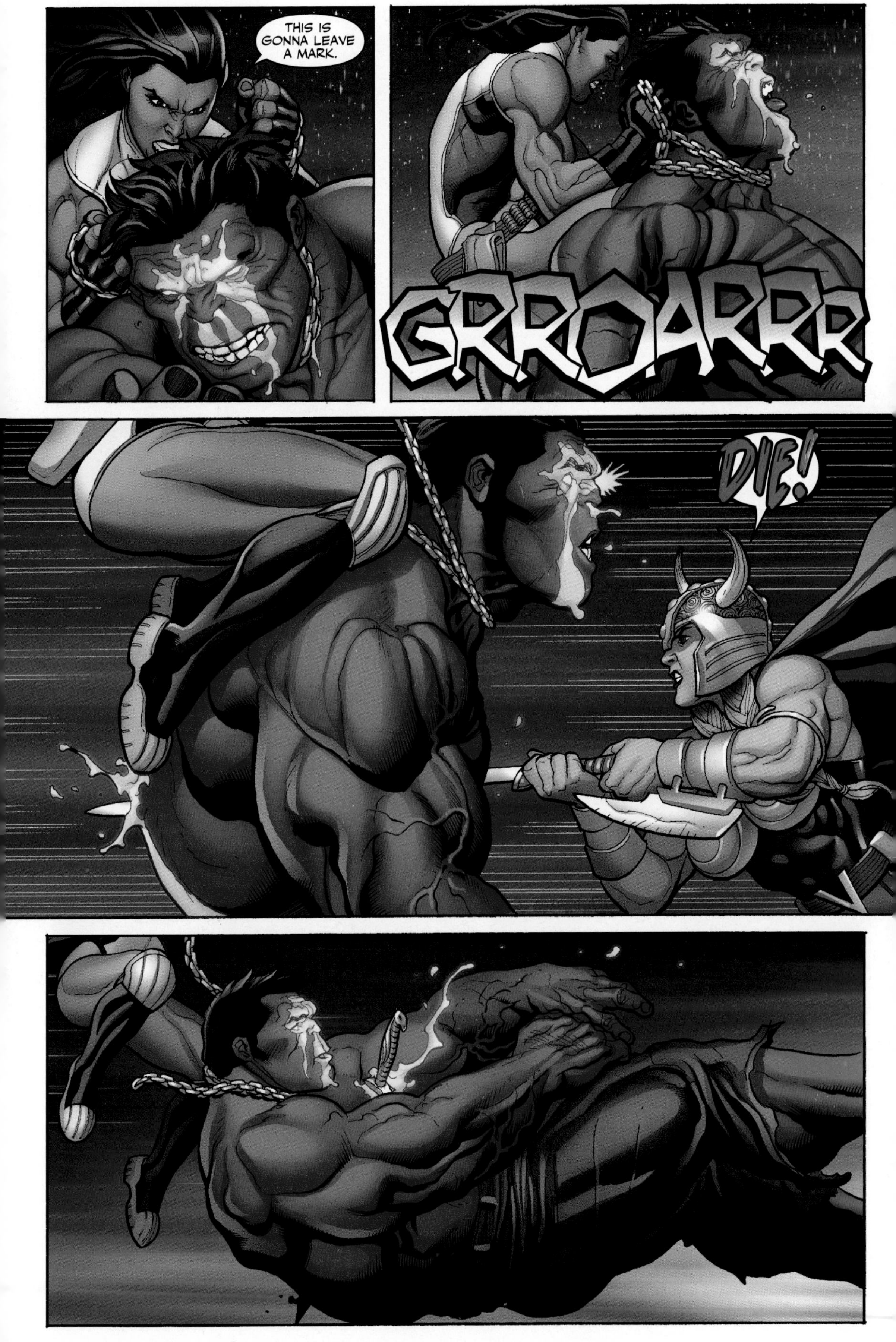
THIS IS GONNA LEAVE A MARK.
GRROARRR
DIE!

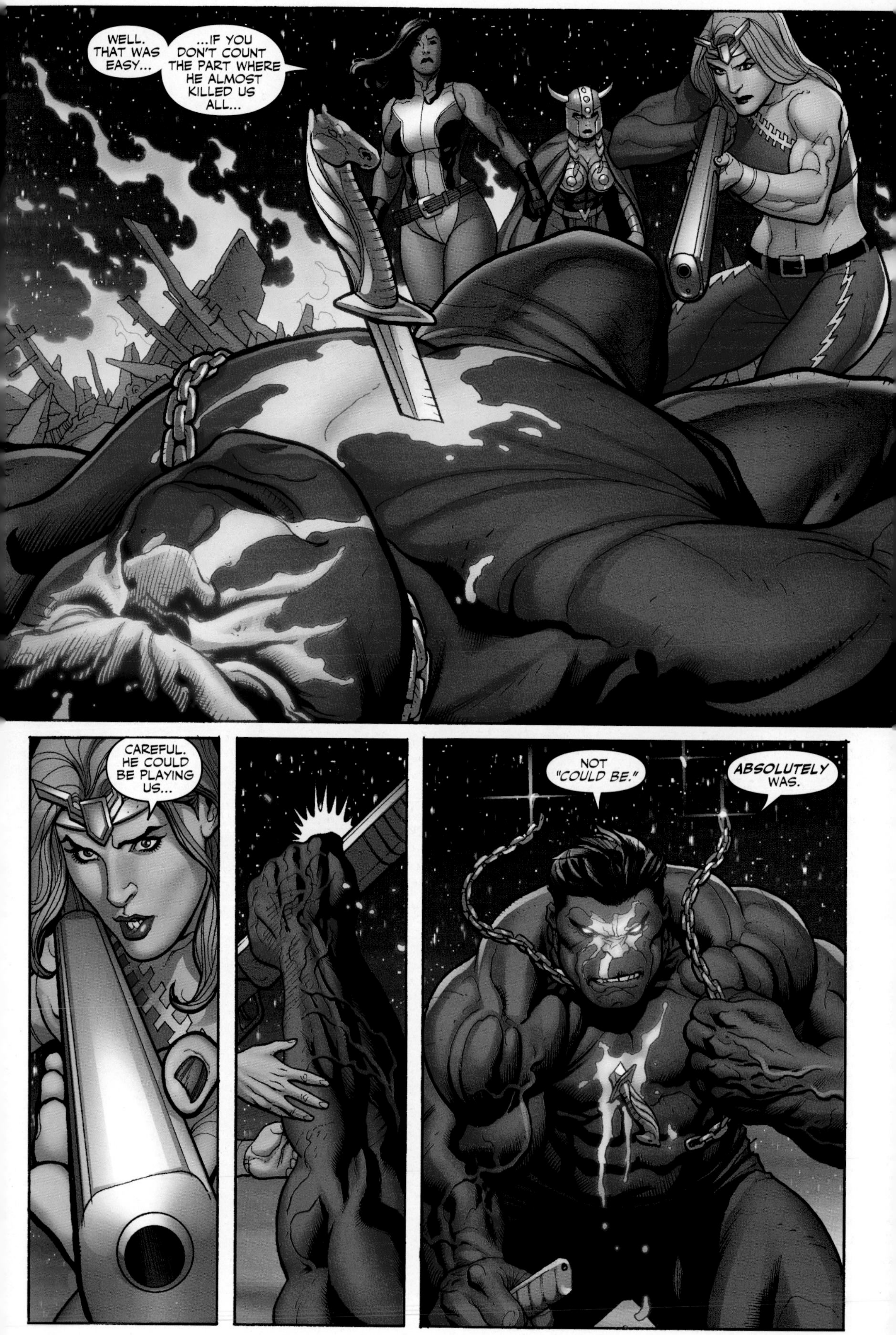
WELL. THAT WAS EASY...
...IF YOU DON'T COUNT THE PART WHERE HE ALMOST KILLED US ALL...
CAREFUL. HE COULD BE PLAYING US...
NOT "COULD BE."
ABSOLUTELY WAS.

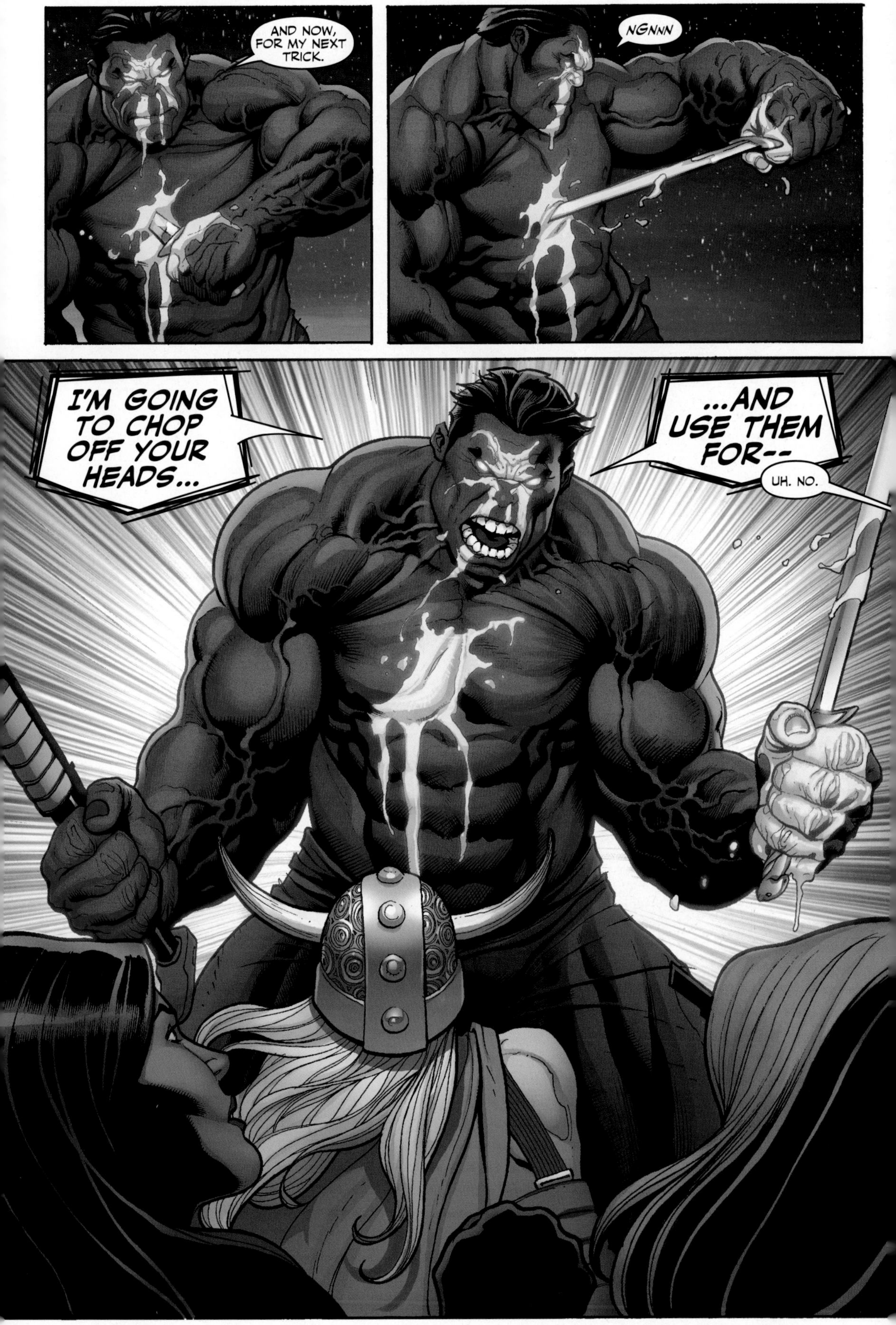
AND NOW, FOR MY NEXT TRICK.
NGNNN
I'M GOING TO CHOP OFF YOUR HEADS...
...AND USE THEM FOR--
UH. NO.

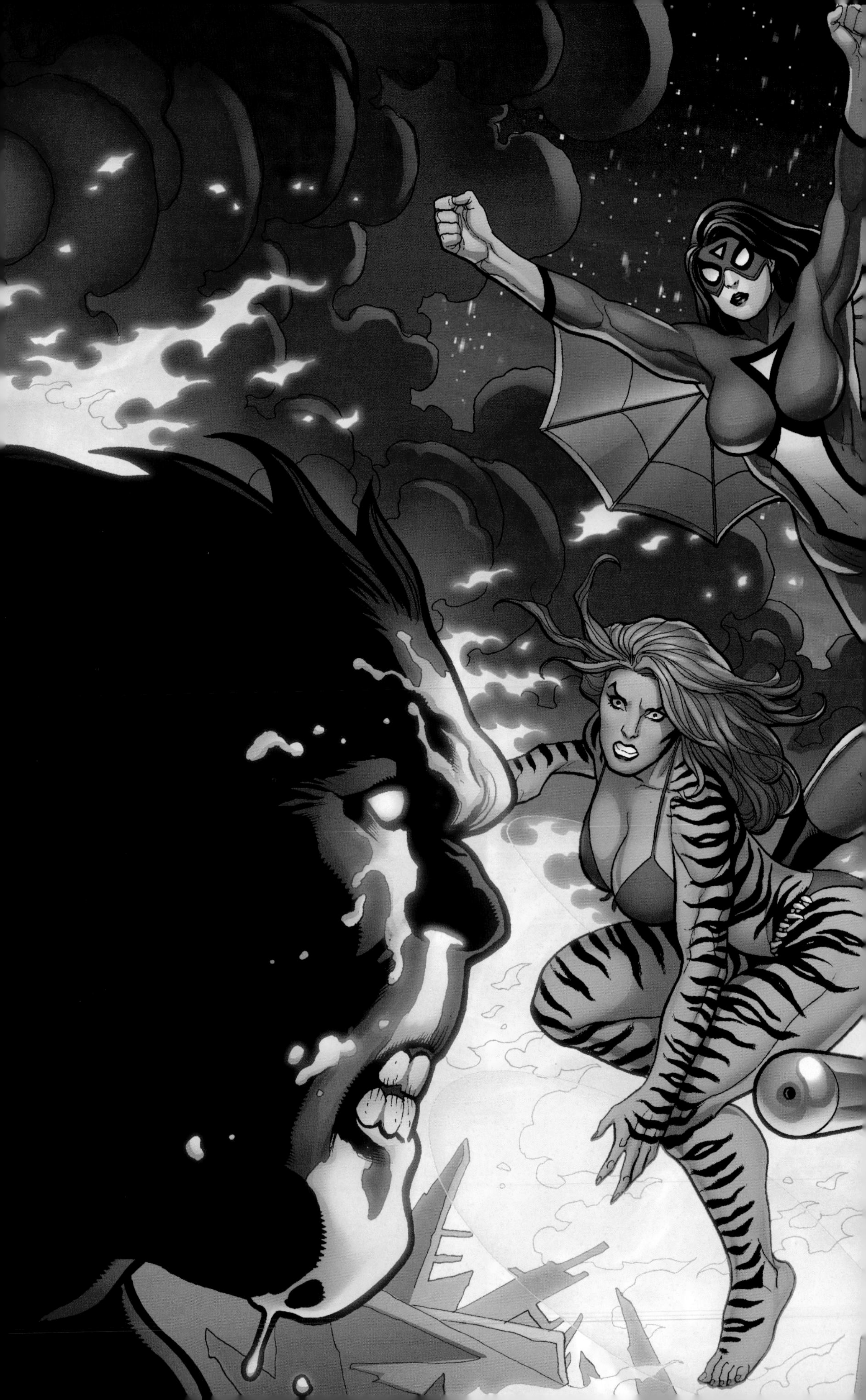

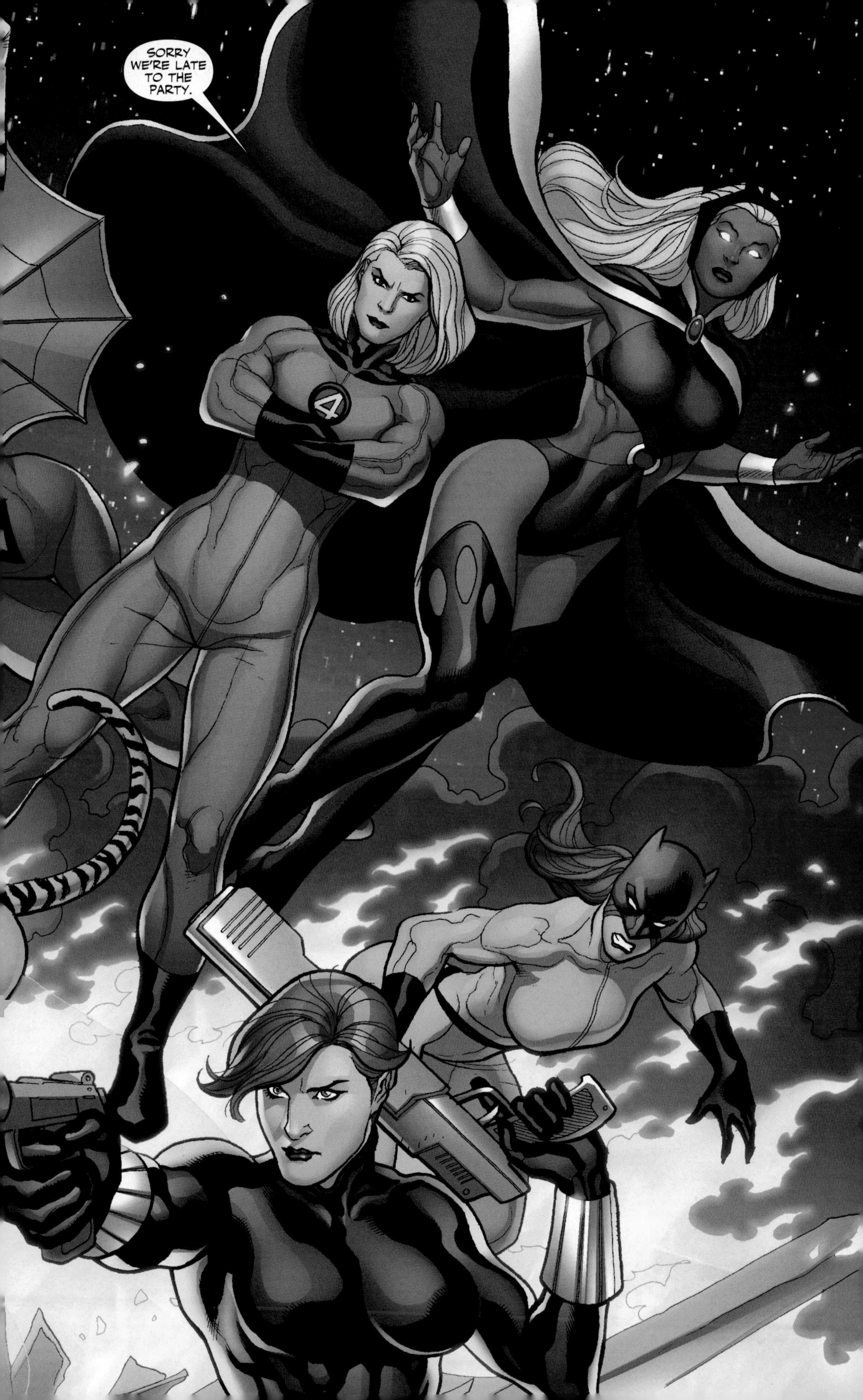
SORRY WE'RE LATE TO THE PARTY.

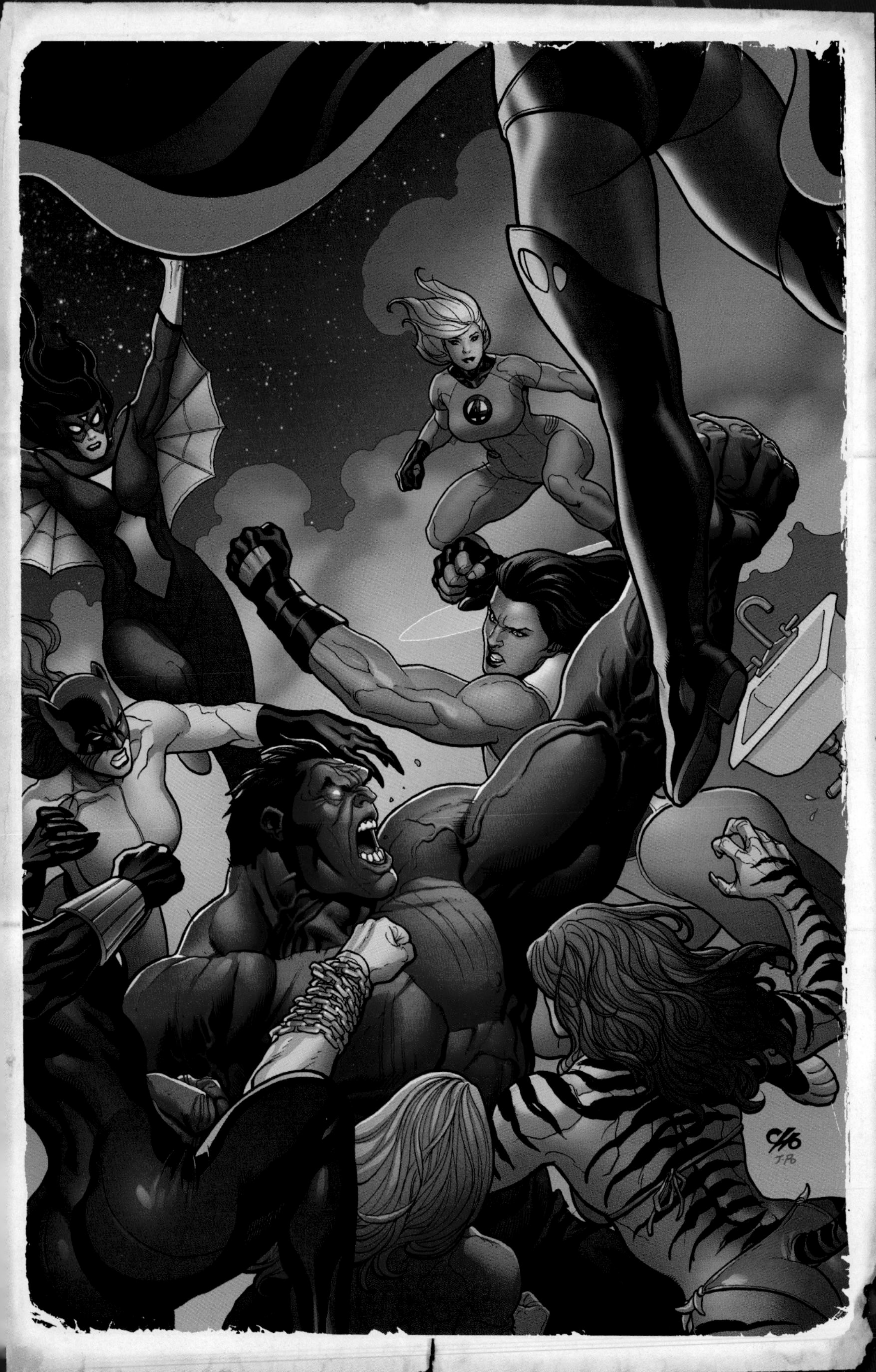

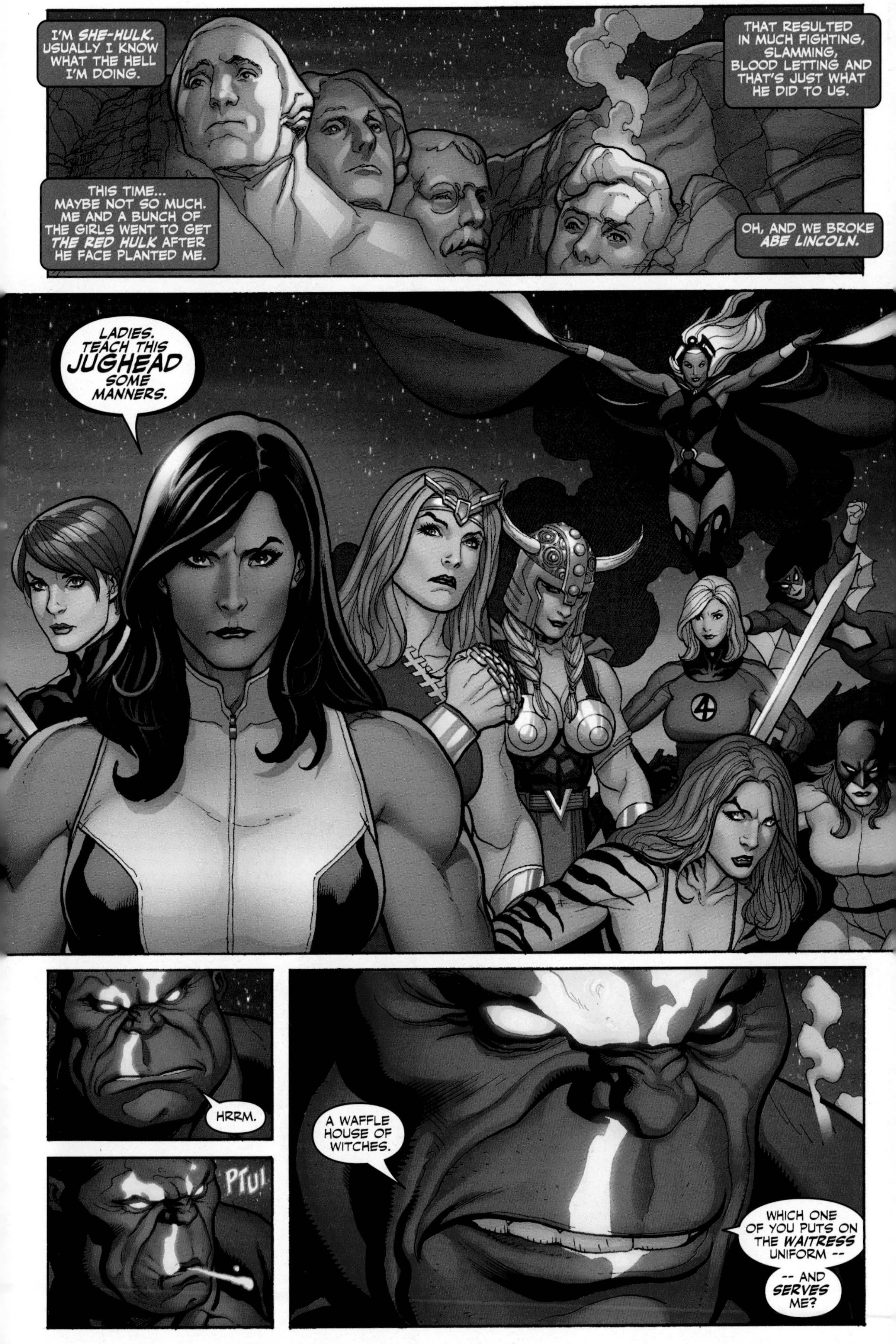
I'M SHE-HULK. USUALLY I KNOW WHAT THE HELL I'M DOING.
THIS TIME... MAYBE NOT SO MUCH. ME AND A BUNCH OF THE GIRLS WENT TO GET THE RED HULK AFTER HE FACE PLANTED ME.
THAT RESULTED IN MUCH FIGHTING, SLAMMING, BLOOD LETTING AND THAT'S JUST WHAT HE DID TO US.
OH, AND WE BROKE ABE LINCOLN.
LADIES. TEACH THIS JUGHEAD SOME MANNERS.
HRRM.
PTUI
A WAFFLE HOUSE OF WITCHES.
WHICH ONE OF YOU PUTS ON THE WAITRESS UNIFORM --
-- AND SERVES ME?

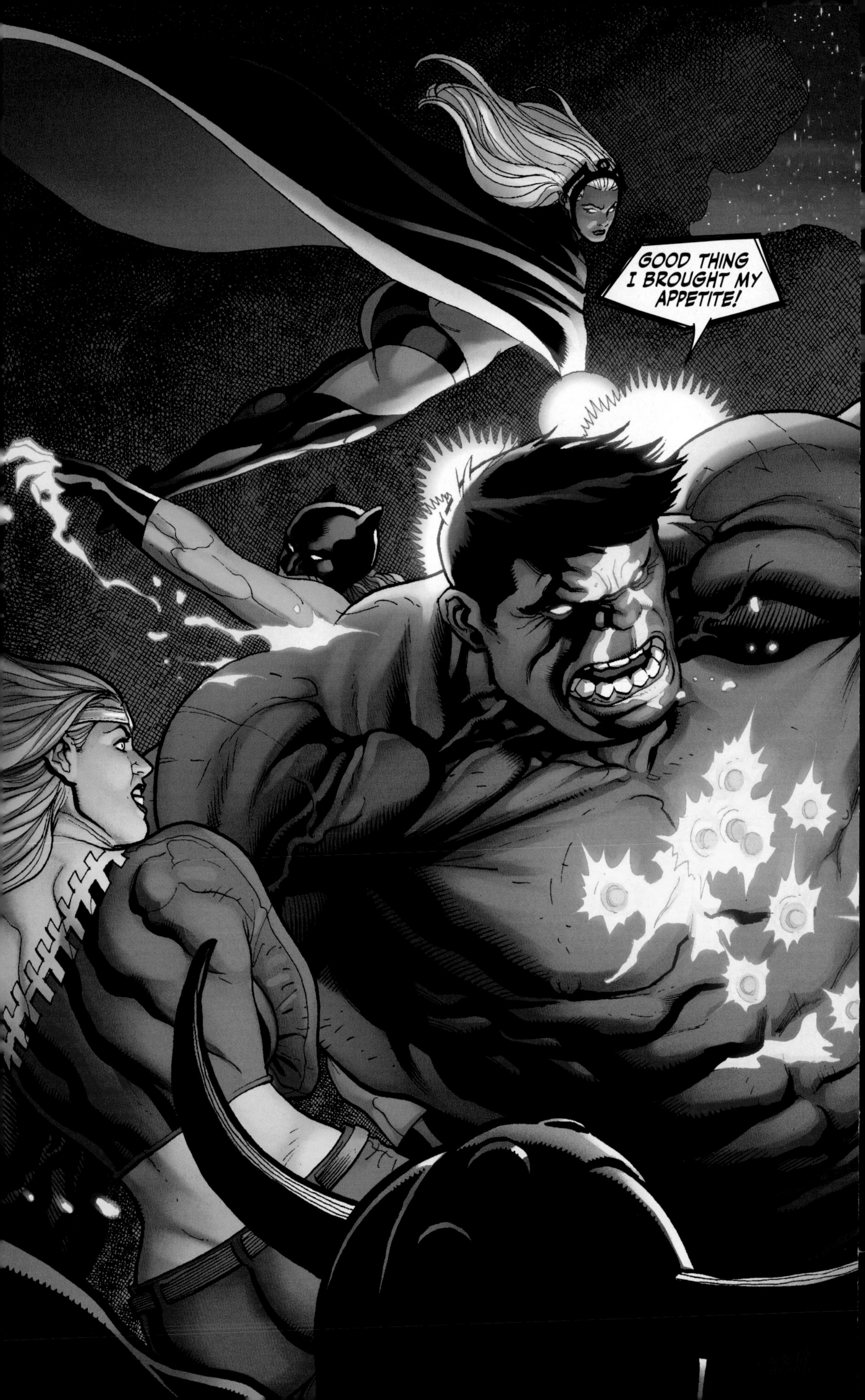
GOOD THING I BROUGHT MY APPETITE!

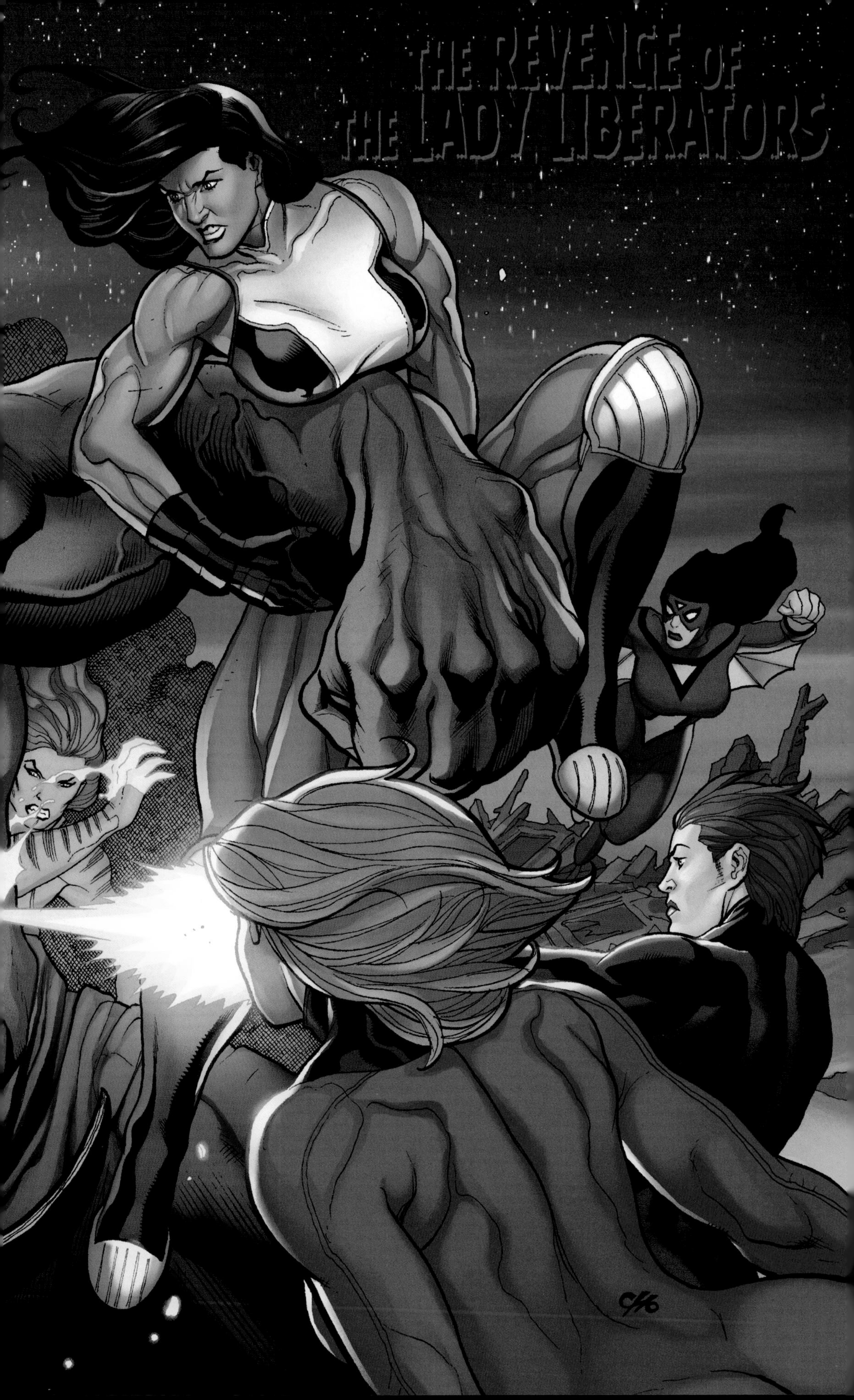
THE REVENGE OF
THE LADY LIBERATORS

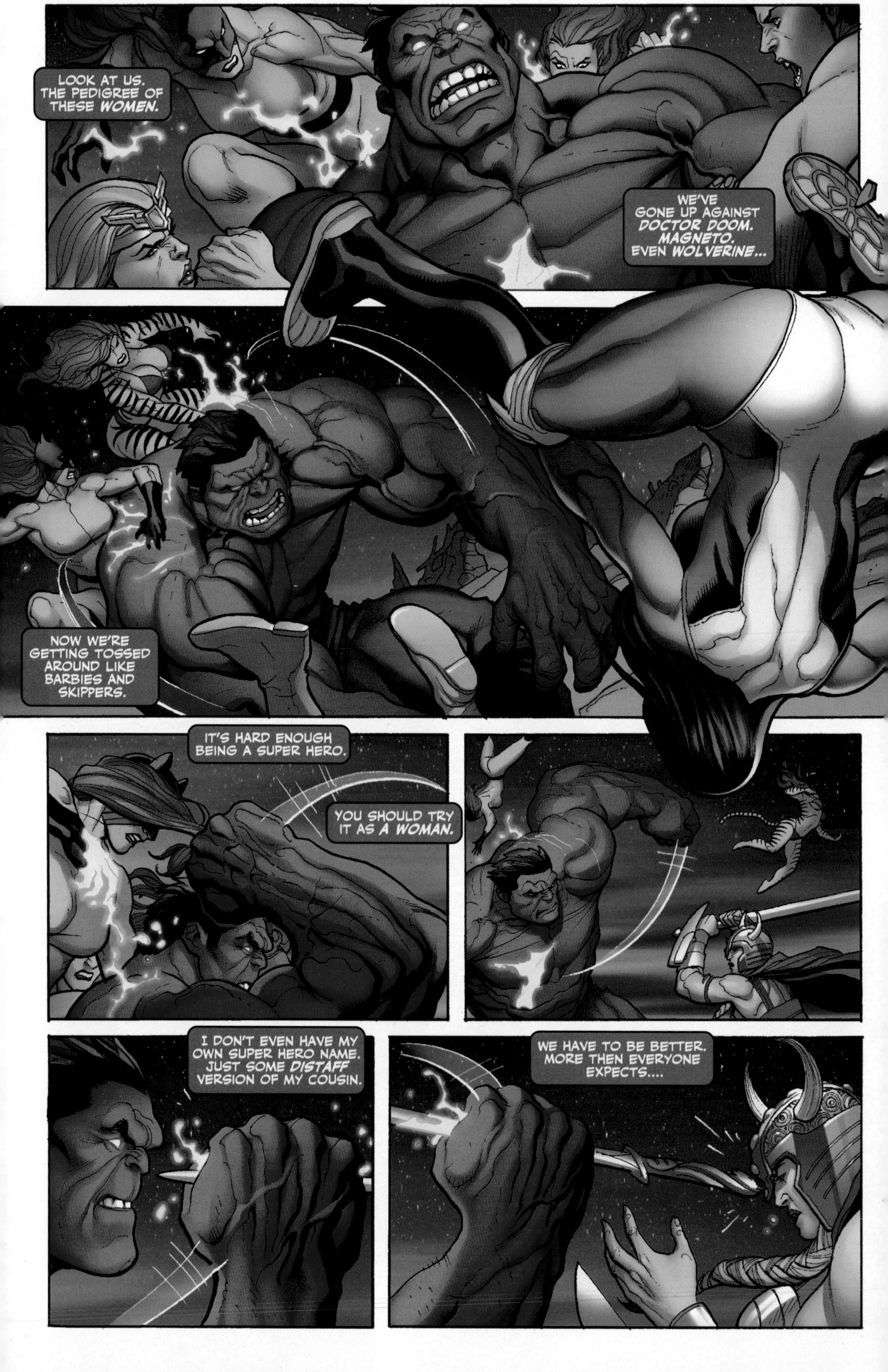
LOOK AT US. THE PEDIGREE OF THESE WOMEN.
WE'VE GONE UP AGAINST DOCTOR DOOM. MAGNETO. EVEN WOLVERINE...
NOW WE'RE GETTING TOSSED AROUND LIKE BARBIES AND SKIPPERS.
IT'S HARD ENOUGH BEING A SUPER HERO.
YOU SHOULD TRY IT AS A WOMAN.
I DON'T EVEN HAVE MY OWN SUPER HERO NAME. JUST SOME DISTAFF VERSION OF MY COUSIN.
WE HAVE TO BE BETTER. MORE THEN EVERYONE EXPECTS....

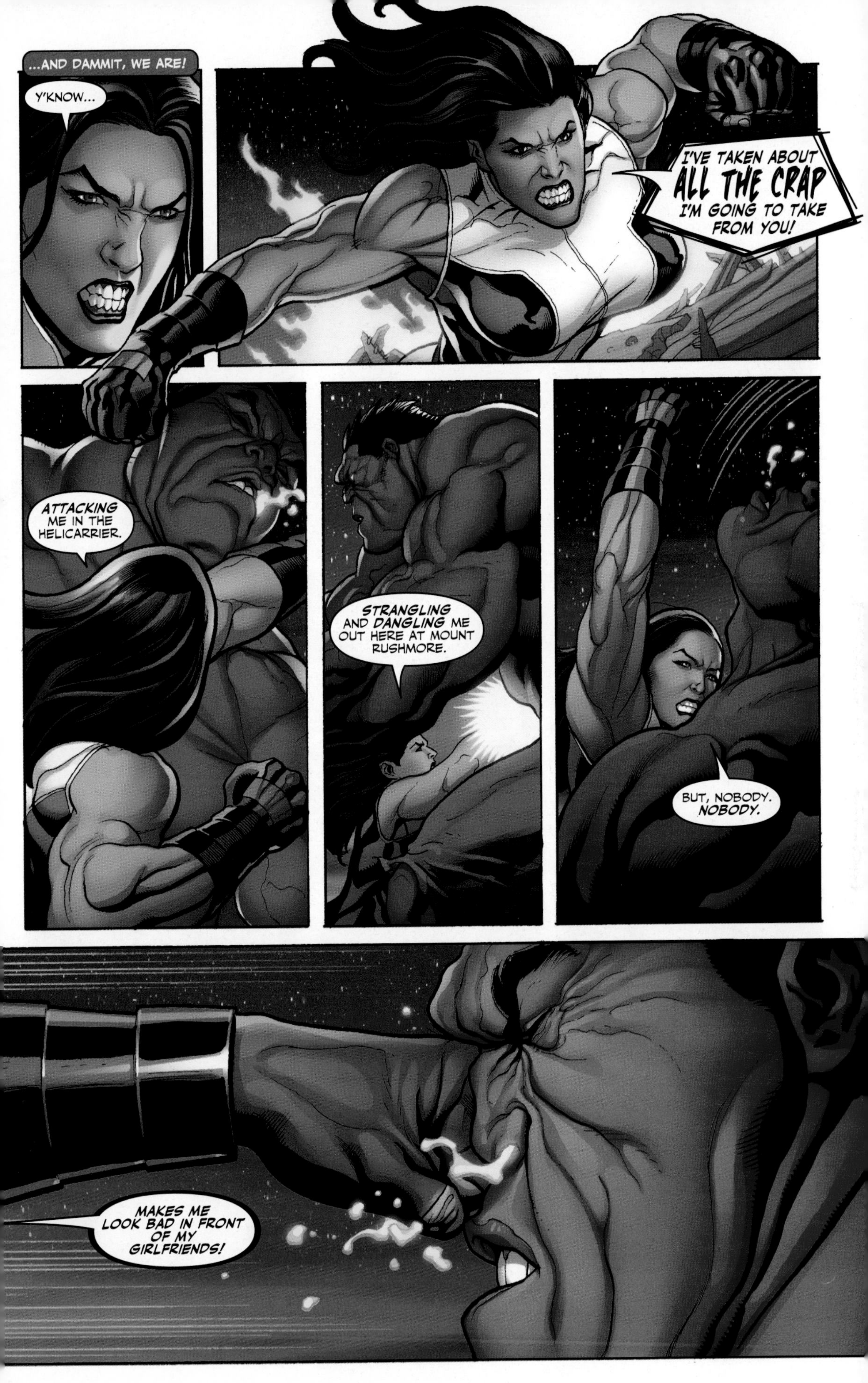
...AND DAMMIT, WE ARE!
Y'KNOW...
I'VE TAKEN ABOUT ALL THE CRAP I'M GOING TO TAKE FROM YOU!
ATTACKING ME IN THE HELICARRIER.
STRANGLING AND DANGLING ME OUT HERE AT MOUNT RUSHMORE.
BUT, NOBODY. NOBODY.
MAKES ME LOOK BAD IN FRONT OF MY GIRLFRIENDS!

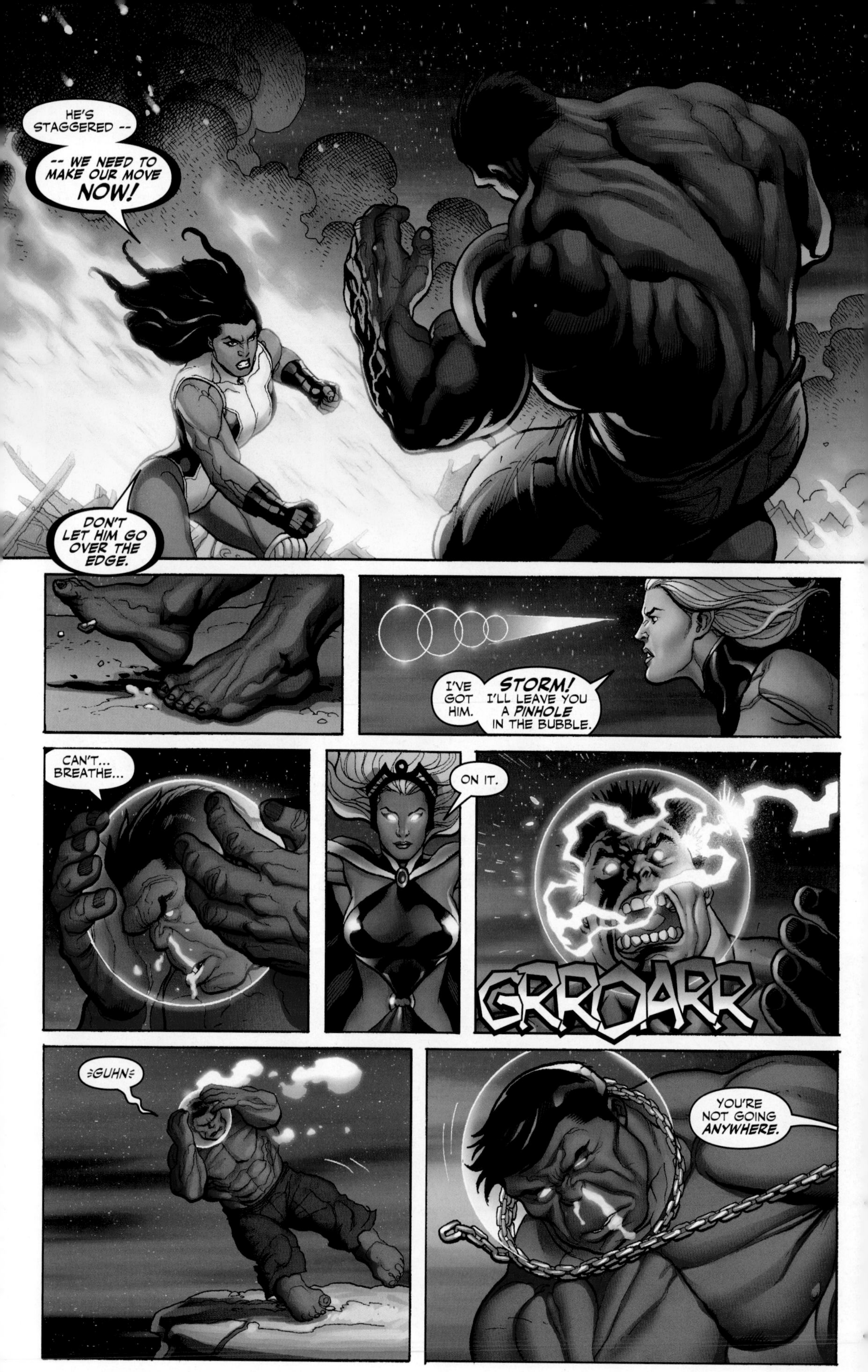
HE'S STAGGERED --
-- WE NEED TO MAKE OUR MOVE NOW!
DON'T LET HIM GO OVER THE EDGE.
I'VE GOT HIM.
STORM! I'LL LEAVE YOU A PINHOLE IN THE BUBBLE.
CAN'T... BREATHE...
ON IT.
GRROARR
GUHN
YOU'RE NOT GOING ANYWHERE.

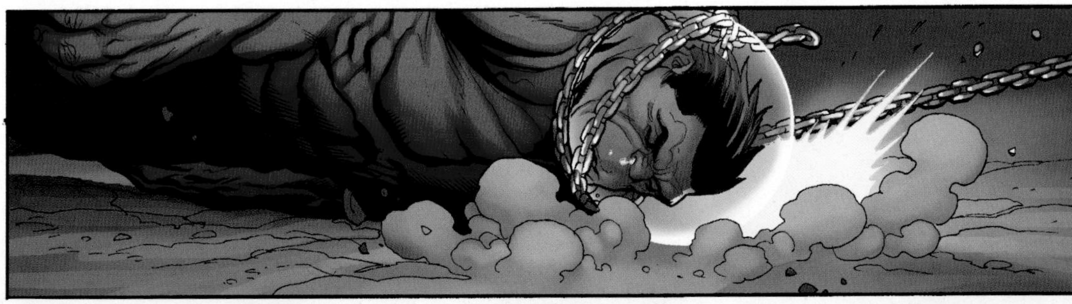

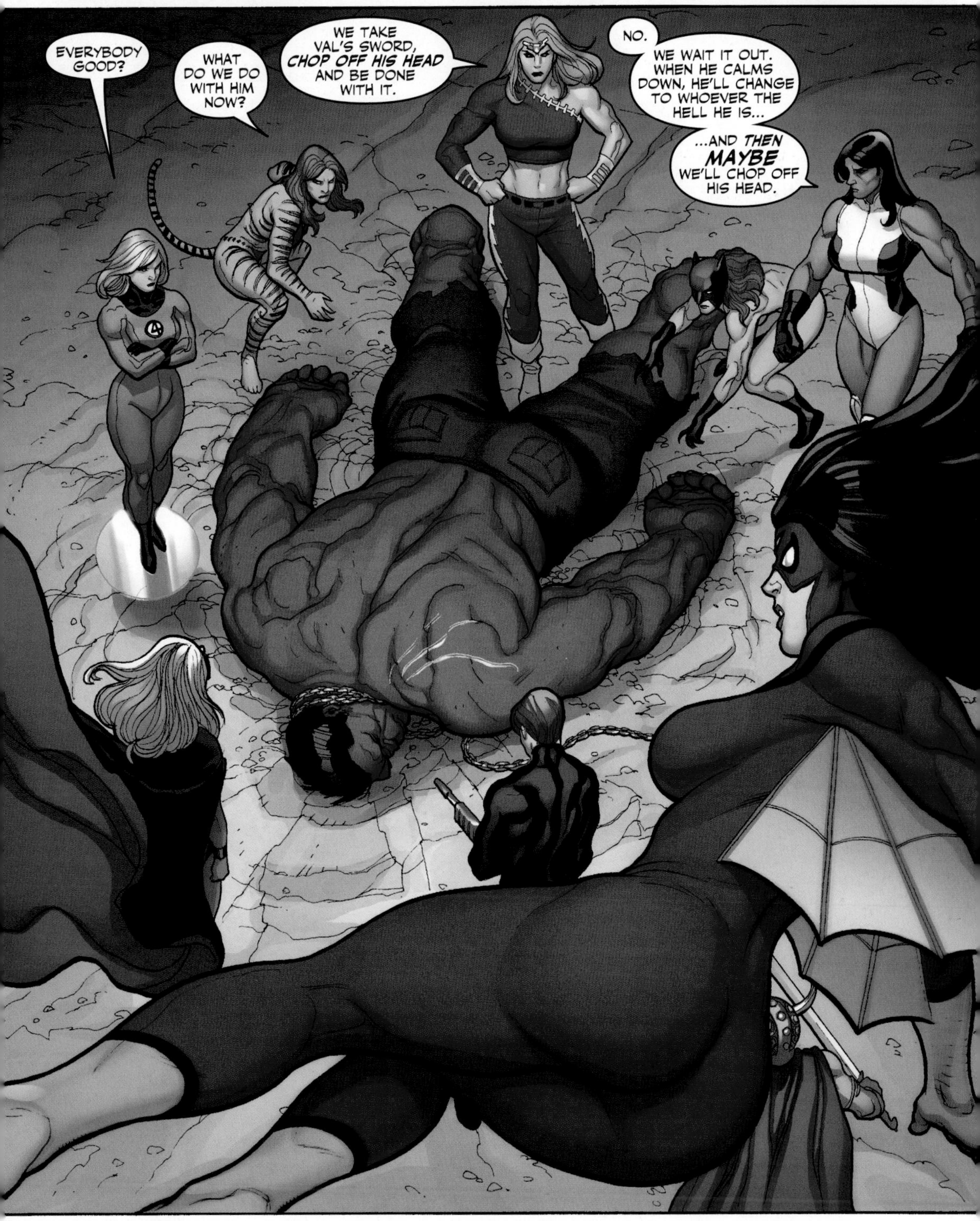
EVERYBODY GOOD?
WHAT DO WE DO WITH HIM NOW?
WE TAKE VAL'S SWORD, CHOP OFF HIS HEAD AND BE DONE WITH IT.
NO.
WE WAIT IT OUT. WHEN HE CALMS DOWN, HE'LL CHANGE TO WHOEVER THE HELL HE IS...
...AND THEN MAYBE WE'LL CHOP OFF HIS HEAD.

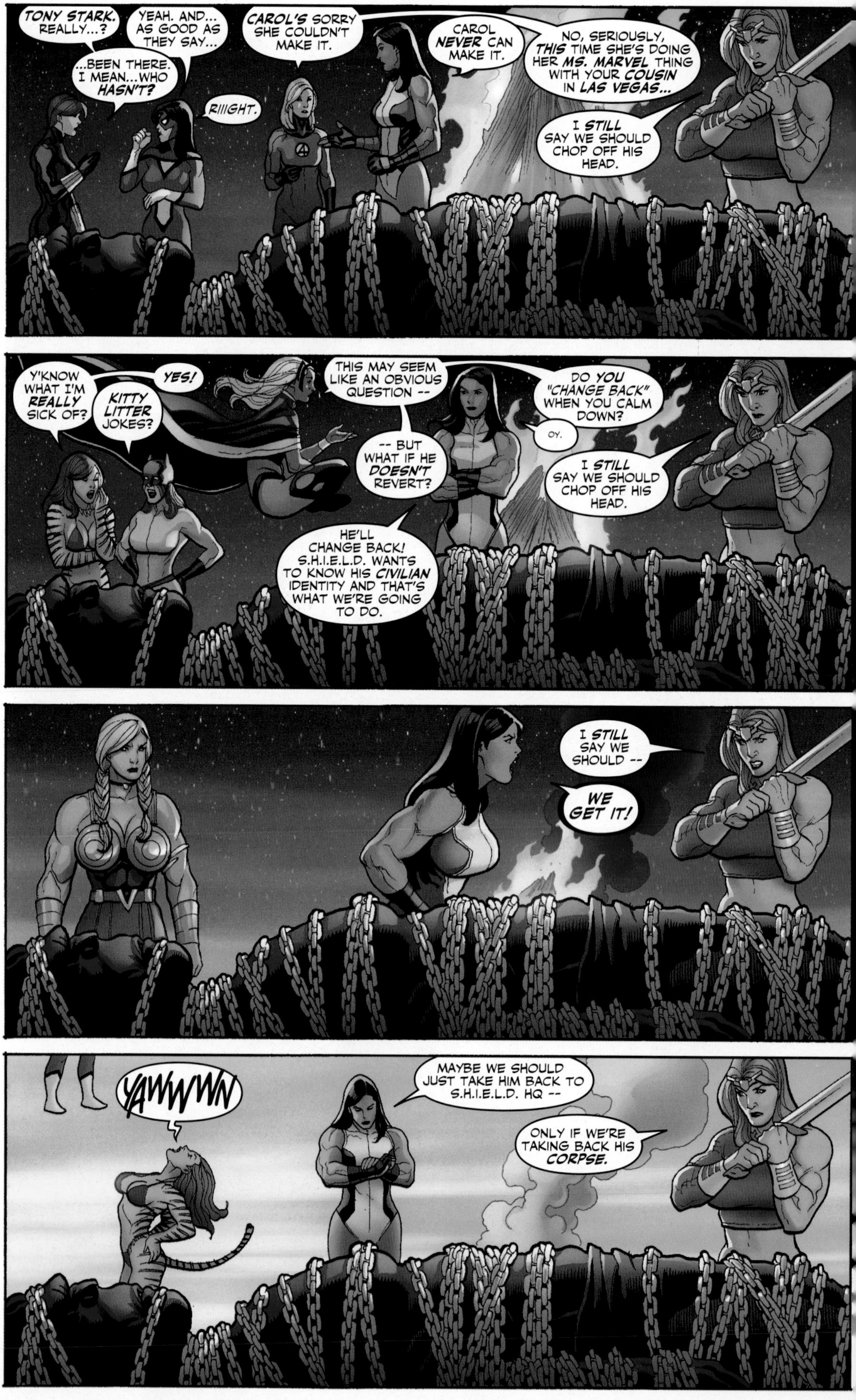
TONY STARK. REALLY...?
YEAH. AND... AS GOOD AS THEY SAY...
...BEEN THERE. I MEAN...WHO HASN'T?
RIIIGHT.
CAROL'S SORRY SHE COULDN'T MAKE IT.
CAROL NEVER CAN MAKE IT.
NO, SERIOUSLY, THIS TIME SHE'S DOING HER MS. MARVEL THING WITH YOUR COUSIN IN LAS VEGAS...
I STILL SAY WE SHOULD CHOP OFF HIS HEAD.
Y'KNOW WHAT I'M REALLY SICK OF?
KITTY LITTER JOKES?
YES!
THIS MAY SEEM LIKE AN OBVIOUS QUESTION --
-- BUT WHAT IF HE DOESN'T REVERT?
DO YOU "CHANGE BACK" WHEN YOU CALM DOWN?
OY.
I STILL SAY WE SHOULD CHOP OFF HIS HEAD.
HE'LL CHANGE BACK! S.H.I.E.L.D. WANTS TO KNOW HIS CIVILIAN IDENTITY AND THAT'S WHAT WE'RE GOING TO DO.
I STILL SAY WE SHOULD --
WE GET IT!
YAWWWN
MAYBE WE SHOULD JUST TAKE HIM BACK TO S.H.I.E.L.D. HQ --
ONLY IF WE'RE TAKING BACK HIS CORPSE.

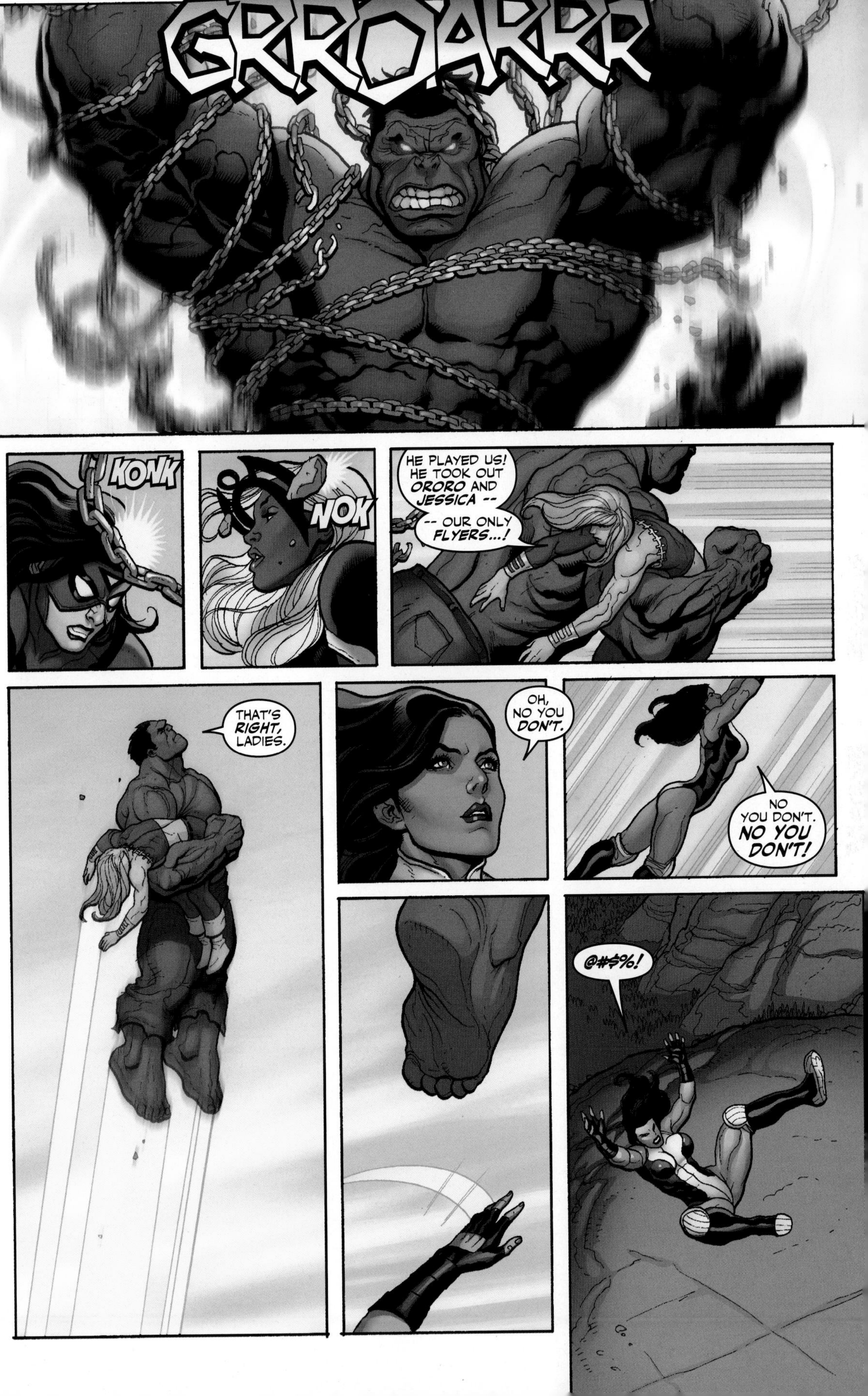
GRROARRR
KONK
NOK
HE PLAYED US! HE TOOK OUT ORORO AND JESSICA --
-- OUR ONLY FLYERS...!
THAT'S RIGHT, LADIES.
OH, NO YOU DON'T.
NO YOU DON'T. NO YOU DON'T!
@#$%!

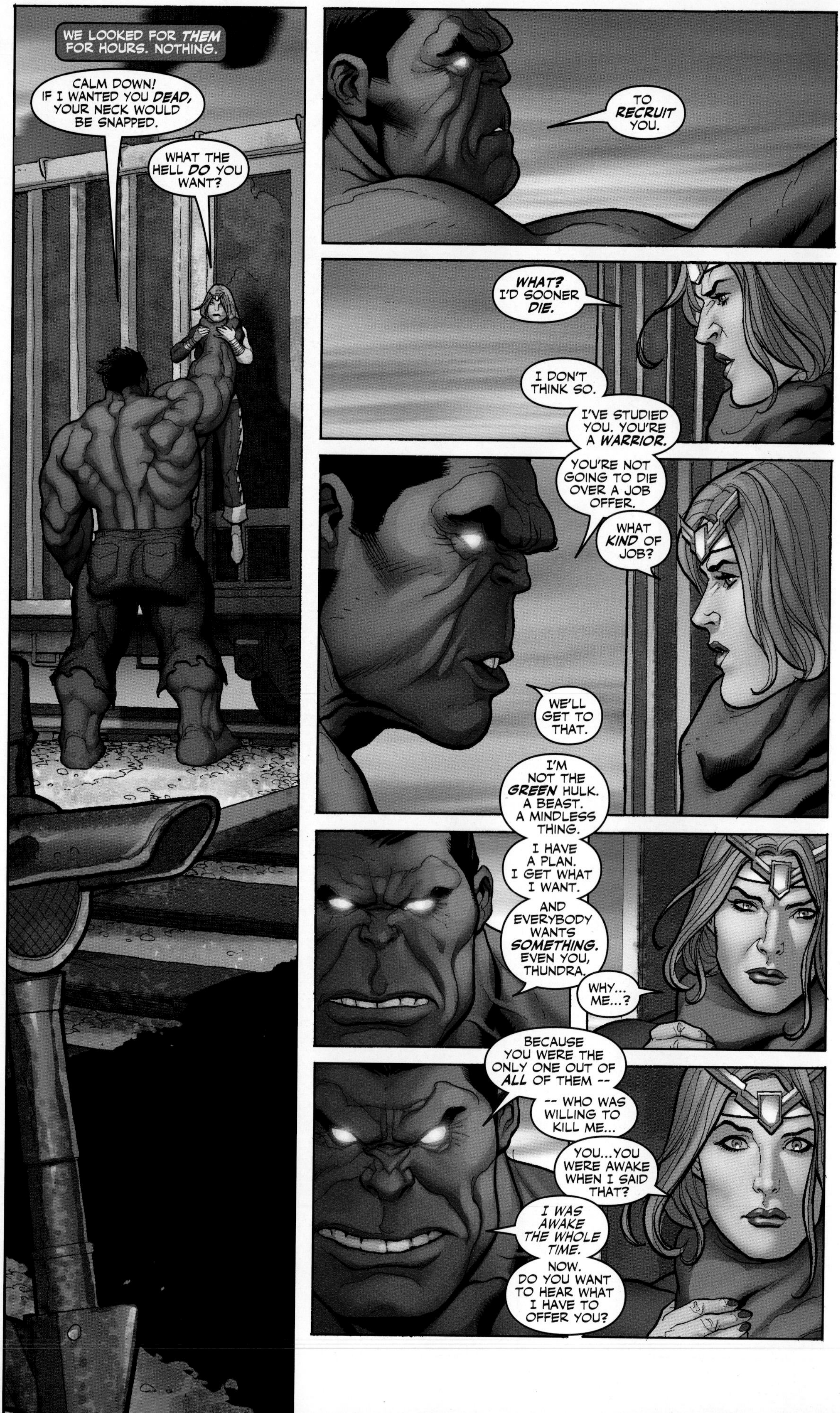

WE LOOKED FOR THEM FOR HOURS. NOTHING.
CALM DOWN! IF I WANTED YOU DEAD, YOUR NECK WOULD BE SNAPPED.
WHAT THE HELL DO YOU WANT?
TO RECRUIT YOU.
WHAT? I'D SOONER DIE.
I DON'T THINK SO.
I'VE STUDIED YOU. YOU'RE A WARRIOR.
YOU'RE NOT GOING TO DIE OVER A JOB OFFER.
WHAT KIND OF JOB?
WE'LL GET TO THAT.
I'M NOT THE GREEN HULK. A BEAST. A MINDLESS THING.
I HAVE A PLAN. I GET WHAT I WANT.
AND EVERYBODY WANTS SOMETHING. EVEN YOU, THUNDRA.
WHY... ME...?
BECAUSE YOU WERE THE ONLY ONE OUT OF ALL OF THEM --
-- WHO WAS WILLING TO KILL ME...
YOU...YOU WERE AWAKE WHEN I SAID THAT?
I WAS AWAKE THE WHOLE TIME.
NOW. DO YOU WANT TO HEAR WHAT I HAVE TO OFFER YOU?

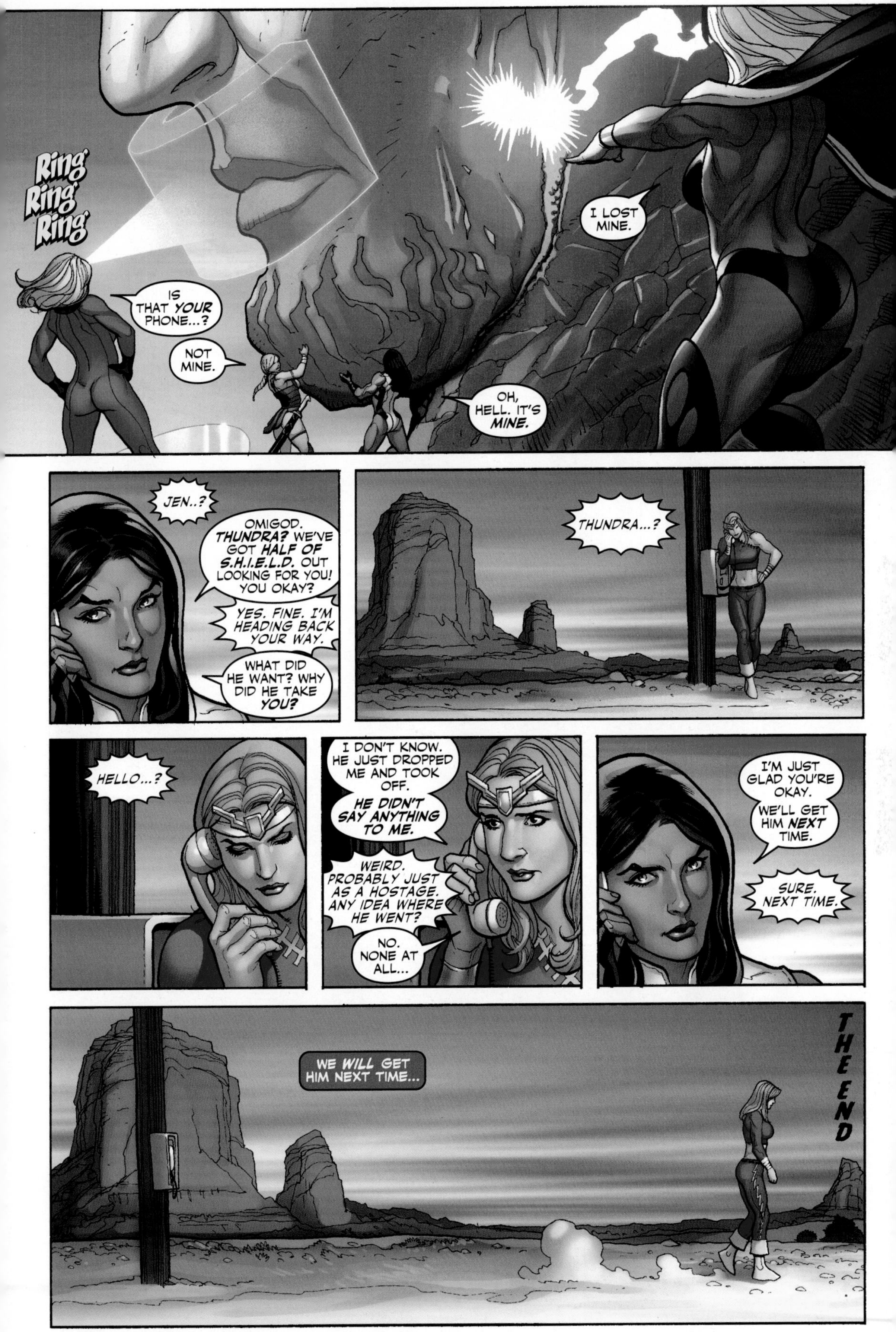
Ring Ring Ring
IS THAT *YOUR* PHONE...?
NOT MINE.
OH, HELL. IT'S *MINE.*
I LOST MINE.
JEN..?
OMIGOD. *THUNDRA?* WE'VE GOT *HALF OF S.H.I.E.L.D.* OUT LOOKING FOR YOU! YOU OKAY?
YES. FINE. I'M HEADING BACK YOUR WAY.
WHAT DID HE WANT? WHY DID HE TAKE *YOU?*
THUNDRA...?
HELLO...?
I DON'T KNOW. HE JUST DROPPED ME AND TOOK OFF.
HE DIDN'T SAY ANYTHING TO ME.
WEIRD. PROBABLY JUST AS A HOSTAGE. ANY IDEA WHERE HE WENT?
NO. NONE AT ALL...
I'M JUST GLAD YOU'RE OKAY.
WE'LL GET HIM *NEXT* TIME.
SURE. NEXT TIME.
WE *WILL* GET HIM NEXT TIME...
THE END

ROUND ★ THREE

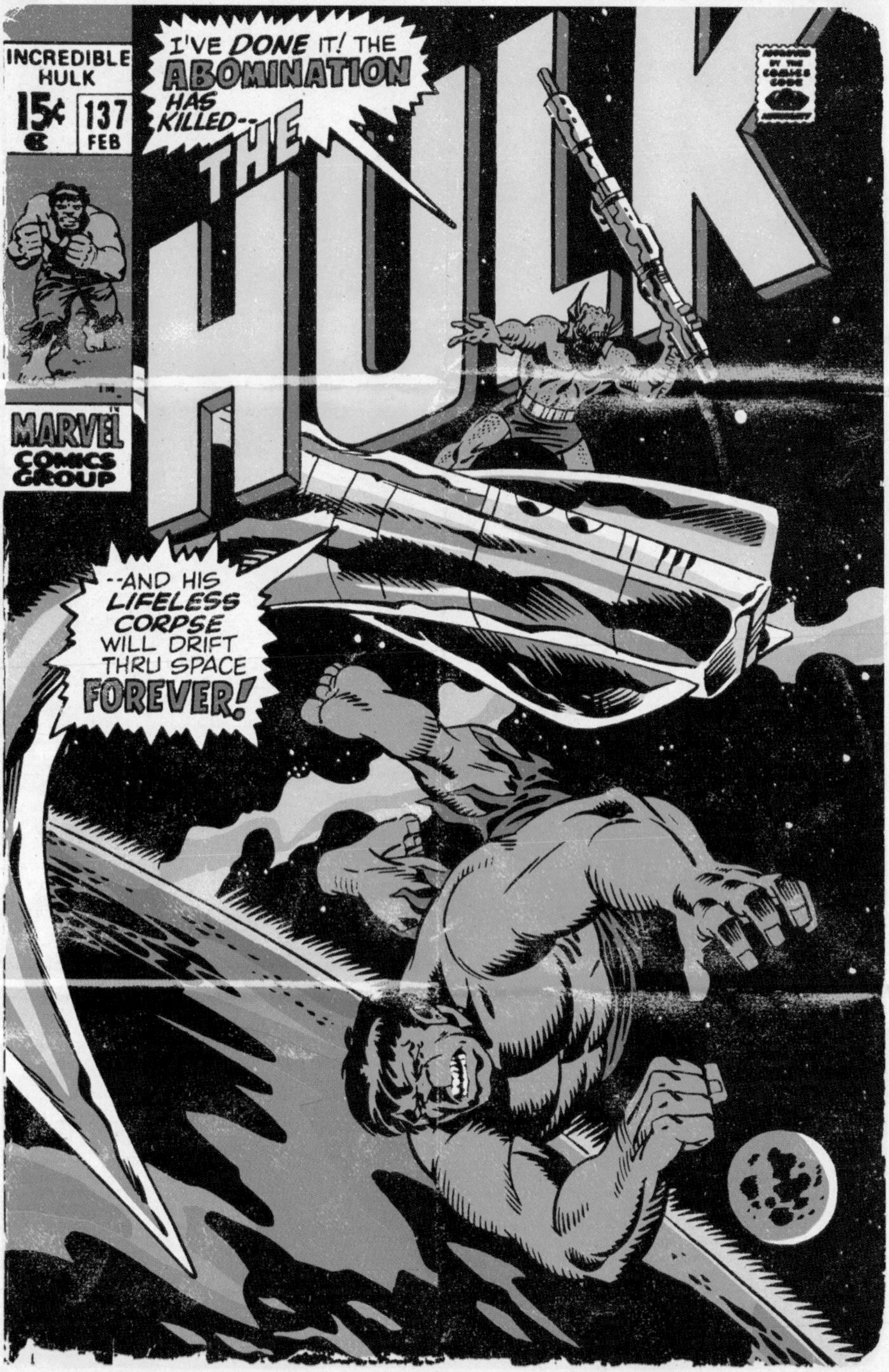
INCREDIBLE HULK
15¢
137
FEB
MARVEL COMICS GROUP
I'VE DONE IT! THE ABOMINATION HAS KILLED-- THE
HULK
--AND HIS LIFELESS CORPSE WILL DRIFT THRU SPACE FOREVER!

THE DEATH AND LIFE OF THE ABOMINATION

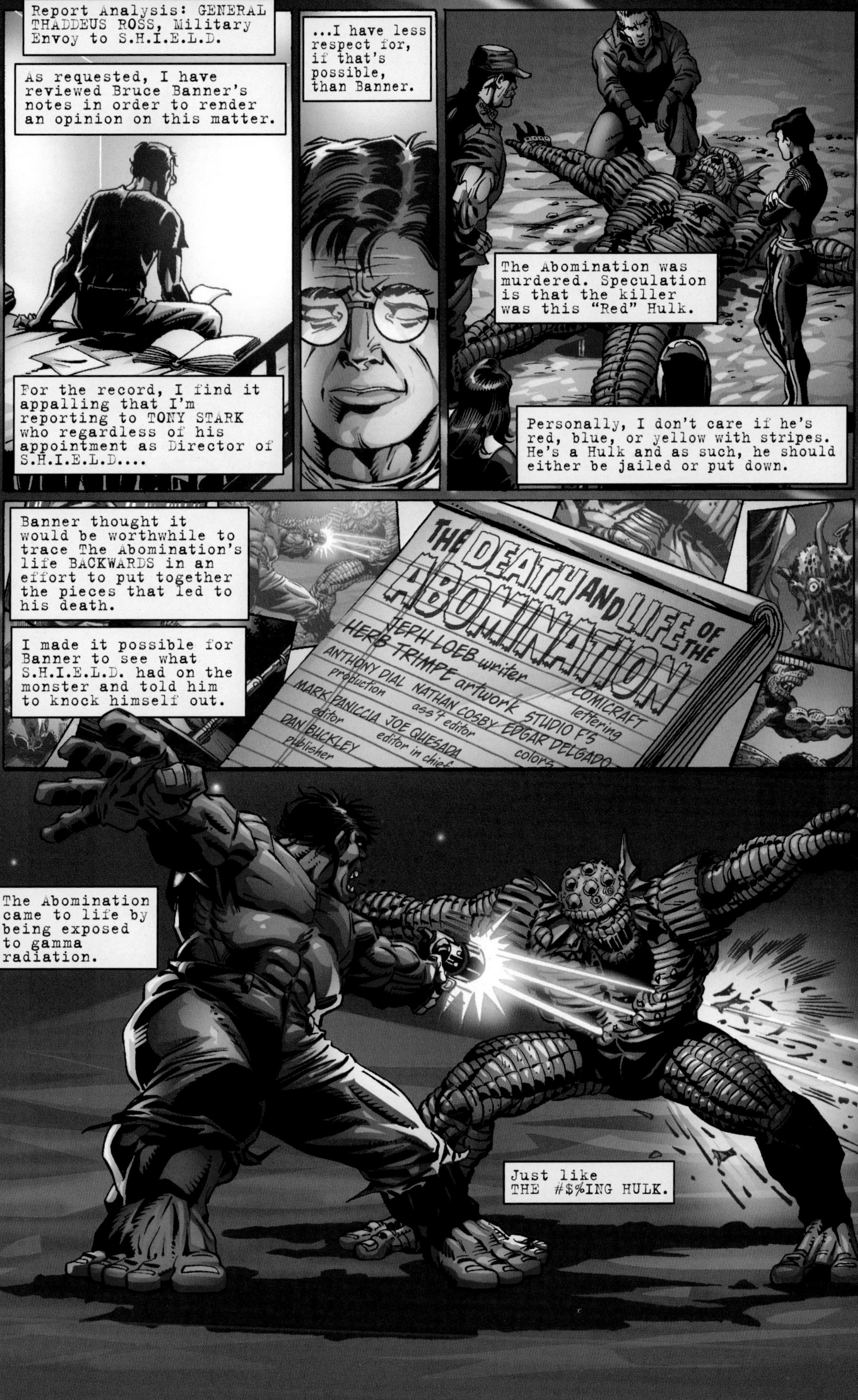
Report Analysis: GENERAL THADDEUS ROSS, Military Envoy to S.H.I.E.L.D.
As requested, I have reviewed Bruce Banner's notes in order to render an opinion on this matter.
For the record, I find it appalling that I'm reporting to TONY STARK who regardless of his appointment as Director of S.H.I.E.L.D....
...I have less respect for, if that's possible, than Banner.
The Abomination was murdered. Speculation is that the killer was this "Red" Hulk.
Personally, I don't care if he's red, blue, or yellow with stripes. He's a Hulk and as such, he should either be jailed or put down.
Banner thought it would be worthwhile to trace The Abomination's life BACKWARDS in an effort to put together the pieces that led to his death.
I made it possible for Banner to see what S.H.I.E.L.D. had on the monster and told him to knock himself out.
THE DEATH AND LIFE OF THE ABOMINATION
JEPH LOEB writer
HERB TRIMPE artwork
COMICRAFT lettering
ANTHONY DIAL production
NATHAN COSBY ass't editor
STUDIO F's EDGAR DELGADO colors
MARK PANICCIA editor
JOE QUESADA editor in chief
DAN BUCKLEY publisher
The Abomination came to life by being exposed to gamma radiation.
Just like THE #$%ING HULK.

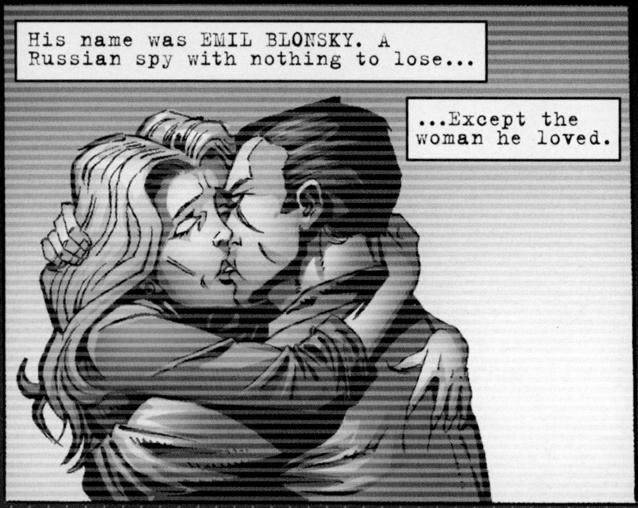
His name was EMIL BLONSKY. A Russian spy with nothing to lose...
...Except the woman he loved.

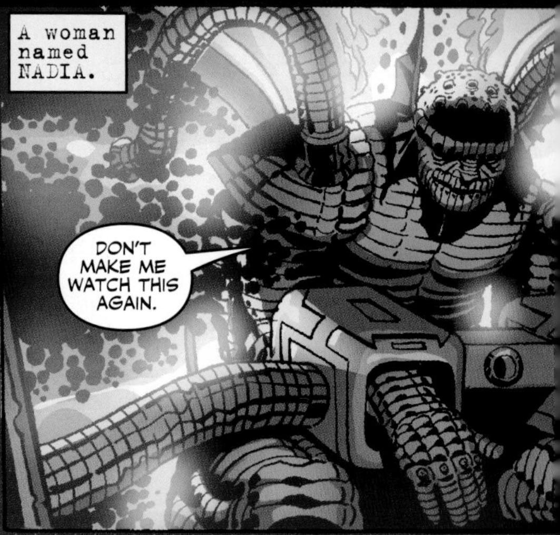
A woman named NADIA.
DON'T MAKE ME WATCH THIS AGAIN.

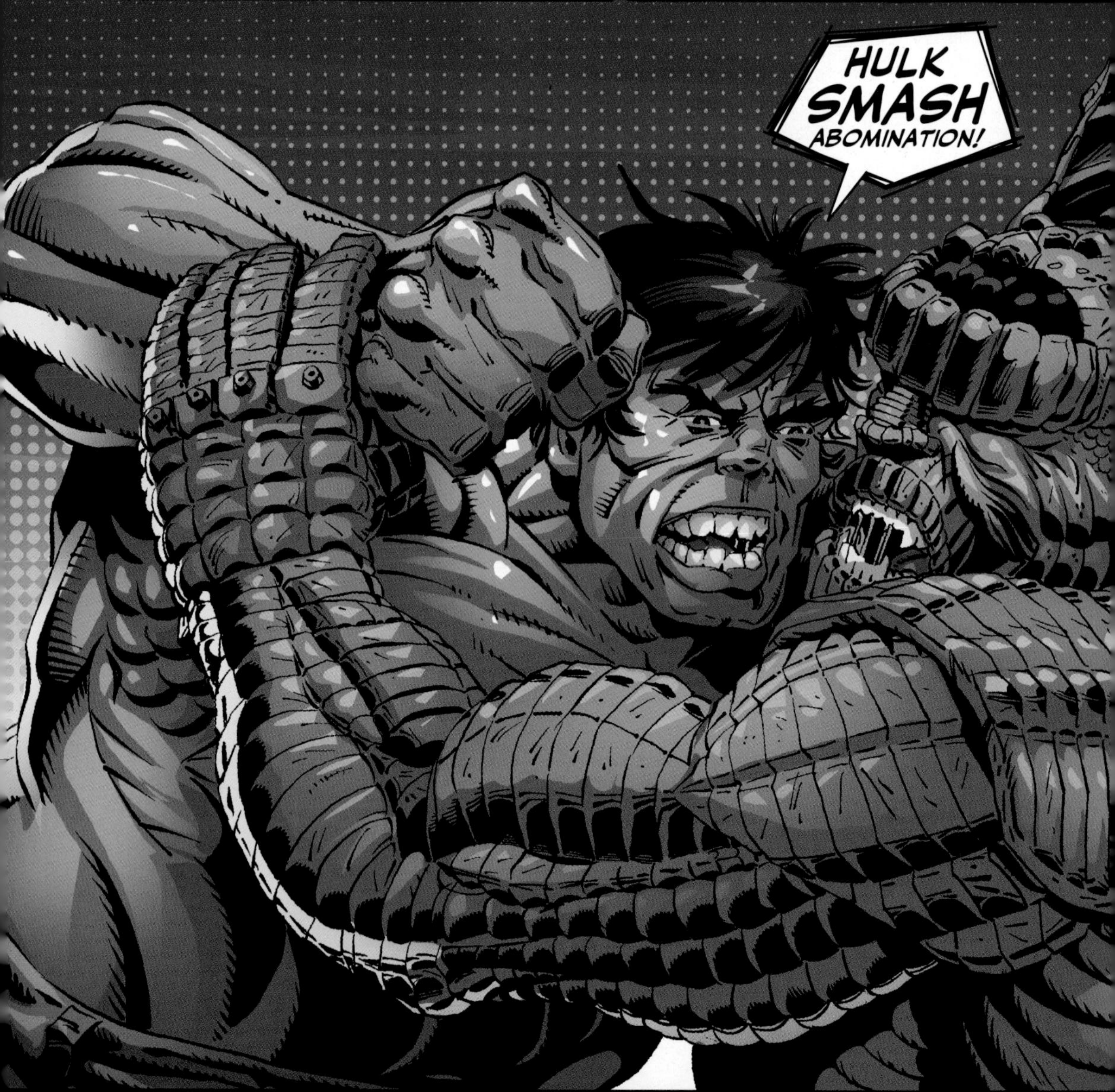
HULK SMASH ABOMINATION!

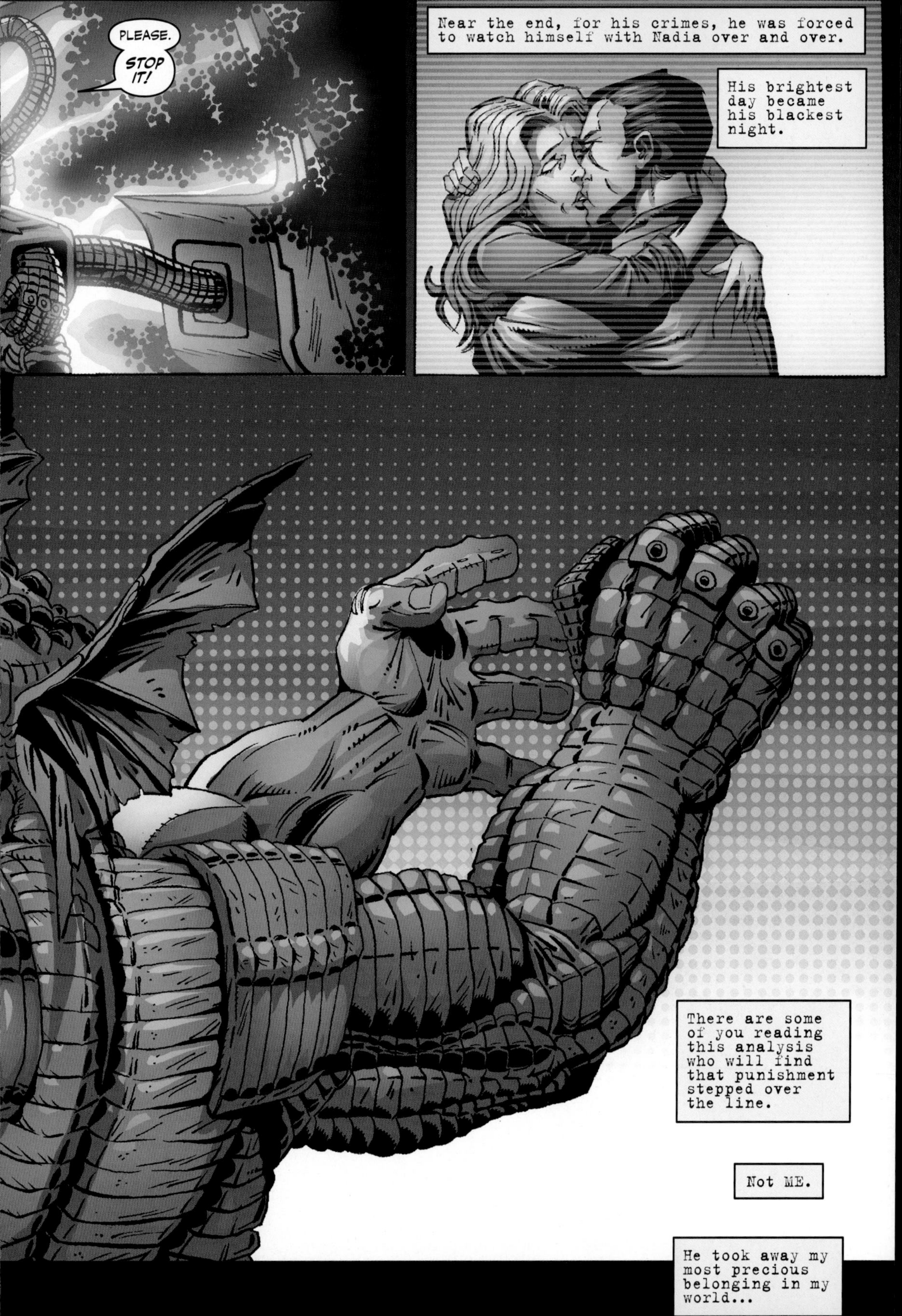
PLEASE. STOP IT!
Near the end, for his crimes, he was forced to watch himself with Nadia over and over.
His brightest day became his blackest night.
There are some of you reading this analysis who will find that punishment stepped over the line.
Not ME.
He took away my most precious belonging in my world...

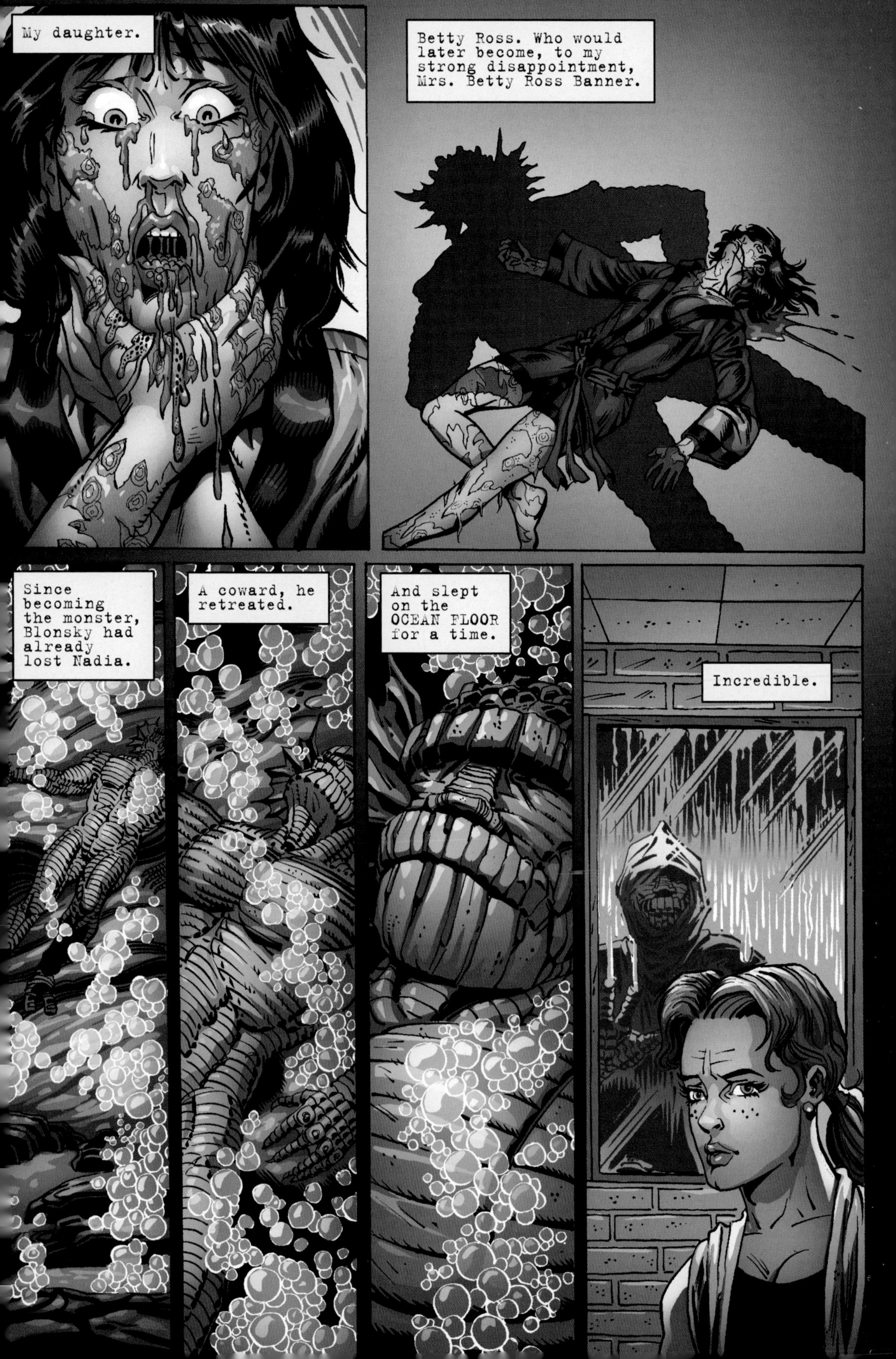
My daughter.
Betty Ross. Who would later become, to my strong disappointment, Mrs. Betty Ross Banner.
Since becoming the monster, Blonsky had already lost Nadia.
A coward, he retreated.
And slept on the OCEAN FLOOR for a time.
Incredible.

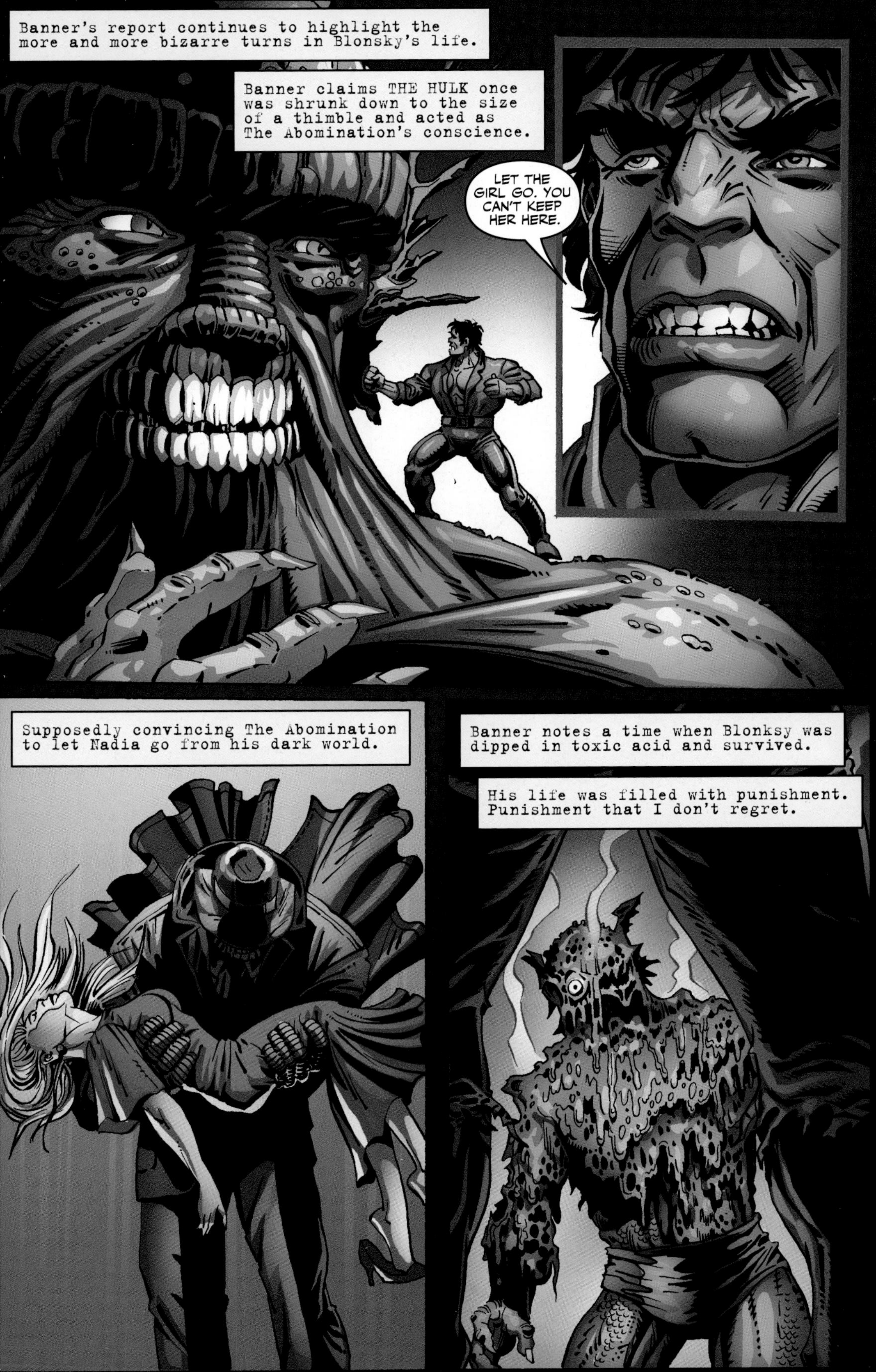
Banner's report continues to highlight the more and more bizarre turns in Blonsky's life.
Banner claims THE HULK once was shrunk down to the size of a thimble and acted as The Abomination's conscience.
LET THE GIRL GO. YOU CAN'T KEEP HER HERE.
Supposedly convincing The Abomination to let Nadia go from his dark world.
Banner notes a time when Blonksy was dipped in toxic acid and survived.
His life was filled with punishment. Punishment that I don't regret.

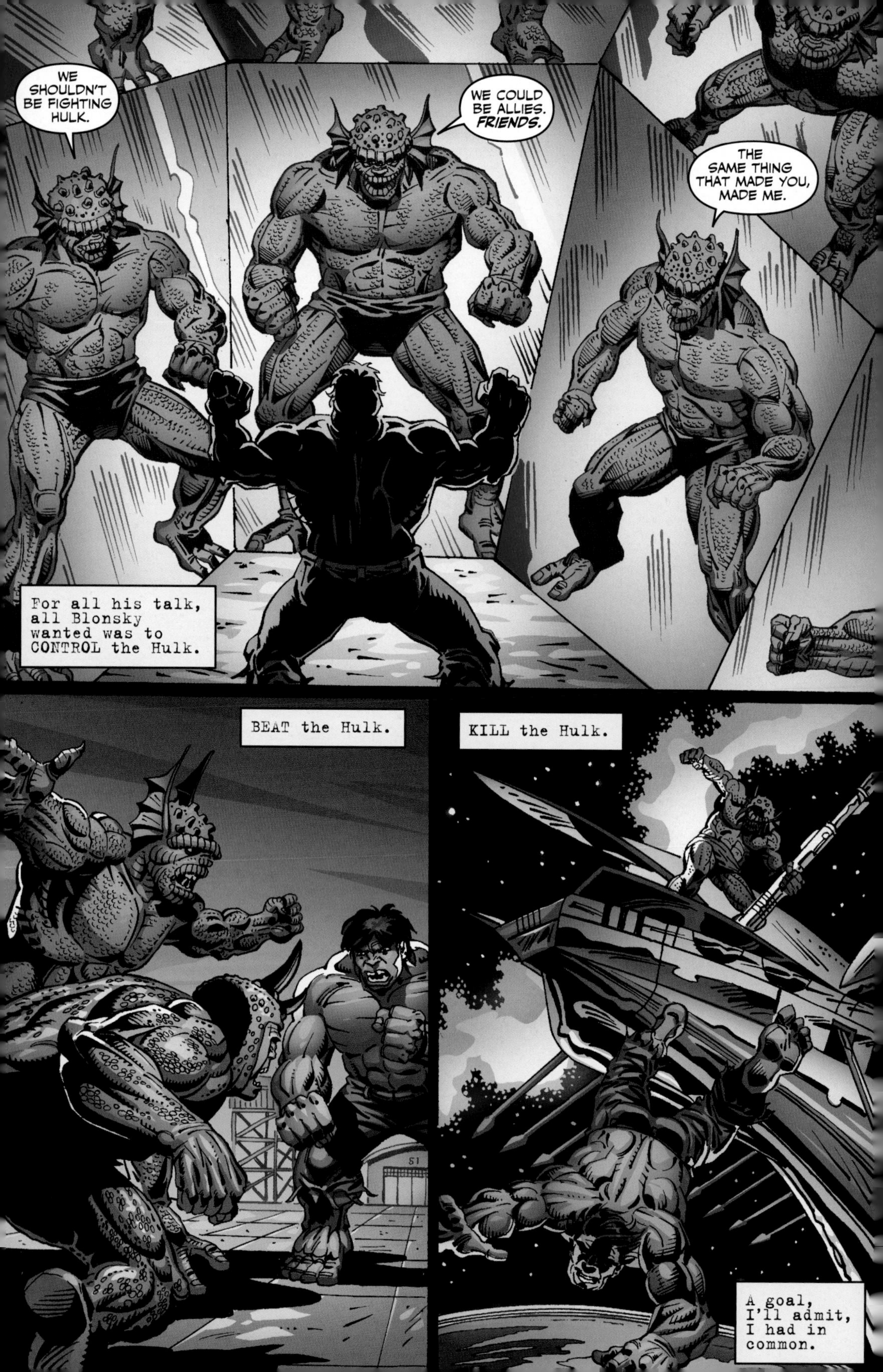
WE SHOULDN'T BE FIGHTING HULK.
WE COULD BE ALLIES. FRIENDS.
THE SAME THING THAT MADE YOU, MADE ME.
For all his talk, all Blonsky wanted was to CONTROL the Hulk.
BEAT the Hulk.
KILL the Hulk.
A goal, I'll admit, I had in common.

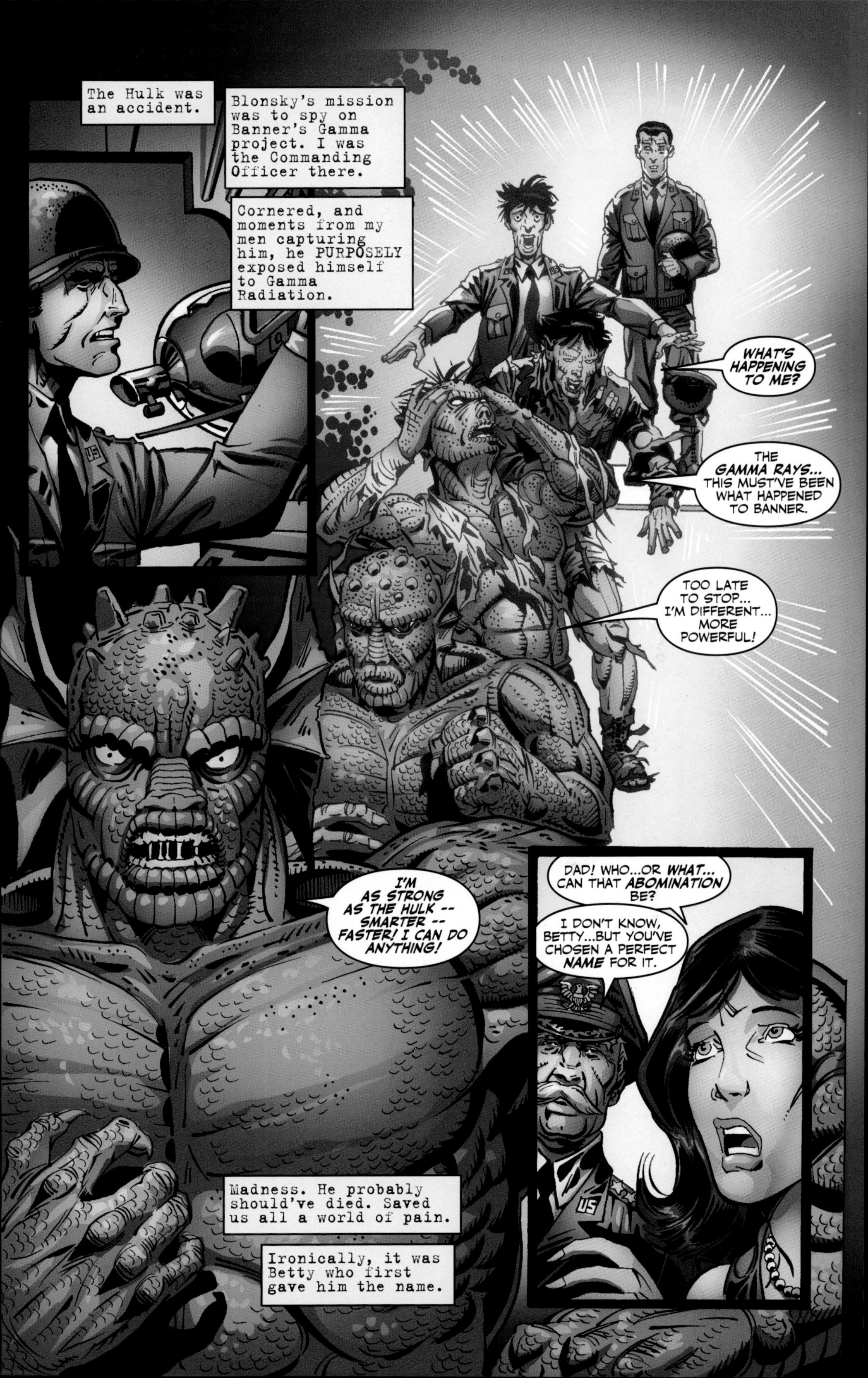
The Hulk was an accident.
Blonsky's mission was to spy on Banner's Gamma project. I was the Commanding Officer there.
Cornered, and moments from my men capturing him, he PURPOSELY exposed himself to Gamma Radiation.
WHAT'S HAPPENING TO ME?
THE GAMMA RAYS... THIS MUST'VE BEEN WHAT HAPPENED TO BANNER.
TOO LATE TO STOP... I'M DIFFERENT... MORE POWERFUL!
I'M AS STRONG AS THE HULK -- SMARTER -- FASTER! I CAN DO ANYTHING!
DAD! WHO...OR WHAT... CAN THAT ABOMINATION BE?
I DON'T KNOW, BETTY...BUT YOU'VE CHOSEN A PERFECT NAME FOR IT.
Madness. He probably should've died. Saved us all a world of pain.
Ironically, it was Betty who first gave him the name.

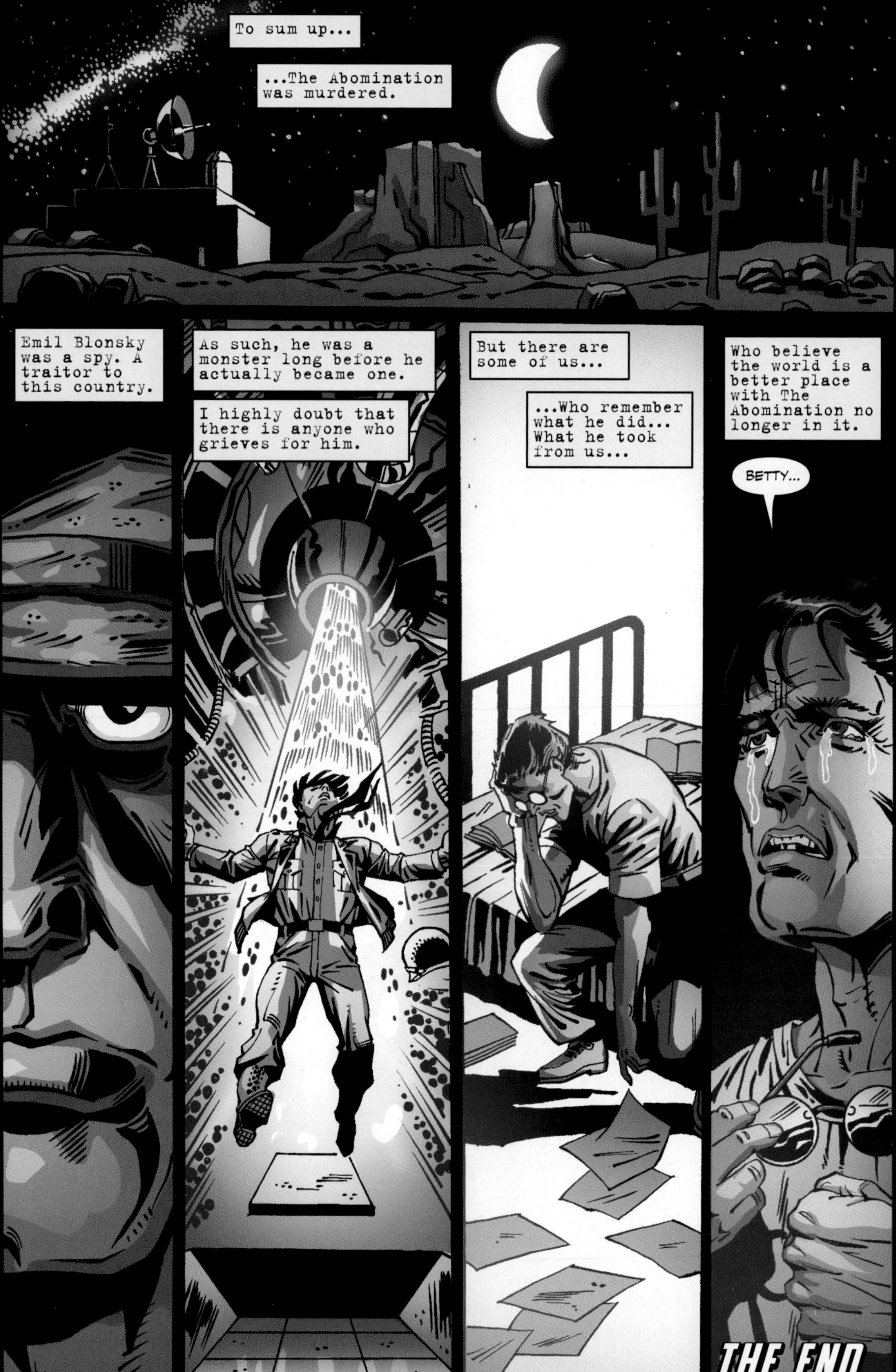
To sum up...
...The Abomination was murdered.
Emil Blonsky was a spy. A traitor to this country.
As such, he was a monster long before he actually became one.
I highly doubt that there is anyone who grieves for him.
But there are some of us...
...Who remember what he did... What he took from us...
Who believe the world is a better place with The Abomination no longer in it.
BETTY...
THE END.

★ EXTRAS ★

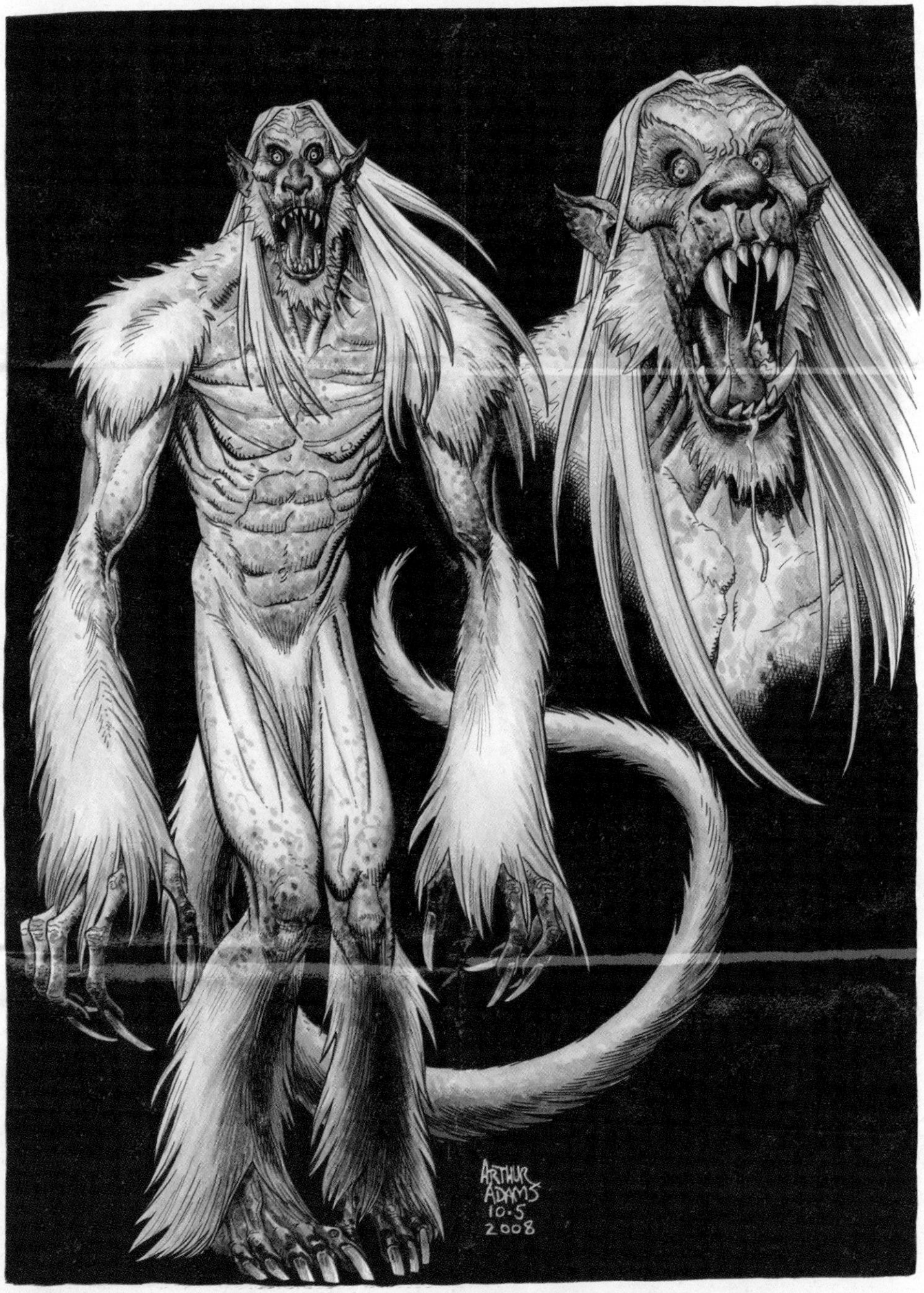
ARTHUR ADAMS
10-5
2008

BONUS FEATURES

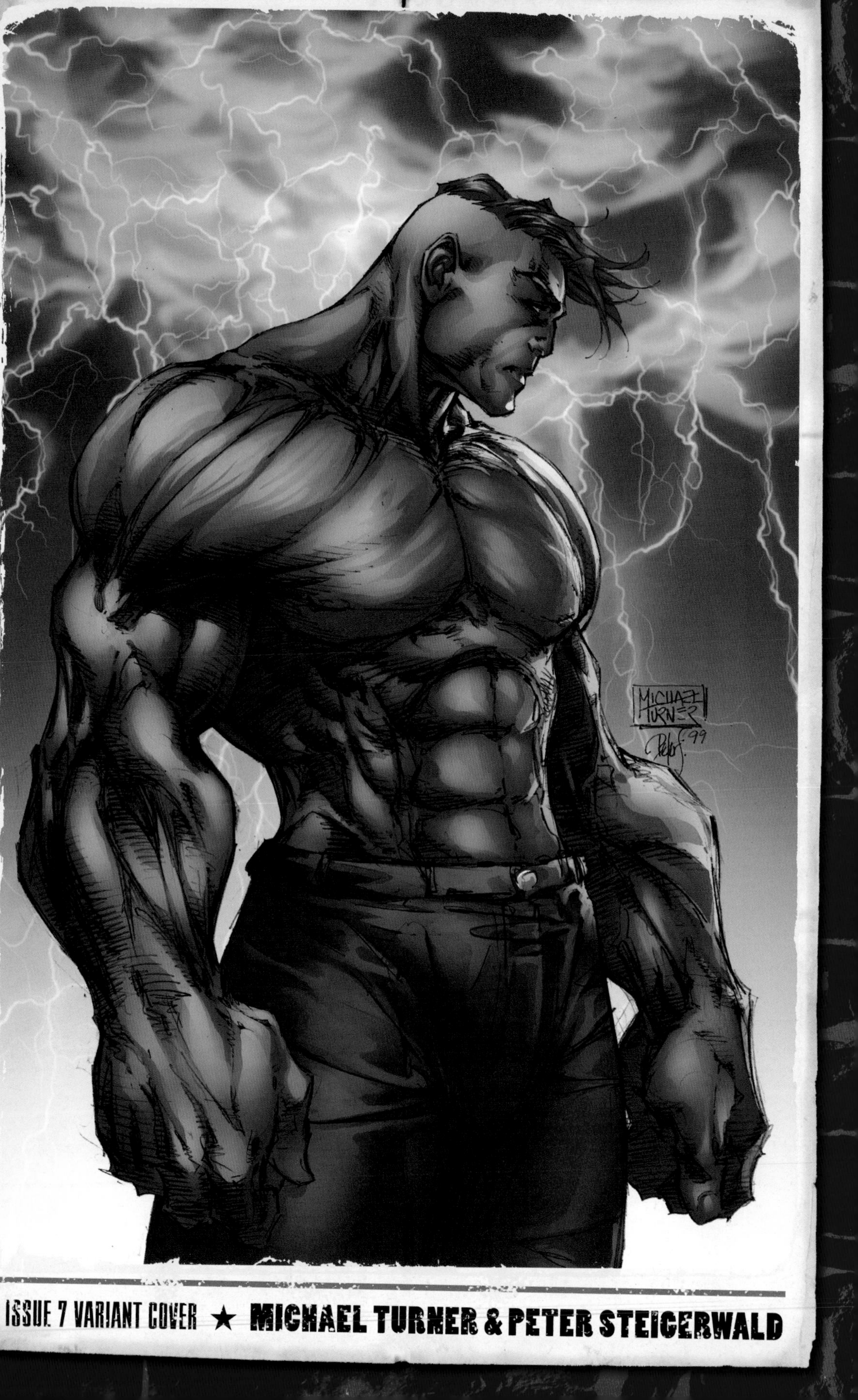

ISSUE 7 VARIANT COVER ★ **MICHAEL TURNER & PETER STEIGERWALD**

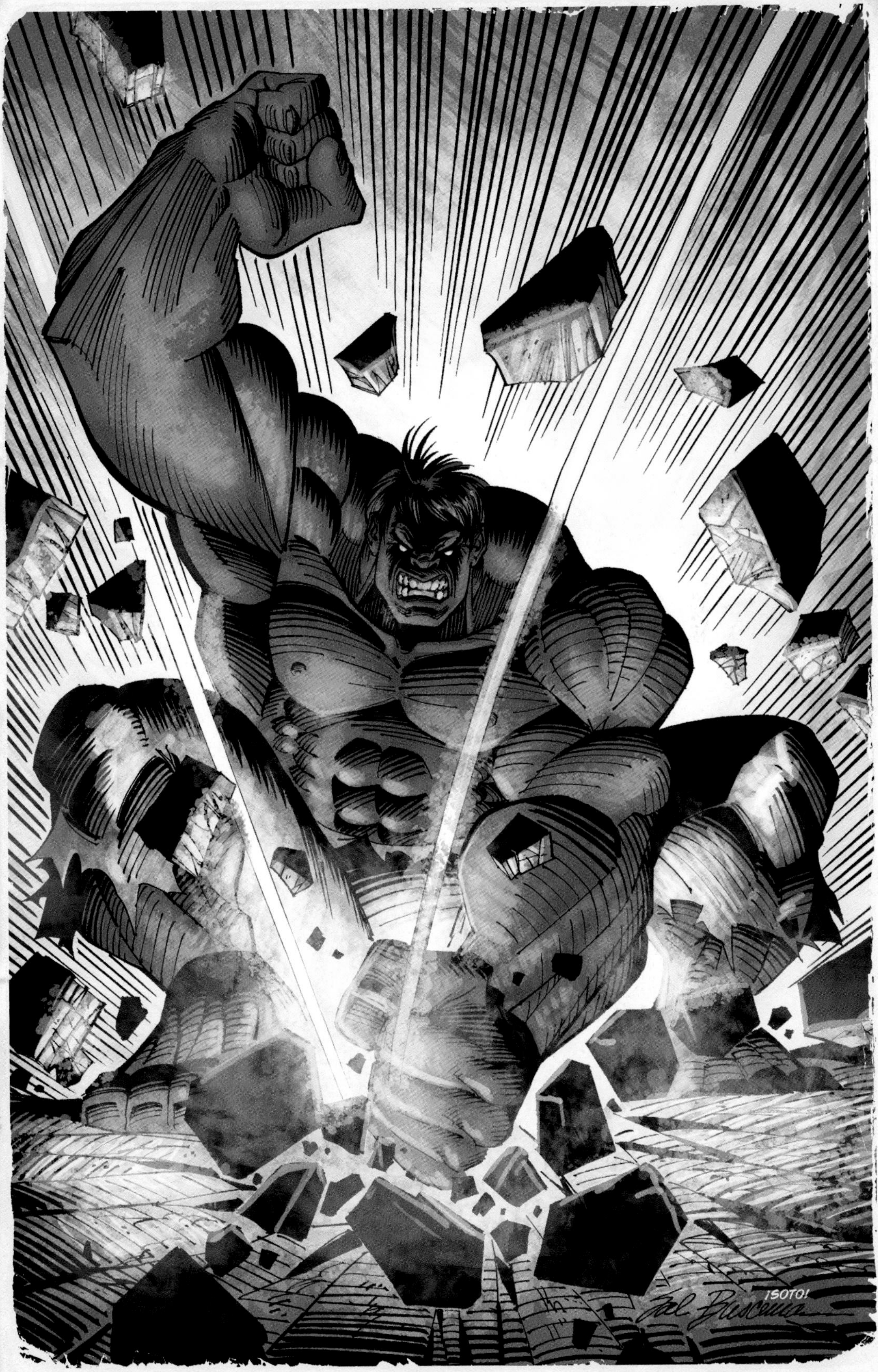
¡SOTO!

ISSUE 8 VARIANT COVER ★ **SAL BUSCEMA & CHRIS SOTOMAYOR**

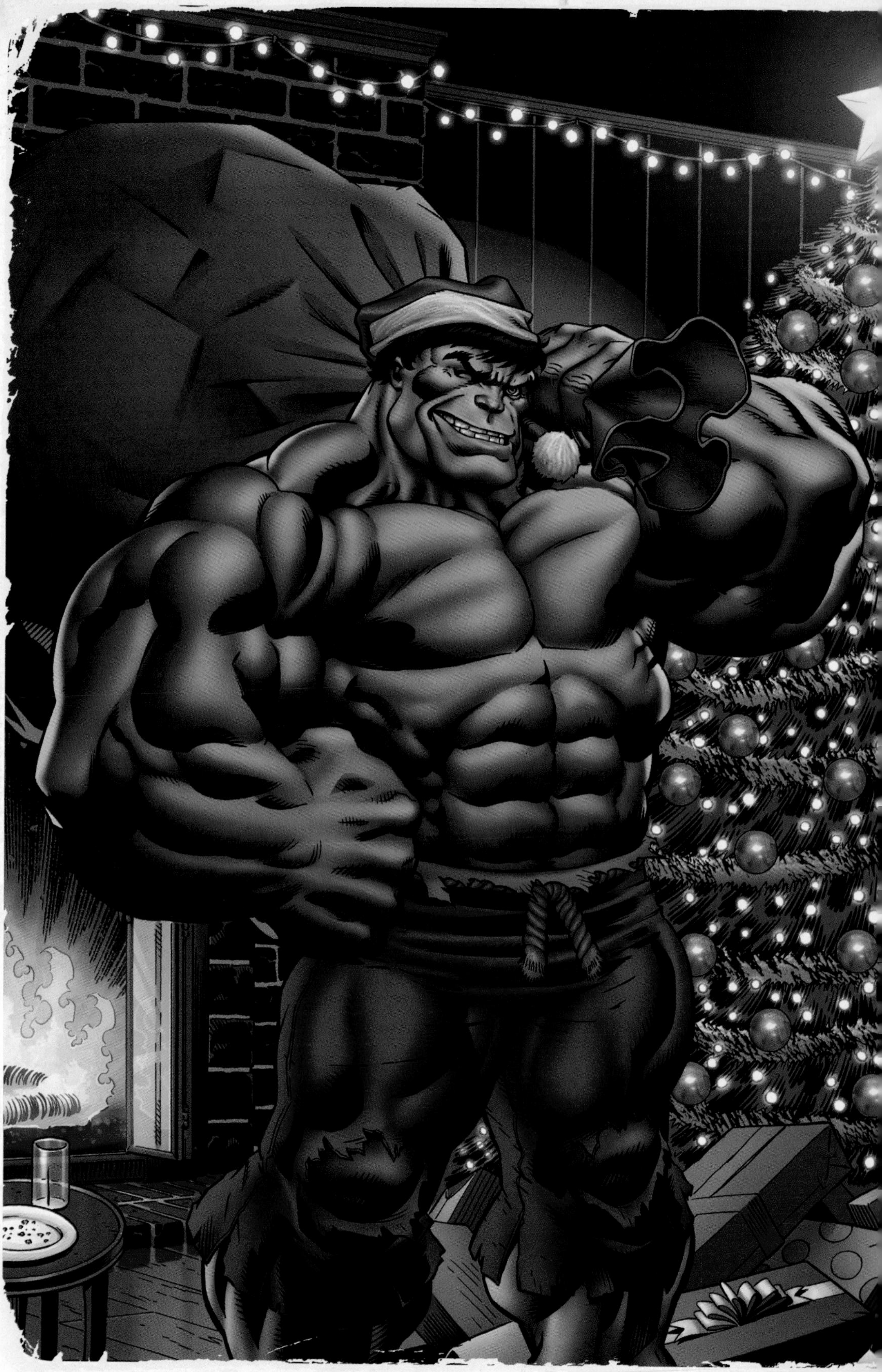

★ ISSUE 9 VARIANT COVER

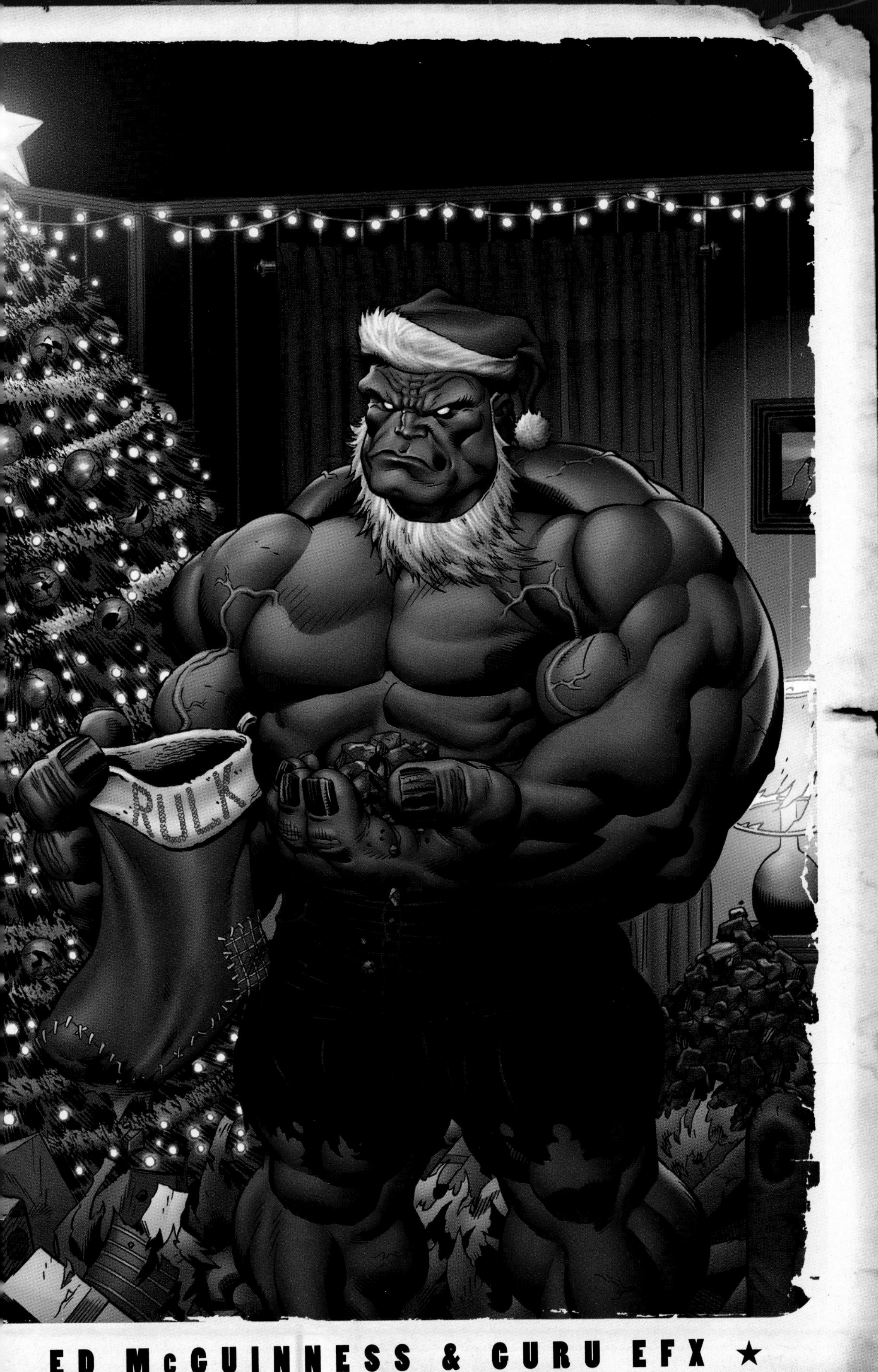
RULK

ED McGUINNESS & GURU EFX ★

MINI MARVELS PRESENTS **HULK WEB** WRITTEN BY **AUDREY LOEB** ILLUSTRATED BY CHRIS GIARRUSSO chrisgcomics.com

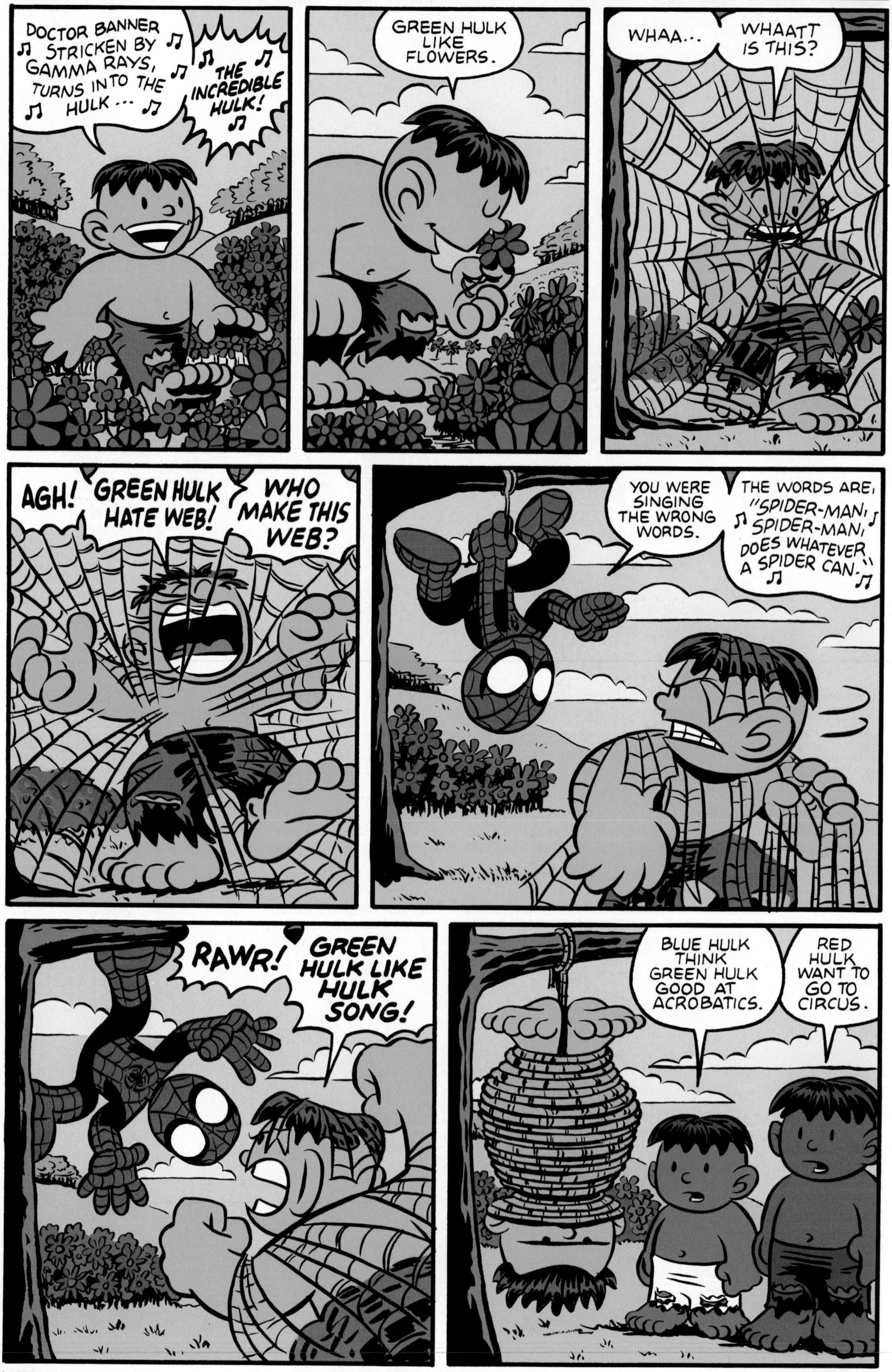

DOCTOR BANNER STRICKEN BY GAMMA RAYS, TURNS INTO THE HULK...
THE INCREDIBLE HULK!
GREEN HULK LIKE FLOWERS.
WHAA...
WHAATT IS THIS?
AGH!
GREEN HULK HATE WEB!
WHO MAKE THIS WEB?
YOU WERE SINGING THE WRONG WORDS.
THE WORDS ARE, "SPIDER-MAN, SPIDER-MAN, DOES WHATEVER A SPIDER CAN."
RAWR!
GREEN HULK LIKE HULK SONG!
BLUE HULK THINK GREEN HULK GOOD AT ACROBATICS.
RED HULK WANT TO GO TO CIRCUS.

NATHAN COSBY - *Editor* **JOE QUESADA** - *Editor In Chief* **DAN BUCKLEY** - *Publisher*

MINI MARVELS PRESENTS **HULK AIRPORT** WRITTEN BY AUDREY LOEB ILLUSTRATED BY CHRIS GIARRUSSO chrisgcomics.com

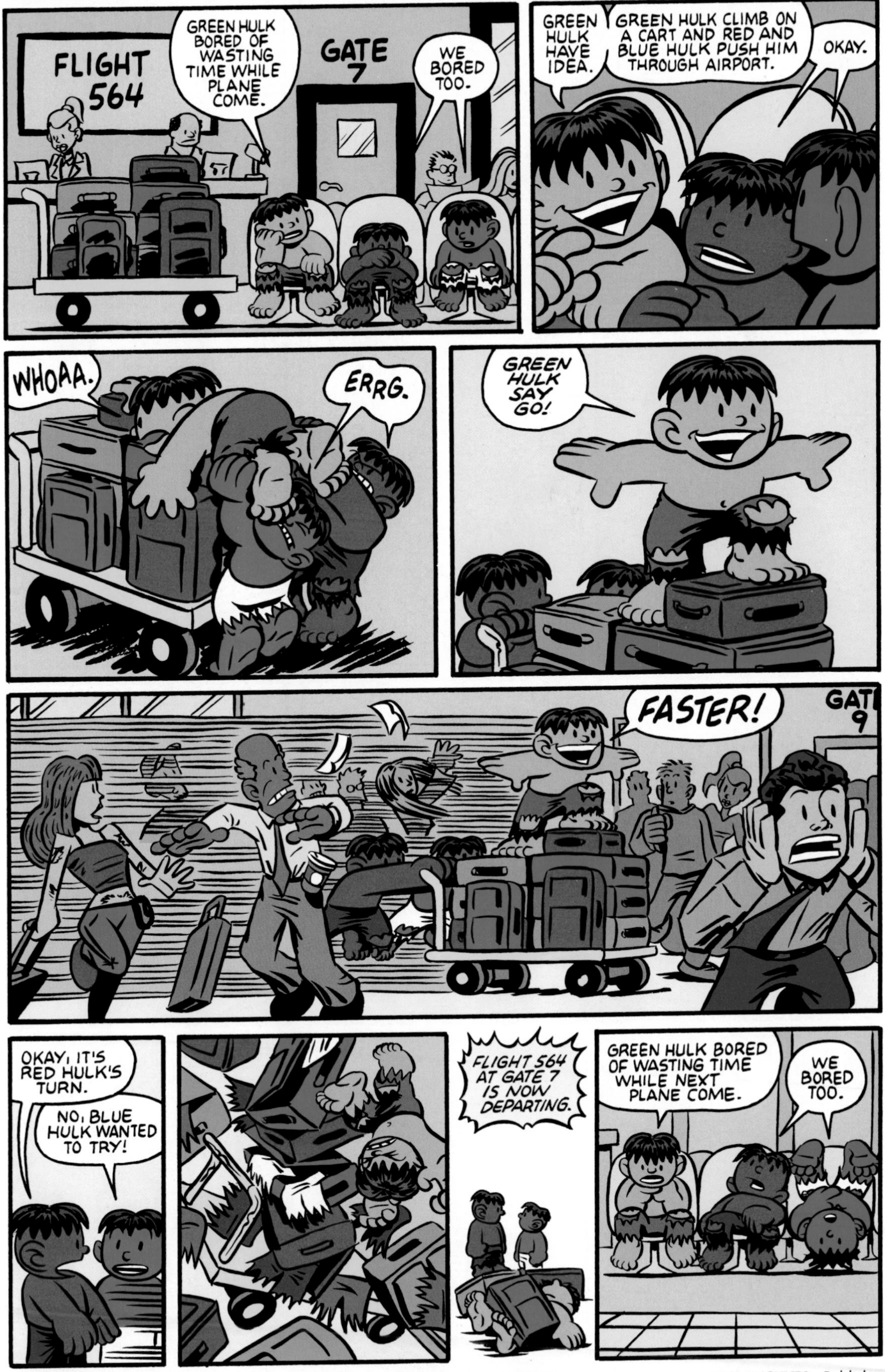
FLIGHT 564
GATE 7
GREEN HULK BORED OF WASTING TIME WHILE PLANE COME.
WE BORED TOO.
GREEN HULK HAVE IDEA.
GREEN HULK CLIMB ON A CART AND RED AND BLUE HULK PUSH HIM THROUGH AIRPORT.
OKAY.
WHOAA.
ERRG.
GREEN HULK SAY GO!
FASTER!
GAT 9
OKAY, IT'S RED HULK'S TURN.
NO, BLUE HULK WANTED TO TRY!
FLIGHT 564 AT GATE 7 IS NOW DEPARTING.
GREEN HULK BORED OF WASTING TIME WHILE NEXT PLANE COME.
WE BORED TOO.

NATHAN COSBY - *Editor* **JOE QUESADA** - *Editor In Chief* **DAN BUCKLEY** - *Publisher*

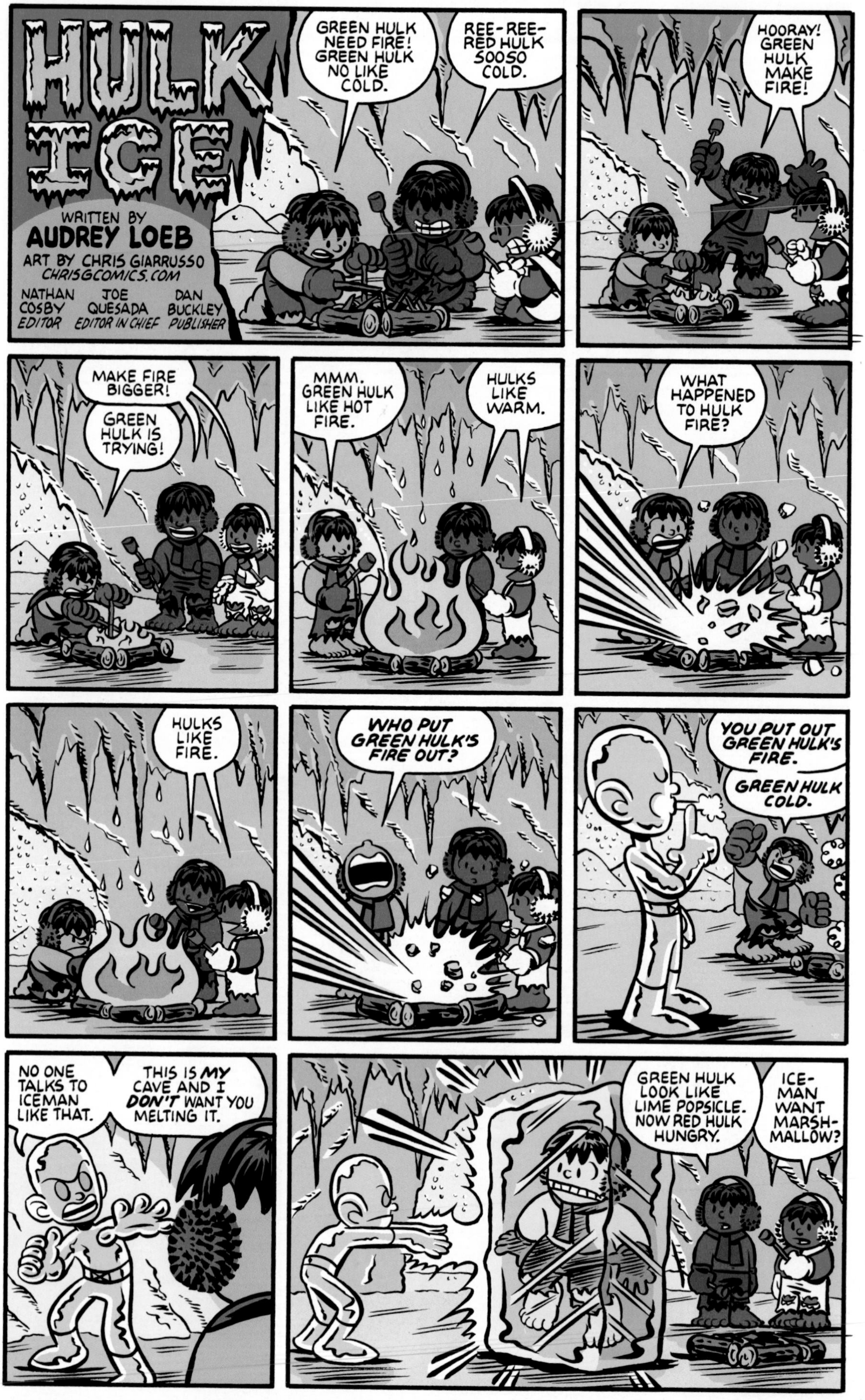
HULK ICE
WRITTEN BY
AUDREY LOEB
ART BY CHRIS GIARRUSSO
CHRISGCOMICS.COM
NATHAN COSBY EDITOR
JOE QUESADA EDITOR IN CHIEF
DAN BUCKLEY PUBLISHER
GREEN HULK NEED FIRE! GREEN HULK NO LIKE COLD.
REE-REE-RED HULK SOOSO COLD.
HOORAY! GREEN HULK MAKE FIRE!
MAKE FIRE BIGGER!
GREEN HULK IS TRYING!
MMM. GREEN HULK LIKE HOT FIRE.
HULKS LIKE WARM.
WHAT HAPPENED TO HULK FIRE?
HULKS LIKE FIRE.
WHO PUT GREEN HULK'S FIRE OUT?
YOU PUT OUT GREEN HULK'S FIRE.
GREEN HULK COLD.
NO ONE TALKS TO ICEMAN LIKE THAT.
THIS IS MY CAVE AND I DON'T WANT YOU MELTING IT.
GREEN HULK LOOK LIKE LIME POPSICLE. NOW RED HULK HUNGRY.
ICE-MAN WANT MARSH-MALLOW?

ARTHUR ADAMS

★ SKETCHBOOK ★

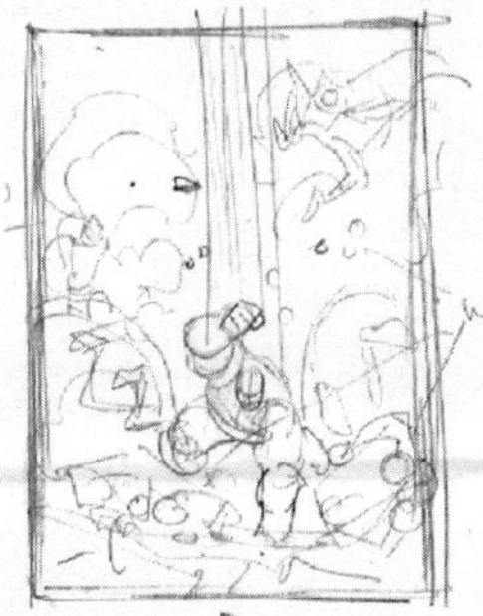
WEN
2

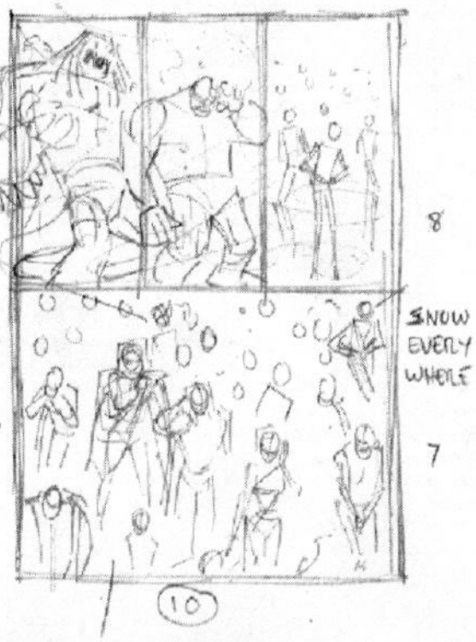
8
SNOW EVERY WHOLE
7
10

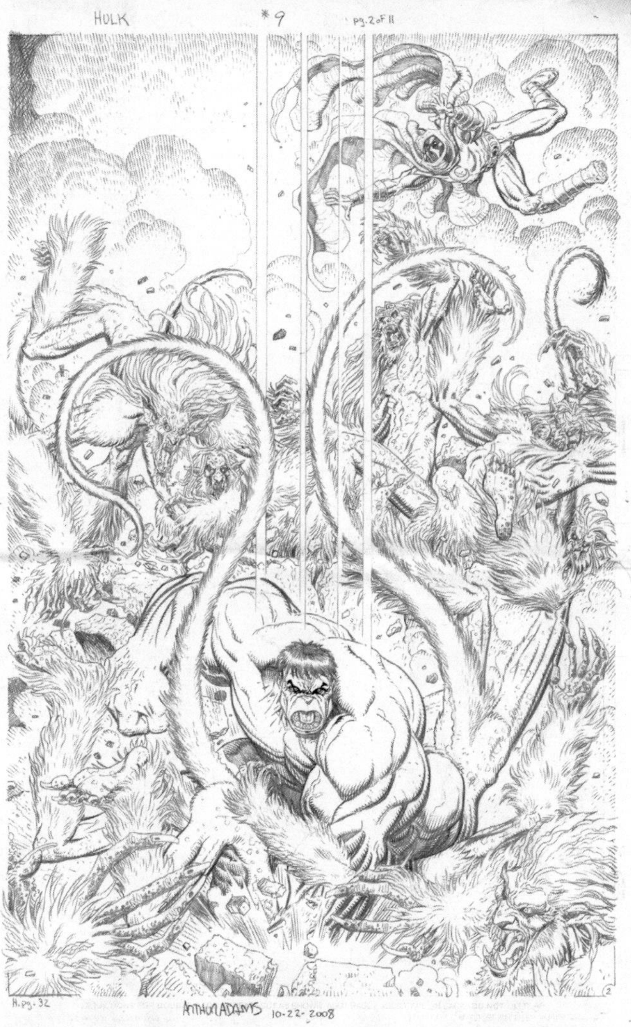
HULK
#9
pg. 2 of 11
H.pg. 32
ARTHUR ADAMS
10-22-2008

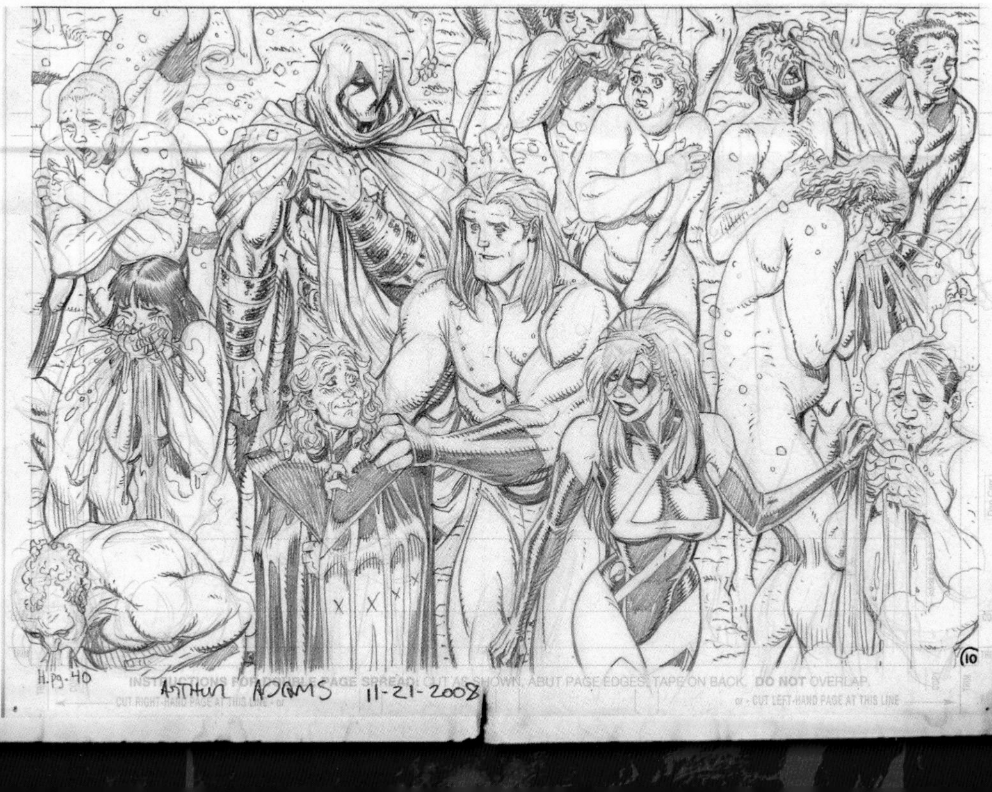
10
H.pg. 40
INSTRUCTIONS FOR DOUBLE PAGE SPREAD: CUT AS SHOWN, ABUT PAGE EDGES, TAPE ON BACK. DO NOT OVERLAP.
ARTHUR ADAMS
11-21-2008

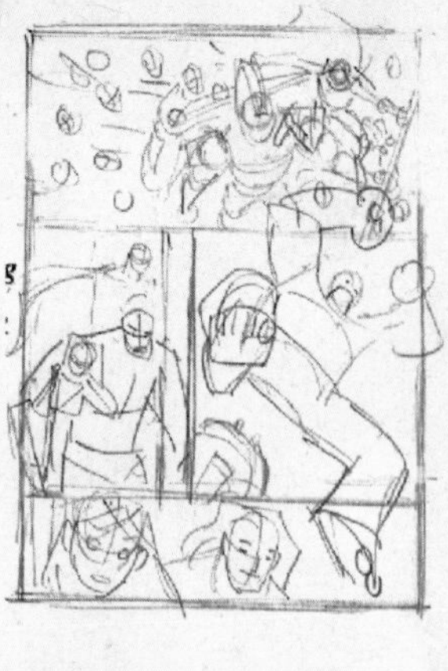

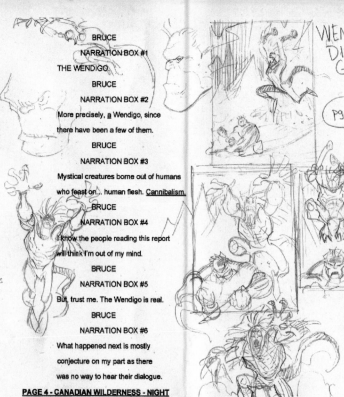

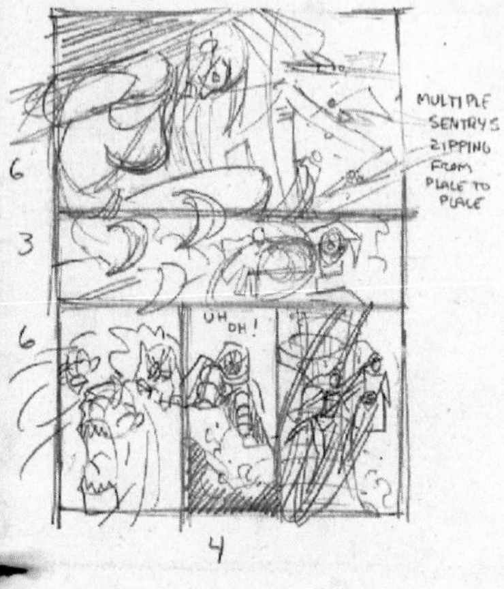
MULTIPLE SENTRYS ZIPPING FROM PLACE TO PLACE
6
3
UH OH!
6
4

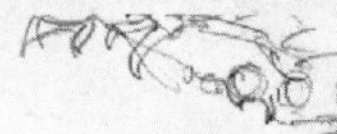

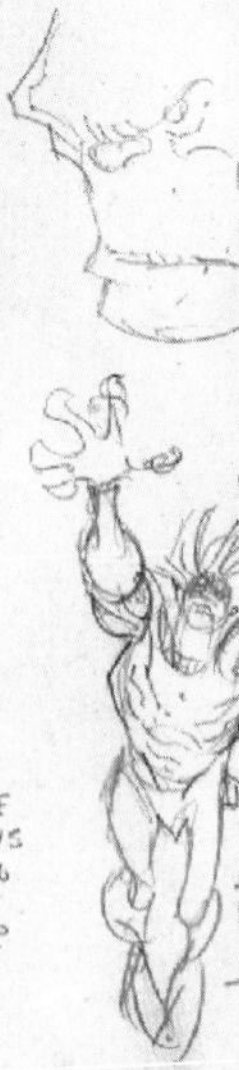

BRUCE

NARRATION BOX #1

THE WENDIGO.

BRUCE

NARRATION BOX #2

More precisely, a Wendigo, since there have been a few of them.

BRUCE

NARRATION BOX #3

Mystical creatures borne out of humans who feast on... human flesh. Cannibalism.

BRUCE

NARRATION BOX #4

I know the people reading this report will think I'm out of my mind.

BRUCE

NARRATION BOX #5

But, trust me. The Wendigo is real.

BRUCE

NARRATION BOX #6

What happened next is mostly conjecture on my part as there was no way to hear their dialogue.

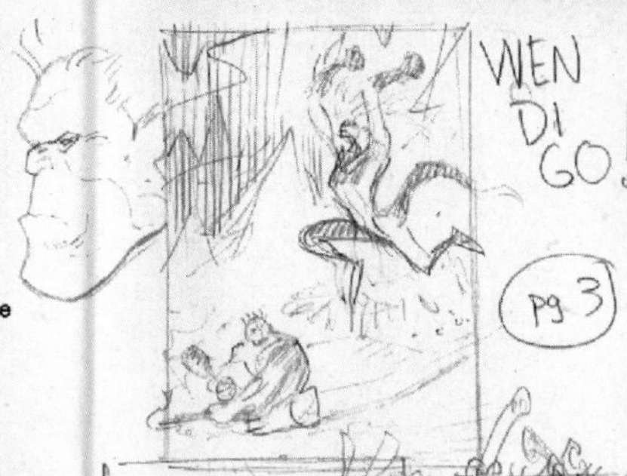
WEN DI GO!
pg 3

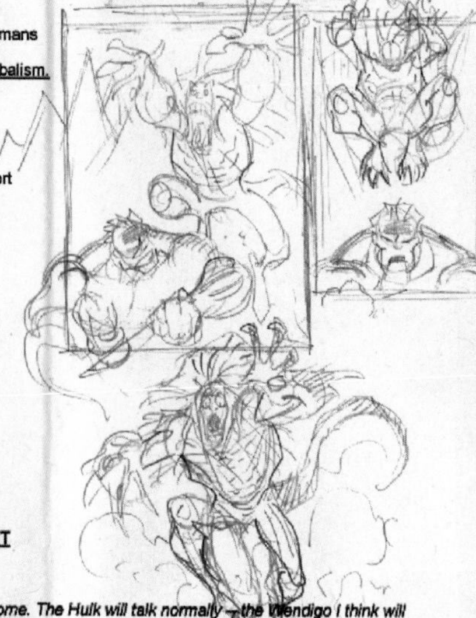

PAGE 4 - CANADIAN WILDERNESS - NIGHT

Panel one

Note: From this point on -- the dialogue is to come. The Hulk will talk normally -- the Wendigo I think will only growl like a monster.

So, to begin, the Wendigo BITES the Red Hulk's shoulder, bleeding him, trying to tear off flesh.

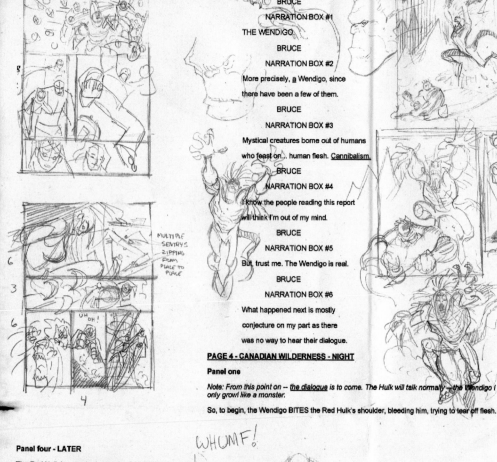

Panel four - LATER

The Red Hulk is crouched around a CAMPFIRE -- roasting the deer meat on a MACHETE type knife. There's blood on the white snow from the kill. Messy stuff.

BRUCE

NARRATION BOX #7

He was presumably on his way to Russia by way of the Bering Straight.

BRUCE

NARRATION BOX #8

We don't know enough about this Hulk to know if he gets tired.

BRUCE

NARRATION BOX #9

But, apparently, he made camp there.

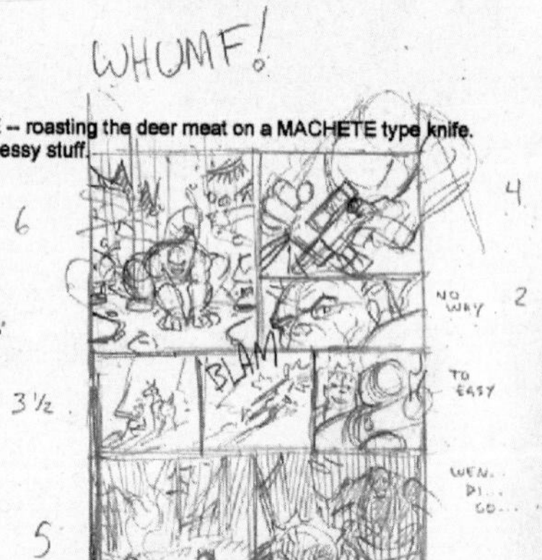
WHUMF!
6
4
NO WAY
2
BLAM
TO EASY
3 1/2
WEN.. DI.. GO...
5
pg. 2

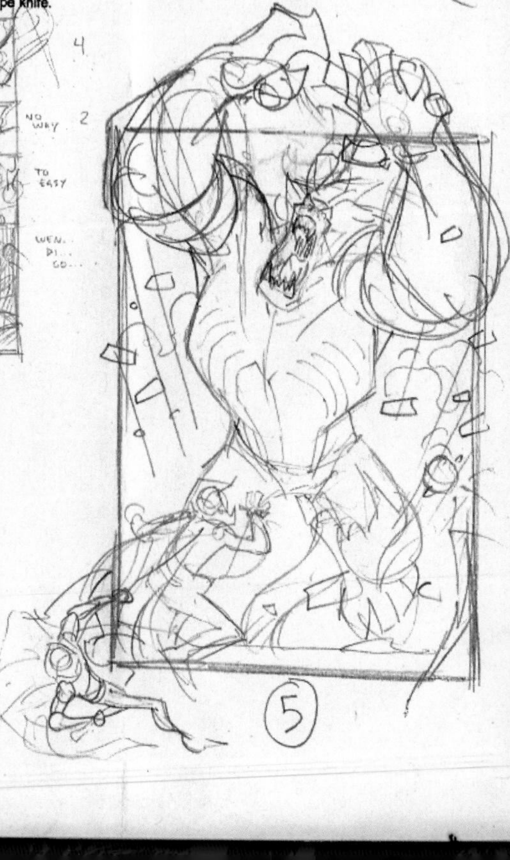
5

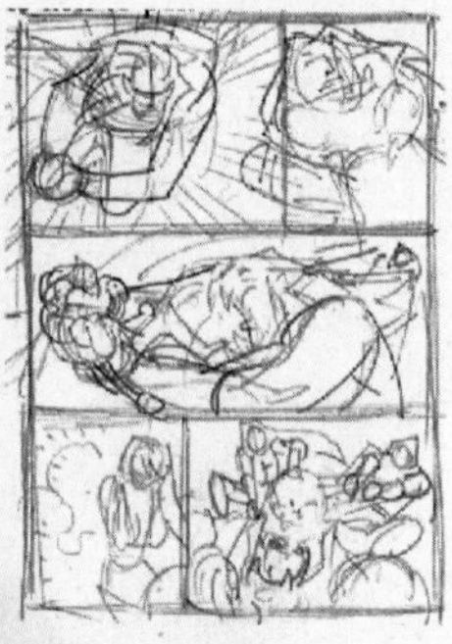

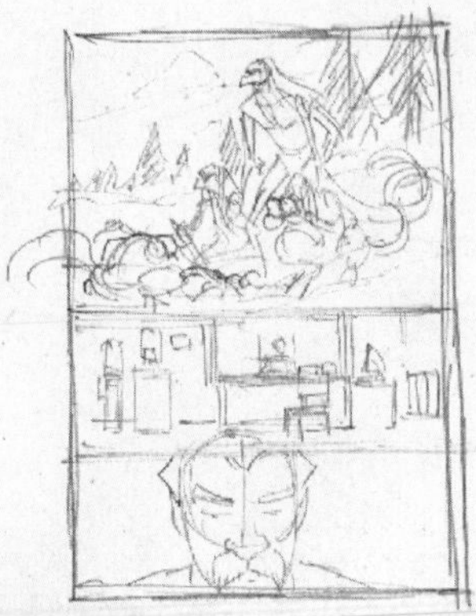

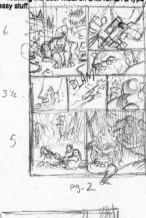

HULK #9 pg. 5 of 11

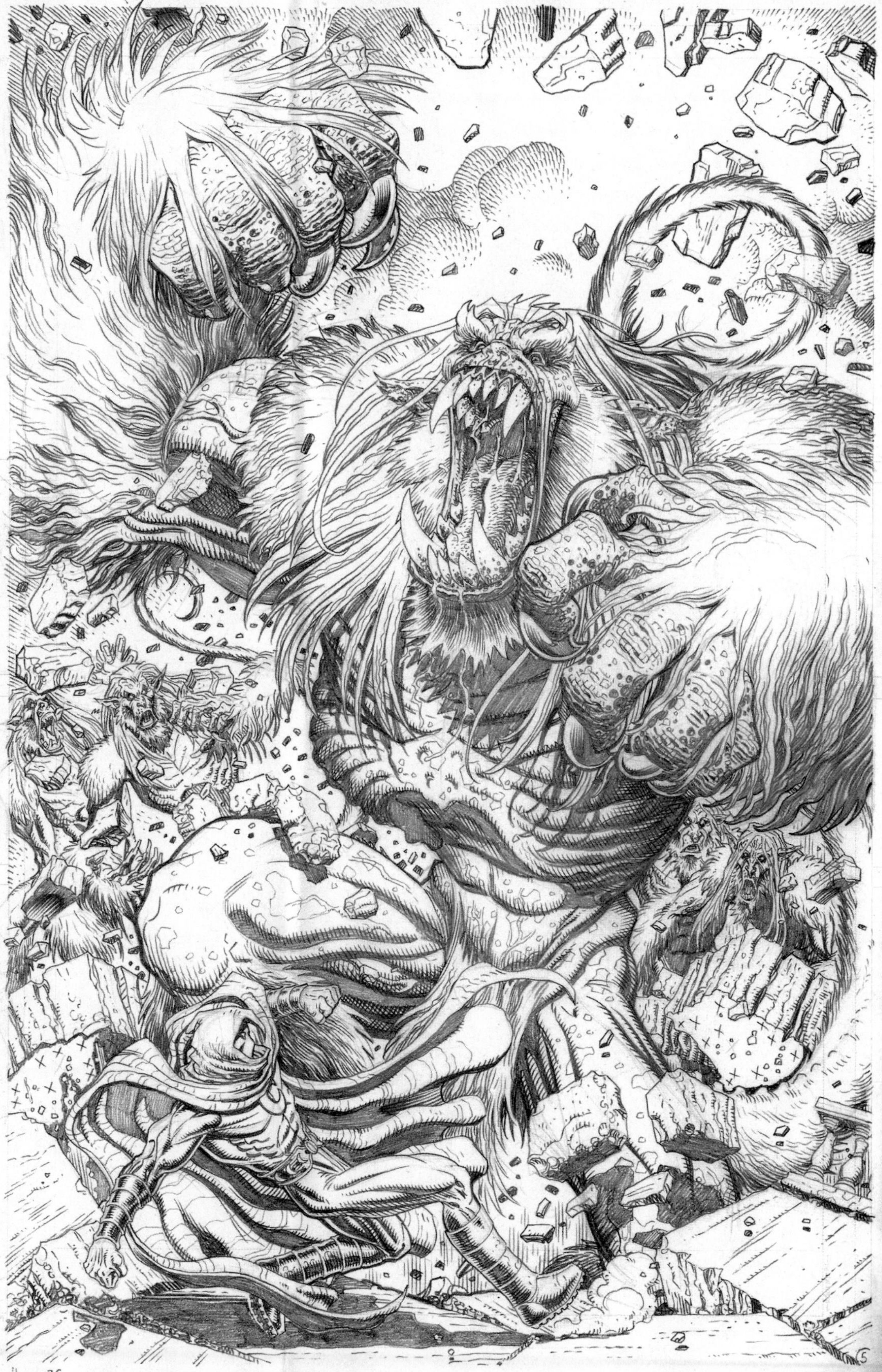

H. pg. 35

ARTHUR ADAMS 11-5-2008

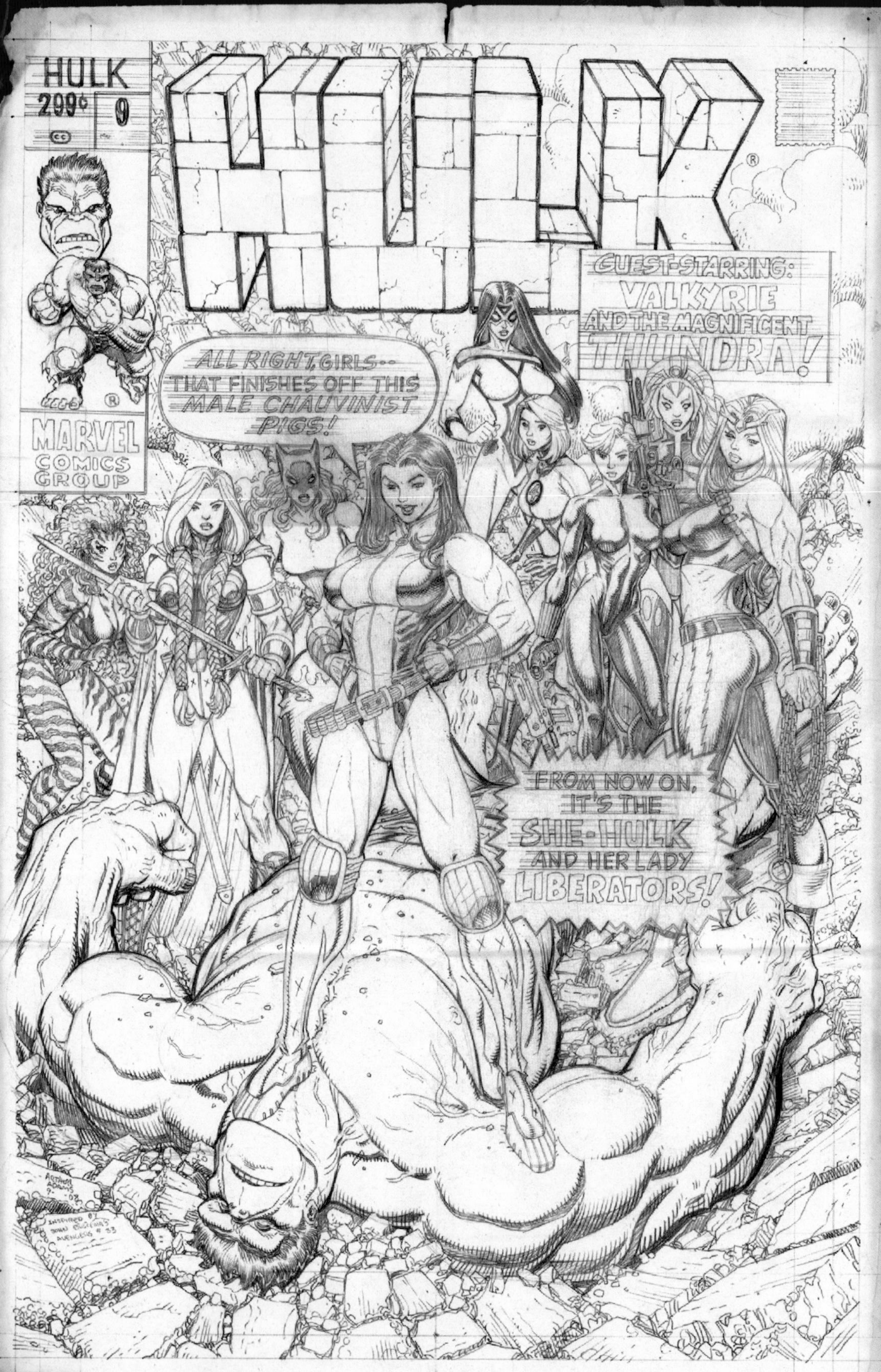
HULK
29¢
9
HULK
MARVEL COMICS GROUP
GUEST-STARRING: VALKYRIE AND THE MAGNIFICENT THUNDRA!
ALL RIGHT, GIRLS-- THAT FINISHES OFF THIS MALE CHAUVINIST PIGS!
FROM NOW ON, IT'S THE SHE-HULK AND HER LADY LIBERATORS!
ARTHUR ADAMS 9-'08
INSPIRED BY JOHN BUSCEMA'S AVENGERS # 33

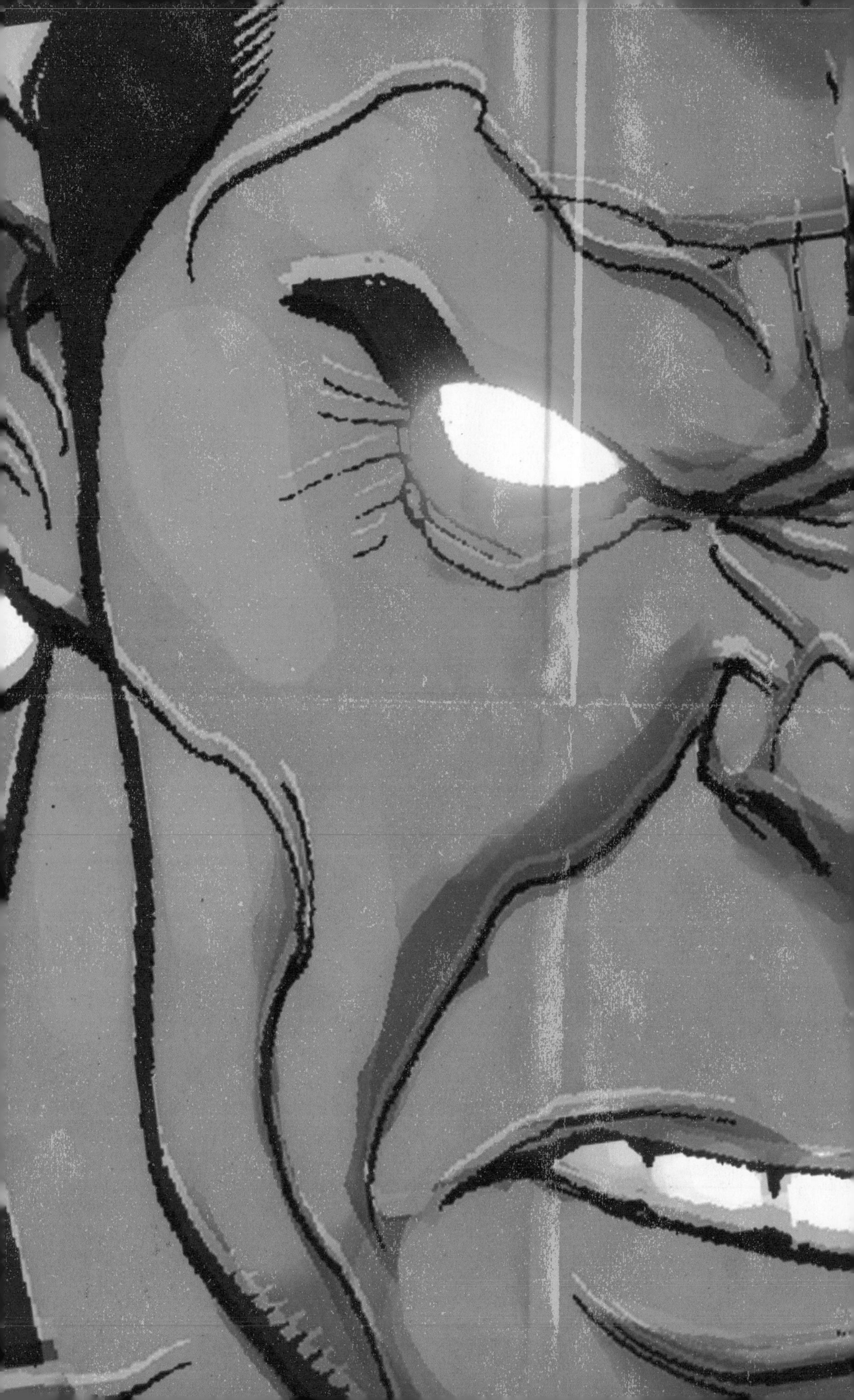